Bad news

MAY 0 4 2011

D0820496

BAD NEWS

BAD NEWS

HOW AMERICA'S BUSINESS PRESS MISSED
THE STORY OF THE CENTURY

EDITED BY

ANYA SCHIFFRIN

THE NEW PRESS

NEW YORK
LONDON

Requests for permission to reproduce selections from this book should be mailed to:
Permissions Department, The New Press, 38 Greene Street, New York, NY 10013.

Published in the United States by The New Press, New York, 2011
Distributed by Perseus Distribution

LIBRARY OF CONGRESS CATALOGING-IN-PUBLICATION DATA

Bad news : how America's business press missed the story of the century / edited by
Anya Schiffrin.
    p. cm.
  Includes bibliographical references.
  ISBN 978-1-59558-549-3 (hc)
  1. Journalism, Commercial--United States. 2. Financial crises--United States. 3.
United States--Economic conditions--2001-2009. I. Schiffrin, Anya, 1962-
  PN4784.C7B33 2010
  070.4--dc22
                                                                    2010035640

The New Press was established in 1990 as a not-for-profit alternative to the large,
commercial publishing houses currently dominating the book publishing industry.
The New Press operates in the public interest rather than for private gain, and is
committed to publishing, in innovative ways, works of educational, cultural,
and community value that are often deemed insufficiently profitable.

www.thenewpress.com

Book design and composition by The Influx House
This book was set in Janson Text

Printed in the United States of America

10 9 8 7 6 5 4 3 2 1

For André and Leina

CONTENTS

PREFACE

Anya Schiffrin

The roots of this book begin for me in Hanoi in the late 1990s. I was there for the first two years of the Asian financial crisis, and it was interesting to report in a place where the media were controlled by the Communist Party and government. Banking was an important part of my beat and, like other countries in Asia, Vietnam was in the middle of a banking crisis with a number of state-owned banks that were saddled by large amounts of nonperforming loans. The government was so afraid of bank runs and loss of confidence that the Politburo passed a law early in 1997 making nonperforming loans a state secret. We worked in an atmosphere of secrecy, and it made getting information difficult and meant that Vietnamese reporters were unable to report on much of what they found out.

When the U.S. financial crisis started, I saw some points in common. There was the fear of undermining confidence by printing bad news accompanied by pressure from government and, in some cases, readers not to do so. There was a collapse in advertising revenues—which preceded the crisis but was aggravated by the economic downturn. There were the ensuing layoffs and staff cuts that made journalists fear for their jobs and perhaps more afraid to stand out from the rest of the pack.

At the same time, new opportunities opened up: if you are a business journalist, you toil away doing routine earnings and stock market stories that are buried on the back pages. But during a crisis everyone is interested in business and the economy. For those journalists, there is also the chance to write stories that are usually shunted aside—detailed explanations of different financial instruments and the chance to write about how real people are affected. We began to see all kinds of reporting that we would not normally see in the business pages.

These were the impressions I had, and when we began doing research on the effects that economic crises have on the media, I found there was very little written on the subject. What is available are a lot of articles written by journalists and media critics after bubbles burst. Both the dot-com collapse of the late 1990s and the demise of energy giant Enron ushered in a period of soul-searching and questioning about why the crisis was not predicted earlier.

I wanted to produce a book that would look not just at the mistakes the press made in the run-up to the crisis, but also at the coverage that took place during the crisis. I wanted to highlight some of the good reporting that emerged as well as some of the omissions and hopefully unearth some suggestions for how business and economic reporting could be improved in the future.

This book covers all of those topics. The first two chapters, by me and Joseph E. Stiglitz, give an analytical framework for understanding business journalism. I've drawn on the academic research in the field, and Stiglitz has applied some of his theories of asymmetric information to the coverage we've seen. Dean Starkman looks into the press coverage leading up to the crisis and examines why it was so weak in many cases. Ryan Chittum investigates the coverage during the crisis while Moe Tkacik analyzes the way television in the modern era contributed to the bubble. Peter S. Goodman talks about his experiences trying to bring in the stories of real people to his beat and how he used their (often very sad) experiences to supplement the macroeconomic reporting he did at the *New York Times*. Chris Roush defends the business press and puts much of the criticism into historical context. Stephen Schifferes describes the experiences he had working for the BBC. And we finish with Bob Giles and Barry Sussman from the Nieman Watchdog Project who describe to us what good coverage can look like.

The role of the press during this past crisis is likely to be studied for years to come and taught in our universities and journalism programs. I hope this book will add to the discussion.

ACKNOWLEDGMENTS

I would like to acknowledge the Roosevelt Institute in New York and Andrew Rich for supporting this book, as well as the April 6, 2010, conference at Columbia University from which this book originated.

1

THE U.S. PRESS
AND THE FINANCIAL CRISIS

Anya Schiffrin

The financial crisis of 2008 and 2009 came at a time when American journalism was already imploding. Beset by job losses and the migration of advertising revenue to the Internet, traditional media was in a decline that seemed irreversible. Major newspapers like the *Los Angeles Times, Chicago Tribune,* and the *New York Times* cut jobs and offered buyouts to many of their staffers.[1] Well-known magazines such as *Newsweek* changed their format in an effort to boost revenues but still shrank in size.[2] Condé Nast's glossy business magazine *Portfolio* and Dow Jones's *Far Eastern Economic Review* were shut down. Bloomberg bought *BusinessWeek* in the autumn of 2009, and then began to slash its staff, replacing the *BusinessWeek* writers with those from Bloomberg. Across the country, newspapers folded, including the *Rocky Mountain News* and the print edition of the *Seattle Post-Intelligencer.* Television stations struggled for ad revenue, and wire services cut staff. An estimated thirteen thousand newspaper jobs were lost in 2008 and fifteen thousand more in

I would like to thank Leslie Norton, Sheridan Prasso, and Dean Starkman for the comments they made on early drafts as well as Herbert Gans for his important work.

2009, according to Paper Cuts. Newspaper circulation continued the declines of 2007 and 2008, falling an average of 10.6 percent in a six-month period of 2009 as compared to the previous year. In the same period, advertising revenues showed their biggest decline since the Great Depression.[3] The *New York Times* called 2009 "the worst year the newspaper business has had in decades."[4]

"As almost everyone knows, the economic foundation of the nation's newspapers, long supported by advertising, is collapsing, and newspapers themselves, which have been the country's chief source of independent reporting, are shrinking—literally," wrote Leonard Downie Jr. and Michael Schudson in their report, "The Reconstruction of American Journalism," published on the *Columbia Journalism Review* Web site in October 2009. "Overall, according to various studies, the number of newspaper editorial employees, which had grown from about 40,000 in 1971 to more than 60,000 in 1992, had fallen back to around 40,000 in 2009."[5]

The problems that beset the industry took a toll on the reporting that took place during the crisis. Afraid for their jobs and struggling with fast-moving and complicated events, reporters struggled to keep up with the most complicated story that many of them had ever covered—all the while worrying about their own futures. Sometimes reporters were even personally involved, suffering from financial troubles while covering the story. The most famous case was that of former *New York Times* writer Edmund L. Andrews, whose book *Busted* chronicled his own troubles keeping up with his mortgage payments even while he was covering the economy from Washington, DC.[6] After the book appeared, Andrews was criticized for being too close to the story he was chronicling.[7]

As journalists were attempting to cover the collapsing economy, the pundits and the public criticized them for not seeing the crisis coming and for ignoring its warning signs. American journalists viewed the situation as unprecedented even though it was eerily similar to the one faced during the financial crisis that rocked much of Southeast Asia in 1997–98. That crisis, half a world away from the United States and less severe, was of only peripheral concern to most Americans, but it took a heavy toll on much of that region for several years. The experience of Southeast Asian journalists during that crisis was similar to what reporters would face in the United States a decade later—heavy declines in advertising, job losses, and pressure from sources not to write depressing stories that would undermine confidence in the economy.

This chapter is not an exhaustive look at the coverage before the crisis began (which we can date to the problems in the mortgage market in 2007). Nor will I provide a close textual analysis of the coverage during the crisis. Those subjects are covered in subsequent chapters by Dean Starkman and Ryan Chittum. Rather, I want to look at some of the broader research that has been done on the press, and in particular on the business press, and explain some of the larger themes that have been researched by media critics and academics. I supplemented my reading of the academic research with some of my own research—done with colleagues—on coverage of the stimulus package. I also interviewed some twenty-five working business journalists.

There has been very little academic research done on how business journalism fares during economic crises but what has been done suggests that during crises, reporters become more dependent on their "sources"—their contacts at the firms in key public and private institutions—for information. The pace at which the stories unfold means that reporters do not have the time to do broader investigative reporting, or to turn to academics or even former "insiders" for more analytic perspectives. At the same time, these sources dry up because they are afraid that publicizing bad news will make things worse. If the sources are available, their focus—even more than usual—is on "spin," trying to shape the coverage of the story as it develops.

One of the maxims of U.S.-style capitalism is that transparency is critical to well-functioning markets, but so is confidence. In this crisis, transparency and confidence came into conflict. Honesty in appraising bank losses from declining housing prices would have presented a bleak picture of the economy's prospects. That would undermine confidence, further freezing consumer spending and making the economy weaker.

Public officials often see part of their role as being civic boosters and glossing over problems as part of the job. When things are going well, it is an easy task that does not contradict the evidence that they see. But in a crisis, there is a need for obscurity, dissemblance, or dishonesty (with different public officials drawing the line differently). In retrospect, it's hard to know whether inaccurate official statements were deliberate attempts at manipulation or arose from genuine misunderstanding. In this respect, Fed Chairman Ben Bernanke's remarks are of particular interest, as he repeatedly attempted to reassure the nation that the problems of

the subprime mortgage market were contained and that the economy's prospects were positive. For example, with the economy on
the brink of recession in March 2007, Bernanke testified before the
U.S. Congress and portrayed the declining GDP growth rate as
a sort of settling-in. "Economic growth in the United States has
slowed in recent quarters, reflecting in part the economy's transi-
tion from the rapid rate of expansion experienced over the preced-
ing years to a more sustainable pace of growth," he said. "Thus far,
the weakness in housing and in some parts of manufacturing does
not appear to have spilled over to any significant extent to other
sectors of the economy." He went on: "Employment has continued
to expand as job losses in manufacturing and residential construction have been more than offset by gains in other sectors, notably
health care, leisure and hospitality, and professional and technical
services, and unemployment remains low by historical standards."[8]

In November 2007—a month before the date that the National
Bureau of Economic Research later identified as the beginning of
the recession in the United States—Bernanke could still sound upbeat.[9] "Since I last appeared before this Committee in March, the
U.S. economy has performed reasonably well," he testified before
Congress. "On preliminary estimates, real gross domestic product
(GDP) grew at an average pace of nearly 4 percent over the second
and third quarters despite the ongoing correction in the housing
market." Bernanke described the crisis as being of possible long-
term benefit: "Recent developments may well lead to a healthier
financial system in the medium to long term," he said, though he
qualified that, in the short-term, "these events do imply a greater
measure of financial restraint on economic growth as credit becomes more expensive and difficult to obtain."[10]

By December 2008, even as he acknowledged that the financial
"crisis has become global and is now affecting a wide range of financial institutions, asset classes, and markets," Bernanke sounded
a positive note in a speech about the government's efforts to lower
the federal funds rate, saying that its "policy response stands out
as exceptionally rapid and proactive." He predicted a gradual economic strengthening. "Although the near-term outlook for the
economy is weak, a number of factors are likely over time to promote the return of solid gains in economic activity and employment in the context of low and stable inflation," he said.[11]

But if officials felt under pressure not to be too gloomy lest
they contribute to a general loss of confidence, the same was true

of reporters. Their training requires them to cover the news no matter how bad it is. But they are afraid that their coverage will cause share prices to fall and consumer confidence to evaporate, and will push the economy into a downward spiral. Like journalists in China and Vietnam who have internalized government/Party instructions to write stories that will help promote economic growth, U.S. journalists were afraid of making things worse.[12] In March 2009, some cheery data gave rise to a series of articles about "green shoots" suggesting the economy was due to recover despite the fact that unemployment was still high and retail sales were still weak. When asked why subeditors kept putting optimistic headlines over stories that reported on gloomy economic news, one *Financial Times* reporter hinted that the editors had internalized the prevailing administration line and winkingly described them as "People's Daily headlines"—a reference to the cheery headlines often found in China's government-controlled media.

An article in the *New York Times* in September 2008 described the journalists' dilemma well. "We're very careful not to throw words around like 'meltdown' and 'free fall,'" said Ali Velshi, senior business correspondent at CNN. "If someone wants to say the markets are in free fall, we'll discuss it first," he said, and the outcome is most likely to be a change in wording. Marcus W. Brauchli, the new executive editor of the *Washington Post*, said that covering Wall Street differed from any other industry. "When financial institutions are suffering a crisis in faith about themselves, journalists are inherently a little bit more prudent and cautious."[13]

Just as the credibility of the administration and the Fed was undermined by their ever-rosy forecasts, so too for the media. Some reporters I interviewed said their in-boxes were full of angry e-mails from readers who accused them of putting air in the bubble as the economy grew throughout the nineties and then kicking the economy as it went down. Most of the journalists interviewed said the letters they got did not affect their reporting, but one said it did make him more careful about the words he used. One journalist shared with us some of the angry letters he received. Two of the letters are excerpted here:

> Your article . . . on worsening estimates of the US economy is unnecessarily alarmist. By all means, report the news, but in this time of difficult economic conditions, psychology is a critical part of whether the country can recover soon or not. In

that setting, reporters such as yourself using overheated rhetoric become part of the problem. . . . This is serious. Please write
in more neutral terms. It is going to be challenging enough to
fix things as it is. We don't need journalists making it worse.

The media and the President have turned this into a self-
fulfilling prophecy. Who could possibly want to spend anything more than necessary when we are being told we are
in an economic "catastrophe"? The people who do have jobs
don't want to spend for fear of not having a job next week
or next month. We need someone with some confidence out
there telling us that we will get through this and that things
will improve.

While the top writers in the field rose to the occasion and
produced a string of significant work as the crisis unraveled (more
about them later), many others were simply overtaken by events
and hesitant about how to report them. The U.S. business reporter
in 2008 was exhilarated by the chance to cover such an important
and dramatic story but also afraid and uncertain. No one knew for
sure how bad the crisis would get. There had been coverage of a
bubble in the housing market, but the world of credit derivatives
and credit default swaps was largely unreported—beyond the occasional story of its immense size (in the trillions of dollars). Such
numbers added mystery to what was going on. How could the value
of this supposed insurance product come to exceed the world's entire GDP many times over? Who was buying and selling these derivatives? Were they really insurance products? If so, what reserves
had been set aside? All that was clear was that these products were
highly profitable—and that the industry players were so politically
powerful that the sellers had managed to get legislation ensuring
that the sellers would not be regulated (either as insurance products or as gambling products), and that they would receive priority
treatment in bankruptcy.

While the usual "sources" became less available and/or less
reliable, even those without self-interest became less helpful.
Reporters and editors have no choice but to rely on the experts. But
many of the so-called experts had failed to see the crisis coming.
Lots of economists did not believe that things would get as bad as
they did. And so, caught in the fog of events, the coverage reflected
the confusion felt in the broader economy.

Many journalists feel upset and guilty about their coverage before and during the crisis. They knew they fell short and they agonized about it:

> The reality: We committed journalistic malpractice on a grand scale. We wrote glowing accounts of the heroic masters of the universe, epitomized by endless reverential profiles of the likes of Jack Welch of General Electric, and, until the roof fell in, Ken Lay of Enron. We asked far too few questions about derivatives and risky changes to the banking system, instead following mergers and slick new securities like star-struck sportswriters. We helped pimp the stock market as working Americans were giving up their pensions and embarking on a risky—and now ruinous—experiment.
>
> —Jon Talton, economics columnist for the *Seattle Times*, in a widely quoted blog post in March 2009[14]

The History of the Business Press

The difficulties journalists faced in reporting the Great Recession were a logical extension of the limitations of the entire genre of business reporting. Academics and journalists have long criticized business/economic reporting for its cheery, pro-business stance. Chris Roush describes the history of some of this criticism later in this book. Media critics on the left such as Rory O'Connor and Danny Schechter have accused business journalists of being "embedded" with the community they cover, pushing an ideology of U.S.-style free market capitalism.[15] However, although these criticisms have intensified over the last couple of years, they are not new. In his book on the history of the financial press, Wayne Parsons writes that even in the nineteenth century the business press helped shape public opinion in favor of the free market: "Clearly the historical importance of the financial press does not lie so much in its contribution to the development of a literary form as in its role in defining a capitalist language and culture: free markets, individualism, profit and speculation. Not only did the publication of information facilitate the growth of the internationalization of markets, it also assisted in no small way in the promotion of capitalist culture."[16]

Before taking aim at the business press, it's important to remember that the field was never really meant to provide public interest reporting. Rather, it is grounded in a historic tradition of providing financial information to investors and business people. The establishment of the business press predated the establishment of political newspapers. Business news sheets have been around since the sixteenth century. They were published in Venice and Antwerp and provided information about "price currents, bills of entry and rates of exchange and marine lists."[17] In the eighteenth century in London, *Lloyds List* began publishing information on shipping and, not much later, newspapers began printing information to help British shareholders make investment decisions about their holdings in the colonies. These were notoriously unreliable and often pushed specific stocks. This lack of information led to many investors in the UK being cheated as it was hard to know exactly what was going on in the colonies. Information was critical but in short supply. As well as being unreliable, the early business press was ideological. *The Economist*, founded by James Wilson and shaped by editor Walter Bagehot, pushed the ideas of laissez-faire economics and Adam Smith, just as it does now. In the nineteenth century, Dow Jones and Reuters both founded business news sheets. The business press continued to grow throughout the twentieth century and expanded rapidly in the eighties and nineties as investment in the stock and other markets grew and investors needed more information.

Academics Describe the Business Press

The academic literature on the business and economic journalism of the eighties and nineties argues that—like its ancestors—it was mostly aimed at helping investors make business decisions. In trade and specialized business publications, explaining economics or the workings of business to the general public was not part of the mandate.

Of course, the general-interest newspapers and television/radio stations were aimed at a more general readership, and their coverage was broader and less technical. However, most business and economic reporting was done by the financial newswires and specialized news outlets. They developed their own vernacular, their own standards, and their own way of framing the issues. Share price was the most important indicator, and events were considered news if they were "market moving." Accordingly, news that affected corporate profitability, and therefore share price, was given top priority. Labor, the environment, and macroeconomic news mattered if those topics affected company earnings and share prices. It goes without saying that larger questions such as fairness, corporate social responsibility, or even the desirability of the free market were not often covered by the average business/economic reporter. All of this was not the result of newsroom censorship. It was simply that these issues were viewed as marginal and largely irrelevant.

Overseas, business reporting was also rooted in support of the American free market system. U.S. reporters living abroad covered the ins and outs of trade agreement negotiations and privatizations and macroeconomic reforms often without questioning the broader social benefits. To a large extent, business reporters around the world adopted this attitude. Reporters from each country reflected the prevailing views of their country and represented back to those at home what was going on through a national lens: in a sense, American reporters described the world as it might be seen by the typical American, were she or he to be on the scene. But because American business reporters were reporting to the American business community, they typically became imbued with the same belief system that dominated that community. They did not attempt to reflect even the dominant perspectives within the foreign community. Localized political interests might be reported on, but mainly as they affected American economic interests, and with a presumption that when there was a clash, "we" were in the right, and "they" were either parochial or captured by "special interests." The growth of the international capital markets and the spread of Washington consensus-style economic liberalization served to promote the free market gospel globally. It provided a framework within which journalists could assess "good" versus "bad" economic policy. Journalism training carried out by organizations like the World Bank Institute and the Reuters Foundation in places like Africa also inculcated these ideas even as it attempted to raise the standards of ethics, reporting, and writing.

Apart from the innate ideological bias in business/economic reporting, there were also a number of other limitations inherent in the genre, which gave rise to criticism of the job the media was doing. Some of these are inherent to journalism—a job that requires reporters to write about a wide range of topics on tight deadlines—and some of these are particular to business journalism.

Academics studying the profession have critiqued the firmly held convention in U.S. reporting that stories need to include "real people." This meant that much of the coverage before the crisis was personality-driven. And because of journalists' well-known proclivity toward promoting mainstream thinkers and personalities, the press wrote mostly about those in power. The likes of *Fortune* magazine and *Portfolio* published profiles of corporate titans. U.S. Federal Reserve Chairman Alan Greenspan was lionized for a decade.

Columbia Journalism Review's Dean Starkman has collected a list of some of the most egregiously fawning press coverage of the U.S. banks and companies that later had serious financial problems. Among his favorites is a 2006 piece from *Fortune* magazine about Lehman Brothers' head Dick Fuld entitled "The Improbably Power Broker: How Dick Fuld Transformed Lehman from Wall Street Also-ran to Super-hot Machine." *Fortune*'s 2004 piece about Merrill Lynch CEO Stan O'Neal and a 2003 piece about Washington Mutual's plan to "turn the banking world upside down" are also on Starkman's list. Just a few years after these articles, Merrill and Lehman had collapsed, and Fuld was widely blamed for his company's shady accounting practices.

Says media critic Mark Frazier, "Even the quality press was in awe. . . . During the recent upward spiral, journalistic complicity and self censorship was compounded by an adulatory cult of the chief executive."[18]

While they often have the most knowledge, the dangers of relying on insiders is clear. These business sources who were profiled so glowingly were part of the financial community, and so the information they gave reflected their agendas and pro-market biases. A few well-known examples come to mind: the dot-com boom of the 1990s was hyped by the media, and then–Federal Reserve Chairman Alan Greenspan was described as the "maestro" who could do no wrong. Particularly telling was the press coverage of the repeal, in the late nineties, of the Glass-Steagall laws. These laws had been put in place after the Great Depression that began in 1929 in order to help prevent another crisis. The laws were aimed at preventing American banks from becoming too big and mandated the separation of commercial from retail banking. When the laws were repealed in the late nineties, the U.S. media heralded the change. Reporters invariably referred to the laws as outdated "Depression-era regulation." Little reporting was done on the possible dangers of doing away with Glass-Steagall. In fact, the end of Glass-Steagall ushered in the rise of the megabanks that took the risks that caused the collapse of the subprime mortgage market. As monopolies grew, competitiveness declined, leading to poor decision making and the erosion of quality in the banking sector.

In the years before the crisis, many journalists largely ignored the economists who saw the coming crisis and warned of a growing bubble in real estate, created in part by the Fed's interest-rate policies and failure to rein in the frothy housing market. After Greenspan's reputation collapsed and he apologized for his mistakes, reporters turned to his critics for guidance. A LexisNexis search of references shows that once the crisis began, bearish economists like New York University's Nouriel Roubini, Yale University economist Robert Schiller, and Nobel laureate Joseph E. Stiglitz were quoted much more often in the mainstream press as journalists gave more space to their disheartening opinions. However, the coverage often dwelt on the fact that they had predicted the crisis. Detailed coverage about macroeconomics—for instance, about why the bears had been right and the mainstream wrong—was still lacking. It is perfectly natural for journalists to pile on once an event has spotlighted the need for alternative views, but the sudden interest in these economists suggests that the press moved in a pack and failed to set the agenda before the crisis occurred.

As well as identifying the tendency toward groupthink, media critics and academics also argue that the time pressures and scoop-driven, short-term focus inherent in much of journalism often lead to incomplete reporting. After interviewing about twenty-five working business journalists, we found that nearly all felt guilty about how superficial their coverage was before the crisis.

"We spent so much time trying to explain what a CDO and the other derivatives were that we never actually stood back and said 'this won't work. You can't be leveraged thirty times.' Partly it's because you are not supposed to editorialize, so you write the story that explains what is going on and then the column that actually gives your opinion. Well, we wrote the stories, but somehow we never got to write the columns," said an editor responsible for bond market coverage at a U.S. financial newswire.[19]

Technical Knowledge
Academics and journalists alike have long commented that there is another weakness inherent in the profession of business/economic journalism; it is a field that requires a great deal of technical knowledge, with some notable exceptions, and few reporters have PhDs in economics or know enough to write insightfully on the subject. The massive expansion of business news in the 1980s and the 1990s meant that young reporters, who often didn't have much

training, were sent out into the field without the ability to truly evaluate the subjects they wrote about. Instead, they wrote glowing articles about U.S. companies and focused on subjects that were relatively simple to cover: the rise and fall of the stock market and the latest economic indicators. In-depth pieces about macroeconomic policy were less common and alternative view points were often left out altogether. The problem was especially acute at the financial news wires and in the magazines and newspaper sections that focused on personal finance.

After the Enron collapse of 2001, it was widely observed that a close reading of the footnotes of Enron and Citigroup's financial statements would have revealed a number of red flags. And yet, with the exception of Bethany McLean's piece for *Fortune* in March 2001, many journalists didn't look or didn't understand what they had read.[20] Former *Wall Street Journal* editor Paul Steiger has defended the *Journal*'s coverage of Enron, noting that the paper ran very critical stories in October 2001.[21] However, those stories were the exception and were published just weeks before Enron, on November 8, filed documents with the Securities and Exchange Commission stating that it was revising its financial earnings over the last five years to show it had a loss of $586 million.[22] To be fair, Steiger has said that the reporters working on the story started in early 2001. In any case, such reporting was unusual. More typical was the coverage that lauded Enron for aggressively creating a new business model. In his piece for *Columbia Journalism Review*, Scott Sherman describes the favorable coverage found in much of the business press about Enron and about the climate of deregulation that allowed Enron to happen. Reading through back issues of *Forbes*, *Fortune*, *Business 2.0*, and *Red Herring*, Sherman said, was like entering a "parallel universe of cheerleading and obsequiousness, a universe where applause obliterated skepticism."[23] He points out that Bethany McLean got her information about Enron's problems from noted short seller Jim Chanos.

The glowing coverage of the dot-com era of the nineties, the massive expansion of personal finance news, and the nonstop market reporting of MSNBC left a legacy in the business press. As newspapers cut back their staff they became more dependent on wire copy, and this wire copy was often fairly superficial.

Presentation and interpretation of data present real challenges, especially when the economy is undergoing rapid change—as is typically the case when the economy is going into a deep recession. The U.S. press coverage of unemployment data in summer 2010 is one example. The Department of Labor provides a number of measures of unemployment. The standard measure asks what fraction of those actively looking for a job have failed to find one. But there is also another, broader indicator: a measure of what fraction of those who would like a full-time job can't get one. There are two differences. The first is that the broader measure includes workers who have stopped looking for a job because they have become discouraged after searching for months and not finding one. The second difference is that the broader measure counts part-time workers who would rather have a full-time job but can't find one. Normally, the two measures move in tandem. But as the economy sunk into the Great Recession of 2008, the gap between the two measures widened markedly, and the broader measure provided a more telling assessment of the weaknesses in the labor market. Moreover, the reported numbers are typically "seasonally" adjusted. In summer, and before Christmas, employment swells; but one wouldn't want to confuse these temporary movements with longer-term, more permanent changes. Again, normally, the adjustments are mechanical and of little interest to anybody but a small group of experts who worry about the right way to do these adjustments. But in a crisis, standard patterns may not prevail. One can't be sure. Thus, in July 2009, the U.S. Bureau of Labor Statistics estimated the actual job loss to be 1.3 million; but the seasonally adjusted job loss was only 247,000. Given that Obama's stimulus package had promised to create only 3 million jobs, the one-month job loss would have represented a major setback, if it were permanent. Articles in the *New York Times* and other publications often failed to explain how job losses were being measured or whether they were corrected for seasonal factors such as the entry of recent graduates into the job market. There were exceptions: David Leonhardt did run a piece in November 2009 explaining some of the numbers—and suggesting that real unemployment was closer to 16 percent and not the 10 percent typically mentioned. The *Financial Times* published a still higher number, without adequately explaining what further corrections they had made. Diversity of views is a good thing and it's reassuring that different newspapers often differ in their interpretations of economic data. But more explanation as to how they arrived at their analysis would have made the coverage less confusing.

Dependence on Sources

When journalists lack confidence in their own understanding of economics, accounting, and business, they often become overly reliant on sources who can—or claim they can—explain these matters. Public relations officers know this and take advantage of it. They put forward the corporate point of view, and business reporters who are on tight deadlines often rely on a quick call to the "flacks" they know for help with information and analysis.

"If you have five hours to write your story and you need information quickly, then who is going to be quoted? The companies that have entire PR machines aimed at putting across their point of view in a very short time," said a senior *Wall Street Journal* reporter.[24]

In his classic work, *Deciding What's News*, sociologist Herb Gans spent several years in the newsrooms of network television stations, including the CBS *Evening News*, NBC *Nightly News*, and *Newsweek* and *Time* magazines, and wrote about how very conventional television reporters were when choosing which sources to quote in their reports. In his taxonomy of how sources are chosen, Gans includes sources who are reliable, can provide the sort of information reporters need, are nearby, and are articulate. A symbiotic relationship develops in which reporters rely on their sources for information and become afraid to alienate them. Gans writes:

> Being on the inside enables beat reporters to gather information that lends itself to dramatic inside stories; but at the same time, they must concentrate on stories that please their sources since angering them may endanger their closeness or rapport, thus ending the reporter's usefulness on the beat. As a result, beat reporters are drawn into a symbiotic relationship of mutual obligations with their sources, which both facilitates and complicates their work.[25]

If the world that Gans describes sounds cozy and insular, then this is even truer for business journalism. It's hard to generalize about the tens of thousands of articles that have appeared in the last two decades, and there is a difference between the business sections of general-interest newspapers, television, and specialized publications. Magazines like *BusinessWeek* prided themselves on covering labor and critiquing big business. Many of the major labor stories on companies like Nike, Liz Claiborne, and Wal-Mart's Kathie Lee Gifford clothing line, as well as the corporate responsibility stories about companies such as oil giant Shell, were published in the business press or the business pages of the mainstream press. The *Wall Street Journal* was awarded a Pulitzer Prize for public service journalism in 2007 for a series on the misuse of backdated stock options. The *Charlotte Observer* was a finalist for a 2007 investigation of the mortgage and housing crisis in North Carolina. In 2008, *Forbes* published an exposé of child labor in India. Bloomberg did a piece on slave labor in Latin America that was published in 2006. Some of these pieces did a tremendous amount to raise awareness about labor conditions in developing countries and, along with efforts by labor activists, involved shareholders and student groups and did a lot to help the corporate social responsibility movement.

However, studies of the business press have repeatedly found that ordinary people are excluded from many of the bread-and-butter stories that compose the daily news diet. Stories about economic indicators, corporate earnings, the financial markets, and banking focus on short-term news, not on the larger social implications of the events being described. For these kinds of stories, the sources that journalists call upon and quote are traders, fund managers, government officials, analysts, businessmen, and endless PR people, often referred to derisively as flacks. Occasionally, an academic or a representative from a trade union or consumer group is included, but that is the exception.

The relationships journalists cultivate can and do lead to scoops and exclusives. But the need to keep supply lines of information open as part of the news-gathering process also breeds a coziness that naturally inhibits hard-hitting, critical reporting.[26] This pro-market mind-set usually leads to the kind of market-rally cheerleading for which television personalities Maria Bartiromo and James Cramer have been so criticized, after both the bursting of the Internet bubble and the most recent crash.

Of course, much of journalism is based on getting access to sources. Sources tell journalists things and journalists report them. Trafficking in information and building up lists of reliable sources is part and parcel of the news business. Even so, media critics and academics have long noted the risks. The danger of dependence on sources is twofold: (a) the risk of being given incorrect information and (b) the risk of becoming dependent on access to sources.

There is an inherent paradox in journalism: journalists depend on sources for access, but any information that is given to them from sources is inherently slanted in some way because usually the person talking to them has an agenda. Sources speak to journalists because they want to influence coverage and hope the reporter will communicate their point of view.

In describing the difficulties he faced writing the biography of economist John Maynard Keynes, Robert Skidelsky, quoting Virginia Woolf, refers to the fact that family members—often widows—control access to important historical papers.[27] These family members only want to release the papers to biographers who will write favorably about their subjects. Because of this, favorable biographies are the norm. The exceptions—such as the Patrick French biography of V.S. Naipaul—generate quite a bit of attention.

In order to get information, journalists sometimes mislead their sources by giving the impression that they are more sympathetic than they really are.[28]

But more often, reporters shy away from endangering their source relationships and report on them uncritically. This uncritical reporting is endemic to much business writing. There has not yet been an in-depth study of the relationship between sources and reporters in the world of business journalism. But a recent example of the dangers of trusting unreliable sources was described in a series of articles by Jack Shafer at *Slate* and Michael Massing in the *New York Review of Books*, who described how Judith Miller, the senior *New York Times* reporter, pushed for the U.S. invasion of Iraq in part because she uncritically repeated what her sources in the Iraqi exile movement told her. *New York Times* business reporter Andrew Sorkin, who reports on Wall Street, has also been accused of being too supportive of his sources.[29]

Over and over again, business journalists say they feel the same pressures as do political reporters.

"Pressure against negative reportage can take many forms—journalists and publications whose views are critical, may, for example find they receive less favorable treatment in terms of access to leaked data about the economy or to exclusive interviews with ministers. Whilst such pressure may be seen as an occupational hazard, the consequences of it in terms of an informed citizenry and democracy are worthy of further research and analysis," Professor Gillian Doyle wrote in a paper published in 2006.[30]

Journalists, even senior writers, are sensitive to pressure from sources even if the threat of losing access is only implicit. "When they lean on you, you think twice about what you will write," said one very senior business columnist.[31]

In *Deciding What's News*, Gans writes that in the newsrooms he observed, reporters who covered specific agencies or beats became "ambassadors" to the newsroom as well as to the public, explaining the agendas of their sources to both their editors and colleagues as well as to their readers. Each time a reporter is given interesting information that reflects unfavorably on the beat she covers, she has to decide whether to use the information or whether to discard it in the hope of getting a better story later. The fear of being scooped by the competition means that sometimes the reporter has to break the news because the wrath of the source is less important than the wrath of the editor. Sometimes, reporters band together and all release the same story, as described so well in *The Boys on the Bus*, the famed account of the 1972 primary campaign involving Hubert Humphrey, George McGovern, and Richard Nixon. In this book, author Timothy Crouse details the pack-journalism mentality, with all the campaign reporters clustering around the veteran AP and UPI reporters to see what they filed before they wrote their stories. Reporters whose stories differed from the rest of the pack got phone calls from their editors asking why they didn't have the same perspective.[32]

During the current crisis, many journalists believe the tendency to groupthink has been exacerbated. There are a few reasons for this: (a) in uncertain times the fear of standing out from the pack is especially acute; this was true as the story unfolded; there was so much uncertainty that it was safer to run with the pack; (b) the need for technical information from government and bankers was greater than ever and reporters didn't want to run the risks of alienating sources and thus falling behind the competition; (c) there was a new administration in place and so opening up supply lines of information was critical (this was not true at the end of the Bush administration—by this time the press coverage was often very critical);[33] and (d) reporters were afraid of losing their jobs and so didn't want to stand out as having different views from their colleagues. There was a very real fear that losing one's job would mean never working in journalism again. In this climate, journalists naturally gravitate toward the center and toward mainstream coverage, which is biased toward Wall Street views. "We are afraid to stick our necks out," said one magazine writer.[34]

But, of course, as anyone who has worked at major news organizations can attest, rank-and-file reporters are hardly autonomous and take their cues from the senior editors. Here it must be said that news management failed in its chief function: to provide the leadership necessary to encourage journalistic risk-taking, to clear space for dissident voices, and to back the badly needed muckraking investigations into major financial institutions.

The cutbacks in newsrooms throughout the country meant that there were fewer people to investigate the crisis as it hit, and senior reporters and editors who remembered previous downturns were put out of work, taking with them valuable institutional memory. Instead of covering breaking news, many magazines began to fill their pages with columns written by government officials and corporate titans. *Newsweek* and *Time* followed the example of *Far Eastern Economic Review*, which cut back on news coverage and expanded columns by experts and government officials. Relying on big names for much of its copy brought about a new dependency on sources. Not only did reporters need access, but the production of their publications depended on getting cooperation from people in government who were writing for them. "We've become much more dependent on our sources," said one senior editor.[35]

Human Interest Stories

While most *business* reporting on the crisis was done from the perspective of how businesses were affected, and most *economic* reporting was done from the perspective of how the *macroeconomy* was (and was likely to be) affected, as the crisis dragged on, more and more "human interest" stories were presented. Accompanying a report on the rising foreclosure rate would be a graphic story of someone who had been preyed upon by a mortgage broker and was about to lose her home and her life savings. In this crisis, finding such moving stories was not difficult. (See, for example, Peter Goodman's chapter.) For many readers, they were more effective in conveying what was going on than the cold statistics.

The Stories Not Written

There was another area that was typically well covered: the politics behind the economics. Would the stimulus package be passed? Who was against? What did it say about the power of the president? Like stories of the big personalities and the poor home owner losing his home, these were part of the drama of the crisis. But between the cold statistics of declining share prices and rising unemployment and these dramas is an analytic wasteland, the key accounts of how the cold statistics become human faces, the interpretations of the facts.

Occasionally, newspapers have gone beyond simply presenting the stories—they have been at the center of the analytics. An example of such coverage was Louis Uchitelle's coverage of the 1993 "jobless recovery" for the *New York Times*. He presented an original analysis of "displacement" statistics—broad measures of job losses which suggested a transformation of the economy, one which did not bode well for those losing their jobs. Many faced long periods of unemployment and, when they were re-employed, it would likely be at much lower wages.[36]

As the 2008 crisis continued, it became fashionable to look at earlier crises to depict where we were—and where we were likely to go. For a normal recession, such an analysis might have made sense. But this was no normal crisis—it was the worst crisis in three quarters of a century. It was not an inventory cycle. It was not the result of the Fed stepping on the brake too hard. It was a financial crisis. These distinctions were critical. A small economics literature had made a great deal of these differences, but such distinctions proved too subtle for most reporters.

Coverage of the Stimulus Package

We decided to put some of the critiques of business journalism to the test by studying press coverage of the stimulus package signed by President Obama in February 2009. Obama had campaigned on the promise to act quickly to stop the U.S. economy from collapsing. As soon as he took office, he put through a $787 billion package aimed at creating jobs and getting the U.S. economy out of the recession. The bill was arguably one of the two most important pieces of economic legislation in the United States in eight years.

We analyzed three months of press coverage, coding 718 articles to see if there was any bias in news articles and op-eds; what the difference was between the different newspapers, magazines, and newswires we covered; and whether they focused on the economics of the package or the political processes, such as whether it would be passed by the Congress and Senate. We also measured the kinds of sources used to see which categories of people were quoted the most often.

Our results were consistent with the academic literature on business journalism. We found that the *Wall Street Journal* and

Chicago Tribune were consistently opposed to the stimulus.[37] They showed a marked preference for tax cuts (as opposed to expenditure increases) and argued that the "Buy America" provisions would lead to more trade protectionism. The weekly *Barron's* (which, like the *Wall Street Journal*, is owned by Rupert Murdoch) was also against the stimulus, but there were only eleven articles published in the time period we looked at. (The result was that the sample was too small to be statistically significant.) The *New York Times* was the most supportive, both in news coverage and in editorials/op-eds. Before the stimulus was passed, much of its coverage was focused on who would get funds and how the money would be spent. In general the press did not look much at alternative ways of stimulating the economy, alternative designs for the stimulus package, or the effectiveness of the stimulus.

However, in July 2009, when the economy did not show much sign of improvement and more articles began suggesting that a second stimulus might be needed, the press began to present more alternatives. But the criticism was not well informed, for example, by the long-standing debate between Keynesian economics and "Hoover" economics. Rather, we noted a rise in the use of business/market sources in the July articles. These sources tended to be critical of the stimulus.

We found that the newswires rarely discussed alternatives to the stimulus (more rarely than did other parts of the media). We also found that wire coverage generally showed the least signs of bias. The exception was the AP coverage, which showed more bias against the stimulus than other newswires but was less biased against the stimulus than were some of the newspapers.

Consistent with our view that "sources" drove stories, across the board, government officials were quoted the most (69 percent of the time), followed by businessmen and market sources (19 percent of the time). Economists were quoted only 14 percent of the time. Interestingly, a Media Matters study in 2009 found that economists made up only 6 percent of guest appearances on cable news programs and Sunday television talk shows about the economic recovery legislation.[38]

The choice of sources affects the bias of coverage. Businessmen who were quoted were largely against the stimulus. As expected, the economists and academics quoted imparted opinion or commentary rather than breaking news.

Conclusion

While the business press did not do a good job in "calling the recession," defenders of the business press have many strong arguments. They point out that there was a lot of good reporting that was ignored. They did no worse than many others, including the Fed. They further argue that the central role of all journalists is to report the news rather than pass judgment on the events that take place. As Dean Starkman points out later in this book, journalists are dependent on information from others—for instance, from government or from regulators and investigators—and since these sources abdicated their responsibilities during the recent boom, there was less information available to journalists.

A lot of very strong reporting has come out of this crisis. Peter S. Goodman has written on the human aspects of the crisis. Gretchen Morgenson warned early in 2007 of the problems at the mortgage lenders Fannie Mae and Freddie Mac. Rick Schmitt uncovered the story of the role of Lawrence Summers, Robert Rubin, and Alan Greenspan in suppressing the regulation of derivatives, overcoming the valiant efforts of Brooksley Born, the former head of the Commodity Futures Trading Commission and a vigorous advocate of regulation.[39] The *New York Times* and Bloomberg have done an impressive job of uncovering the scandals associated with the AIG bailout, despite attempts by the Fed and the Treasury to suppress the public disclosure of this information. Bloomberg's Mark Pittman was another tenacious reporter. In 2007 he tallied the increasing value of the collaterized debt obligations and blasted the rating agencies for downplaying the dangers of the mortgage bonds. *Financial Times* reporter Gillian Tett's coverage in 2007 about the people at J.P. Morgan engineering complex derivatives is worth noting. She also warned in January 2007 about the mispricing of debt and in April 2007 about the role of heavily leveraged U.S. hedge funds in European markets. Alex Blumberg and Adam Davidson at *This American Life* on NPR also did a series called "Giant Pool of Money," explaining the financial crisis in terms that ordinary people could understand. David Faber won awards for his CNBC piece "House of Cards."

Much has been learned since the crisis started, and journalists have had a crash course in recession economics, along with the rest of the country. Whether this will produce long-standing changes within journalism is questionable.

2

THE MEDIA AND THE CRISIS:
AN INFORMATION THEORETIC APPROACH

Joseph E. Stiglitz[1]

The media have rightly been criticized for failing to adequately cover the crisis. Some news outlets (such as CNBC) were active cheerleaders for the bubble as it grew. But even the more responsible press were insufficiently critical in their reports of official views ("there is no bubble, just a little froth";[2] the problem of the subprime mortgages has been contained;[3] the economy is on the way to recovery[4]—just weeks before the economy sank into deep recession).

How do we understand and explain these failures? What should the press have done? In the aftermath of the crisis, governments around the world grappled with the question of how to prevent a recurrence. Some in the financial market have taken the view that crises are inevitable. To impose more stringent regulation would risk dampening innovation—and in the end would be futile in preventing a recurrence. The wiser course is simply to accept such failures as part of the price we have to pay for a dynamic market. So too, some claim the problems are inevitable and inherent in a free and market-driven press.

In the case of the financial system, however, there is a broad consensus that the response of passive acceptance is wrong: we may not be able to prevent crises, but we can make them less frequent, less severe, with fewer innocent victims. But in the case of the press, the question of whether there is anything that can be done to improve significantly the quality of coverage remains unresolved.

I approach the problem from the perspective of the economics of information. The function of the press in our society is to convey information to readers. Information enables readers— whether as consumers, managers, workers, investors, home owners, or voters—to make better decisions. Better individual decisions would have led to better societal outcomes. If home buyers had a better sense that they were buying into a bubble, they might not have been so willing to pay so much, the bubble would thereby have been diminished, and so too the consequences of its breaking. If those running pension funds had a better sense of the risk associated with the financial products that they were buying—the toxic mortgages that polluted the entire global economy—perhaps fewer of them would have been produced, and perhaps America would not be facing the magnitude of the dislocation in its housing markets that it confronts today. If regulators had more of a sense of the bubble that was forming, perhaps they would have been less confident that it was just a little froth, and perhaps they would have done something to softly deflate it.

Of course, each of these parties has a responsibility for gathering the information required to make good decisions. The regulators have large staffs of economists who are supposed to inform them of what is going on in the economy; pension funds are supposed to gather information from a variety of sources before they put at risk the money that has been entrusted to them.

Still, each of these is part of its own "society" and part of a broader society, networks of individuals who share information and come to shared views, often in a too uncritical way. There is often a herd mentality underlying bubbles. Such a herd mentality can be especially strong in groups that do not have the checks and balances that can bring them back to reality—to say, for instance, that a price of $1,000 for a tulip bulb is not sustainable.[5]

A critical press might serve as one of the checks and balances, restoring sanity to markets that have lost touch with reality, providing the crucial pieces of information that might help remind market participants that what is going on is not sustainable.

But one of the central lessons of the modern theory of the economics of information[6] is that while good information is necessary for good decision making, markets for information often work imperfectly. There are incentives for providing distorted information. Market participants may even understand this, but even when all participants are fully rational in their understanding of these distorted incentives, the outcomes can be distorted relative to what would be the case with full information.

The media transmits information. Unlike the "private reports" that inform bankers and investors, the information transmitted is public. As a result, the media plays a key role in shaping widely held perceptions, for example, whether there is or is not a bubble. The media can, accordingly, play a central role in moving the herd—toward a bubble in the years before the crisis and into the deep pessimism that spread around the world after the breaking of the bubble. The fact that the media can and does play this role increases, of course, incentives to shape the media, by those in the markets and in the government, exacerbating the forces leading to distorted information.

Inevitably, the media is also engaged in a process of editing: there is an infinite amount of information that could be transmitted. What it transmits, and how it transmits it, affects beliefs; beliefs affect behavior—and how the economy and society perform.

Because the media has to be engaged in "editing," it is an active participant in the transmission of information and therefore, as we have noted, in the creation of beliefs.[7] Still, it is useful to make a distinction between two different roles: one in which it is (relatively) passive, simply "reporting" on news (or what it decides is newsworthy—itself an act of editing); and that in which it takes a more critical role of analysis. There were failures in both roles. This chapter suggests that these failures were understandable given the incentives and constraints confronting reporters and the media.

Of course, reporters and their editors do not stand apart from the rest of society. They too can easily be swept up in the herd mentality. Indeed, in this crisis many reporters and editors were. Our argument is that, unfortunately, there are at play strong incentives for the media not to serve as part of society's systems of checks and balances, not to "lean against the wind."[8] While the "failures" cannot be fully eliminated, changes in practices and institutions could ameliorate the problems.

Biases in Sources

As Anya Schiffrin points out in her chapter, one of the major problems is that the natural sources for news stories are biased. For the business and financial press, the most important sources of information are the leaders and key personnel at the businesses and financial institutions upon whom they report. For the nonbusiness press, one of the most important sources of information is the government (and especially the "administration"). Both of these sources have strong incentives to provide distorted information.

The Business Press

Businesses want to sell their products and want investors to pay more for their shares. They thus have an incentive to try to present as good news as they can about themselves, their products, their balance sheets, and so forth, consistent with two constraints: fraud laws (they don't want to go to prison) and the loss of reputation (overt errors will undermine credibility). But these constraints are weak. Shortsighted firms care relatively little about their loss of reputation—so long as the returns in the short run are large enough to compensate. Indeed, the crisis has revealed the shortsightedness of financial institutions, and how their shortsightedness has "infected" so much of the rest of the economy, for example, the increased focus on quarterly returns.

Business media naturally turn to business sources. They typically present the accounts as the businesses present the accounts to their shareholders. There are several reasons for this. A natural defense is that it is not their job to assess the accuracy of the accounts. That is the job of the accountants/auditors. If the auditors have approved the accounts after a thorough review, how is a lowly reporter to question it?

Moreover, there is a question of "responsible" journalism—especially when it comes to a firm that might be on the verge of bankruptcy (or facing a liquidity crisis). Announcing that such a possibility exists might precipitate the event. More troubling is that even inaccurate information—that a firm is on the verge of bankruptcy when it is not—can precipitate a bankruptcy when without that "information" it would not occur—a self-fulfilling prophecy.

Making matters more difficult is the threat of litigation. This is especially true in countries like the UK where there are imbalanced libel laws and even an accurate story may be subject to suit.

But there are two further problems. The first is that because business reporters depend on their sources, they have to please those sources. For example, if a reporter covering some company is excessively critical, he risks being denied access to information about the firm's plans for expansion. He will have to rely on publicly available information, and that will put him at a competitive disadvantage relative to rivals who can obtain "scoops."

In the highly competitive world of journalism, access to informants is critical, and a symbiotic relationship between the press and those they cover results—a relationship that does not necessarily serve the rest of society well. There is, of course, a trade-off between the speed at which information is delivered and its accuracy. Unfortunately, accuracy is often hard to assess—it took a long time before the inaccurate reports of those promoting the housing bubble and the banks' "prowess" were exposed; but it is easy to tell who is first with a given piece of information. Moreover, hubris can lead to the view by journalists that as recipients of information they can sort out the distortions and inaccuracies—so long as they can get the information. In a world in which information is power—and money—having information quickly is what matters. Indeed, much of the economic return in the market relates simply to that. The person who knows it will rain tomorrow can buy the umbrella today, while they are underpriced and underutilized. Even if he has no use for the umbrella, he knows that tomorrow, the price will be high. He gains a return simply because he had this information earlier than others. Indeed, there may be no social return to such early information—only a private return.[9] The gains by one party represent losses to another. But the private returns can be high, and the media responds to these private returns, not the social returns.

I have already alluded to the second problem, the "cognitive capture" of the reporter by those that they cover. It is not just that the reporter writes the story that the business wants him to write in order to gain or maintain access—an economic quid pro quo, a nonmonetary exchange—but also that the reporter comes to think like the business he covers. He becomes one of them. Being part of the club does give greater access, but it is more than that. Individuals come to adopt the views and perspectives of those with whom they interact. If they spend all day talking to business people, there is at least a risk that they come to think, at least to some extent, like business people. And if they do that, they may not be able to fulfill their critical role.

Of course, a good business reporter does not have to rely just on "sources." Listed companies have to file accounts that are publicly available. Accounting frameworks give considerable "flexibility"— and many of the financial innovations have been directed at increasing this flexibility—for instance, helping firms move losses and risks off the balance sheet.[10] Still, the tension between trying to minimize reported income for the tax authorities and maximizing reported income for investors can generate useful information that can be analyzed by reporters. One of the criticisms of the press in this crisis (as in the scandals earlier in the decade) is that they made insufficient use of this information, at the very least to raise questions. The fact that, for instance, anyone looking at Citibank's reported balance sheet as it managed its way through the crisis could not have predicted that this was a company on the verge of bankruptcy—net worth held steady year after year—provides evidence (if evidence was needed) of the extent of "manipulation" of the accounts.[11]

Financial Press
Those covering the financial press have an even more difficult job. I described earlier the natural and understandable incentives of businesses: to increase sales (through good coverage of their products) and to increase share value (through favorable coverage of expected profitability.) The incentives of those in the financial markets are not always so easy to decipher. They make money when prices change, but they can make money when prices go up or down, depending on whether they have a long or a short position. Anyone can potentially have a vested interest. No reporter can know whom to trust. But, unfortunately, in their coverage they often do not bring along the necessary dose of skepticism.

This applies both to the coverage of broad economic stories as well as particular events. For instance, the financial press faithfully repeats the adage that it is necessary for governments to reduce their deficits, and unless they do that, all manner of economic ills will follow. Many putting forth these views have large long-term bond positions. They stand to gain if governments pursue policies that lead to lower inflation, which leads in turn to lower interest rates. Bond prices will increase. Those making these pronouncements will, of course, deny that their views have anything to do with their own financial interests.

A story reported in the *Financial Times* in January 2010[12] illustrates the risks to which the media are prey. It reported that the Greek government had undertaken talks with China for financing their bonds. It appears that the story was not true, though a large financial firm as advisers to Greece may have suggested that as a course of action. If so, it was a suggestion that was turned down. It is also widely believed that the story was planted by the financial firm, who had shorted Greek bonds and stood to gain by the story (which resulted in the price of those bonds going down). If the story were true, it was newsworthy. It was a story that, if true, would probably be denied by government officials. Thus, verifying the story (other than by market participants who potentially had incentives to substantiate the story) would be difficult. It seems that the *Financial Times* may have been used.

While this is a dramatic case illustrating the risks confronting the financial press, in more mundane forms, it occurs every day— and it was a central part of the failure of coverage. The financial sector had financial incentives to keep the bubble going, and so had incentives to persuade the press (as well as the regulators) to go along with the prevailing wisdom: there couldn't be a bubble in a modern sophisticated economy (the tech bubble notwithstanding); we were not experiencing a bubble; one couldn't in any case be sure there was a bubble; even if one suspected a bubble, there were no instruments to deflate it—at least no instruments without serious adverse side effects (conventional wisdom held that the interest rate is a blunt instrument, but there were actually many other instruments in the arsenal of the Fed that it *chose* not to use); even if the bubble broke, the consequences would be minimal because risk had been so well diversified and distributed. Accordingly, it was far better to let the markets take their own course and clean up any minor problems that might emerge in the aftermath of the breaking of the bubble. The press repeated uncritically this kind of mantra, little noting that these views reflected the financial interests of those that were promulgating them.

While cognitive capture plays an important role in explaining the failure of the media to adequately cover the events leading up to the crisis, other explanations are required to understand the inadequacies in coverage after the crisis broke. What made coverage of the banking crisis so difficult is that the financial markets (the banks) had worked hard to develop a system of off balance sheet accounts that obscured what was going on; it allowed them to take on more leverage than any responsible bank should have done. But the complexity and nontransparency of the banks made providing an accurate depiction of the situation—or the consequences, for instance, of not bailing out the banks—difficult if not impossible. The press, like Congress, had to rely on banks' assertions that in the absence of the multitrillion-dollar bailouts and guarantees, the financial system (and therefore the economy) would have collapsed.

But again, I believe that they could have played a more critical role. A single Bloomberg reporter, Mark Pittman, looked at the accounts carefully.[13] Only Bloomberg turned to the Freedom of Information Act to uncover hidden details of the bailouts, to find out where the money was really going.[14] Good reporting eventually uncovered that claims by the New York Federal Reserve that French law required AIG credit default swaps (CDSs) to be settled for 100 cents on the dollar were false.[15] There remains no good accounting of why the CDSs had, in fact, to be settled—especially if they were to be settled on such unfavorable terms. Much of what was uncovered by the inspector general and the Congressional Oversight Panel could have been uncovered by good investigative reporting but was not.

The Nonbusiness/Nonfinancial Press

The national press also failed in this crisis. Of course, they do not see themselves as experts in economics and business—that is a responsibility delegated to the business press. Their focus is normally on politics, on the one hand, and "human interest" on the other—covering the stories about the forces shaping the lives of their readers.

The result is that there is a gap in coverage, which only the largest and best-financed media can bridge: economics. While to many, economics is *just* business, there is a marked difference. The latter covers the fortunes of particular firms or sectors. A reporter covering the retail sector may cover what is happening to Wal-Mart, or the sector as a whole. But economics is about the performance of the entire economic system. Normally—when everything is going well—the economic story is fairly boring. The economy grows at say 3 percent a year, a little faster one year, a little slower another. Of course, investors worry intensely about how, say, the

Fed is going to respond, for example, by raising or lowering interest rates. But while for those who have millions at stake, a change in interest rates of one tenth of 1 percent can be a big deal, for most readers, such changes will not affect their lives. It is nice to know that everything is going on as it should be, but for most readers, that is all they want or need to know. It is only in times of crises that economics becomes a matter of everyday concern.

The problem is that it is expensive for newspapers to keep on reserve a reporter ready to provide this exciting coverage at the moment it is needed. And so typically they don't. Some of the coverage is done by business reporters who "convert" from covering the details of firms or sectors to covering the big economic story; some by political reporters who try to cover the underlying economics as they unravel the political implications of the changing scene; and some "human interest" reporters who cover how the unfolding economic tale is affecting the lives of ordinary Americans. But few of these have the training to critically assess the pronouncements coming out of the administration or the Fed or the contrary pronouncements of the critics.

The result is that, too often, there is a "he said, she said" kind of coverage, a simple reporting of the different perspectives, with little balance, let alone analysis. It is as if, in covering a story about the color of the sky, a color-blind reporter gave equal weight to those who claim it is orange as to those who claim it is blue. Of course, it is more complex: it is perhaps more akin to how a reporter in the Middle Ages might have covered the story about the "discovery" that the world is round. With a majority of those interviewed still claiming that the world is flat, it would be natural for the critics to dominate.

This is understandable. What is less understandable is the seeming failure of so many in the press to understand (and convey) the incentives of those in the administration and Fed to provide distorted information. Increasingly, administrations have seen part of their task as "shaping" news coverage (or to use the less polite term, "spinning" the stories). In their quest to keep the poll numbers up, they want voters to believe that the administration is doing a good job, and a key metric for performance is how well the economy is doing. This is especially true in times of trouble, with an administration elected on a platform of restoring an economy that (allegedly) had been badly bruised by the misdeeds of the predecessor.

Here, the press consistently falls for what has come to be called presidential economics, where the performance of the economy under different presidents is compared and contrasted. The reality is that much of what goes on in the economy is outside the control of the administration (or even the Fed); and what is under their control typically affects the economy with a long lag. What we see today is as much the result of what happened in previous administrations as it is of actions taken today. The economic policies of an administration are important, but their effects *typically* take months or years to be fully realized. (An important exception is in the midst of a crisis, a point to which I shall return shortly.)

Thus, the Clinton administration rightly pointed out that the bottom of the income distribution had not been doing well for years, and that their plight had largely been ignored—and sometimes exacerbated—by its predecessors. But the improvement in their plight in the early years of the administration was only partially a result of what the White House did. The administration should have been given credit for the earned income tax credit, which made a big difference in the well-being of many lower income individuals; but the relative improvement in the before-tax income of unskilled workers was the result of complex forces, largely beyond their control.

In seeming to claim too much credit, political leaders also, of course, get too much blame for what goes wrong.[16] Political leaders, perhaps intuitively grasping that they have only limited ability to change the course of events, focus on what they do have some control over—perceptions of those events. This is especially so since they believe (and partially correctly so) that beliefs and perceptions do affect reality: the belief that a political leader is "powerful" can induce those in congressmen to support his position, and thus increase the likelihood of success of his initiatives. Power breeds power (and conversely for powerlessness).

So, too, in economics: the belief that the economy is going well ("confidence") can induce people to spend more, and that will help the economy to do well. In economics, there is a long-standing view that "animal spirits" matter,[17] and more recently, behavioral economists have tried to study the determinants of such animal spirits.[18] Administration pronouncements ("spin") can help induce confidence, in a self-confirming way.

Those in the financial community have always emphasized confidence. And, indeed, one of my long-standing complaints against the financial press is that they have paid too much attention to the financial community's perspectives, for example, in the coverage of crises like that of East Asia. They typically did not even note that most economists disparage the role of confidence except as it affects short-term markets. Standard economic models for half a century have attempted to explain movements in output and employment without any reference to psychological variables such as confidence.

Of course, a statement by a finance minister can affect the exchange rate (or some other variable) for an hour, a day, or even a week. But economists focus on the underlying realities and believe that rational market participants do likewise. There is thus a major gulf between economists' perception of the functioning of the economy and that of the finance (and, to a lesser extent, business) community. Most reporters (including, or perhaps especially, those whose main job is covering finance) seem unaware of this, and this has impaired their ability to cover effectively economic stories, including the story of the crisis.

In March 2009, the Obama administration began talking about "green shoots," the nascent recovery of the economy. It seemed a blatant attempt to enhance confidence, which, it was hoped, together with the stimulus measure that the administration had just passed, would restart the economy's engine. If it worked, the enhanced confidence would reinforce the real effect of the stimulus. There was, of course, a real risk in this strategy: beliefs have to be tied to realities.[19] If the green shoots withered by the early summer, then confidence in the administration and its policies might erode.

The national press covering the administration is in much the same position as the business press covering businesses. They may be aware that those that they are covering have an incentive to distort information, but in covering (or uncovering) these distortions they face several problems.

First, like the business press, they need access. They do not want to lose access, and to retain access they have to provide favorable (or at least not too unfavorable) coverage. Those in the administration work hard to create an artificial scarcity of information so that they have something to trade in return for favorable coverage.[20]

Second, they have a problem of expertise: it is not always easy to challenge the administration's experts. In America's system, the job of challenging pronouncements is given to the members of the opposition party (and allied think tanks). That is why so much of the reportage is of the "he said, she said" form.

Thirdly, there is an element of "responsible journalism." They fear that to suggest that the economy is on the verge of collapse might precipitate the collapse itself.

Economists
While politics is important, and while different political parties had different economic theories—and therefore different interpretations of the likely efficacy of different policies—there needed to be better coverage of the underlying economics.

Here, the press faced an unusual problem. The mainstream of the economics profession had, in a sense, failed as badly as financial markets. They had provided the models used by those in finance which had gone badly awry; they had provided the theories that underpinned the deregulation movement and that provided succor to regulators who did not believe in regulation.[21]

I believe that the press should have taken this fact into account in its coverage of the crisis. It should have leaned more heavily on those who had predicted the crisis—their interpretation of the crisis and the remedies—and been more critical of others. So, for instance, in covering the impact of the stimulus, "Chicago" school economists were typically more skeptical of the effectiveness of the stimulus. But in describing these economists' position, it would have been of relevance to most readers to know that these economists not only did not predict the crisis; their models suggested that unemployment could not exist, or at least persist for long.

The difficulty the media had in turning to economists was thus not just that these were not their ordinary sources, but also that they had a difficult time sorting out different positions.

Market Distortions

Most of this chapter has focused on the distortions in coverage that arise from the distortions in sources—the incentives that most sources have in shaping the news coverage in particular ways. I have also discussed some of the distortions in incentives of the reporters, which limit their drive to uncover these distortions.

But there are also well-known distortions in organizational incentives, which I briefly note. The media is (for the most part) a business, and it has to get subscribers and advertisers. Both of these respond to coverage, in ways that are not always helpful in ensuring accuracy.

Would readers have responded favorably to doom-and-gloom stories that suggested they were about to lose a large fraction of their net worth? Would bankers have responded favorably to business stories that suggested they were irresponsible in their risk management?

Such stories would have been uncomfortable. Revealed preference shows that those who acted as cheerleaders—such as CNBC—did better. The market responded to demands, even if those demands led to poorer quality information. (By the same token, many of those in the financial sector claim that they were just responding to the demand for leverage by their investors.)

In emphasizing the incentives for the provision of distorted reporting, I have perhaps paid too little attention to the countervailing incentives (weaker, admittedly, in a market dominated by shortsightedness): media has an incentive to gain a reputation for accuracy and anticipating stories before they occur. No one wants to have a reputation for being a mouthpiece of industry or finance or the administration. They at least want to seem to be critical.

The critical word, however, may be "seem." Alternative views and voices may be reported, but at the end of the story. An appearance of balance is thereby given, one that pleases the party wanting distorted news—his side gets prominence, and the fact that there is some criticism lends authenticity to the story that it might not otherwise have.

Remedies

Many of the problems that we have described are unavoidable, or almost so. The media is part of our society, and will therefore inevitably suffer to some extent from cognitive capture. If irrational exuberance captures society, it is unreasonable to think that reporters can stand fully apart.

But some of the problems can be alleviated. Part of the problem is a lack of training in *economics*, even for business reporters. And because economic debates are always evolving, the economics training has to be constantly updated. What is required is more than an undergraduate degree—but something different from the technical training afforded by most PhD programs. There needs to be a focus on ideas and policies, not on mathematics. Foundation support for the creation of a summer institute or a program along the lines of the Knight-Bagehot program at Columbia University's School of Journalism, which focuses on training business journalists, could bring this idea into fruition.

We noted, too, how the problem of access in business and finance might undermine reporters' incentives to be critical. Fair disclosure rules—ensuring that any information made available to one reporter be made available to all—will at least mitigate these problems.

So too, in the public sector, stronger and more effectively enforced right-to-know laws may mitigate some of the problems of access there, though to the extent that what matters is *early* access, it may have little effect.

Attempts to identify capture by particular reporters might have a salutary effect, for example, studies that correlate "puff pieces," favorable coverage, and scoops. At the time I served in the Clinton administration, we had a sense of which reporters were "owned" by which members of the administration. If these perceptions could be quantified, verified, and publicized, it might have a chilling effect on this kind of capture.

Finally, there needs to be more independent financing of investigative and analytic reporting, with a recognition that reporting on economics is different from reporting on finance or business, and that such reporting requires specialized training. This problem may be getting worse as the Internet has undermined traditional business models.

Concluding Comments

Certain aspects of the press coverage of the financial crisis were stellar, from the detailed accounts of the collapse of auction-rated securities markets to some of the investigative reporting surrounding the AIG bailout.[22] Yet, overall, the press acted more like a cheerleader as the bubble grew than like a check, like a warning light, like a critic of a set of fallacious ideas that underpinned the bubble. So, too, in the aftermath of the crisis, it has provided both less analysis and less investigative reporting than one might have hoped. Much of the coverage, both in the run-up to the crisis and its aftermath, was biased—reflecting more than distorted perceptions and beliefs of those in the financial sector that had helped create the crisis than the economists who had predicted its end and provided prescriptions for dealing with the havoc left in its wake. Better information might have led to better policies, but market participants had incentives to provide distorted information. The media may have served those interests better than it did the public interest. We have uncovered some of the reasons why this may have been so. Understanding these reasons is helpful in thinking about how we can ameliorate these problems—not prevent them, but at least mitigate the distortions.

3

POWER PROBLEM:
THE BUSINESS PRESS DID EVERYTHING
BUT TAKE ON THE INSTITUTIONS THAT
BROUGHT DOWN THE FINANCIAL SYSTEM

Dean Starkman

The government, the financial industry and the American consumer—if they had only paid attention—would have gotten ample warning about this crisis from us, years in advance, when there was still time to evacuate and seek shelter from this storm.

—Diana Henriques, *New York Times* business reporter, speech at The George Washington University, November 8, 2008

But anybody who's been paying attention has seen business journalists waving the red flag for several years.

—Chris Roush, "Unheeded Warnings," *American Journalism Review*, December/January, 2009

I'm kind of curious as to . . . why it is that people were shocked, given the volume of coverage.

—Nikhil Deogun, deputy managing editor, the *Wall Street Journal*, quoted in "Unheeded Warnings"

For in an exact sense the present crisis in western democracy is a crisis of journalism.

—Walter Lippmann, *Liberty and the News*, 1920

These are grim times for the nation's financial media. Not only must they witness the unraveling of their own business, they must at the same time fend off charges that they failed to cover adequately their central beat—finance—during the years prior to an implosion that is forcing millions of low-income strivers into undeserved poverty and the entire world into an economic winter. The quotes above give a fair summary of the institutional response of the mainstream business press to the charge that it slept on the job while lenders and Wall Street ran amok. And while the record will show this response is not entirely wrong, one can see how casual business-press readers might have a problem with the idea that final responsibility for failing to stop escalating dangers in the financial system has somehow shifted to them.

Dang, Margaret, we blew it again.

It is understandable that the business press would want to defend its record. But it is equally understandable, I hope, that some readers might want to see some support for these claims. You know the old journalism saying, "If your mother says she loves you . . ." etc.

For if the institutional response is correct, and all was done that could be done, then journalism has even bigger problems than Google and Craigslist. In the best case, if this response is to be believed, the financial press faces the problem of irrelevance—all that newsprint and coated paper, those millions of words, the bar graphs, stipple portraits, glossy photos of white guys, the printing presses, delivery trucks, and Yale degrees, is worth about as much as a New Century share.

Lippmann, I think would understand the problem. Without facts, the public is powerless. With them, well, it can lick Countrywide and Goldman Sachs put together. In his book, *Liberty and the News*, Lippmann wrote: "Everywhere today men are conscious that somehow they must deal with questions more intricate than any church or school had prepared them to understand. Increasingly, they know they cannot understand them if facts are not quickly and steadily available." Without them, he says, there can be no liberty.

He was talking about a crude and corrupt press that manipulated public opinion around World War I. We're dealing with a
financial press that is neither of those things, but is nonetheless a
battered and buffeted institution that in the last decade saw its fortunes and status plummet as the institutions it covered ruled the
Earth and bent the government. The press, I believe, began to suffer from a form of Stockholm Syndrome. Now, it is in the awkward
position of telling its readers they were insufficiently attentive to
what it wrote.

I can think of several reasons why this is a bad approach,
optics-wise. For one thing, it sounds a bit like telling customers they didn't read the documents carefully enough, just what
Ameriquest used to say about it Pay-Option ARMS. Don't go
there, press friends.

For another thing, readers could answer that while it is true
that they may have missed warnings, they do recall hearing mes-
sages that didn't sound like warnings at all. Anyone "paying at-
tention" might have thought that the most important thing about
Washington Mutual on a given day was that its "Creative Retail
Approach" had turned the "Banking World Upside Down" (*Fortune*,
3/31/03); that Lehman Brothers was "Trading Up" (*Wall Street
Journal*, 10/13/04); that Ken Lewis had become the "Banker of
America" by "Ignoring His Critics" (*Fortune*, 9/5/05); that Angelo
Mozilo was merely pugnacious ("The Mortgage Maker vs. the
World," *New York Times*, 10/16/05); that Citigroup was "Cleaned
Up" (!) though "Falling Behind" (*BusinessWeek*, 10/05/06); and, ad-
ditionally, that Goldman (drum roll) had "Sachs Appeal" (honk)
(*Forbes*, 1/29/07).

Nothing about mortgage boiler rooms and CDO factories
there, no matter how carefully you read.

Finally, if reader inattention is really the problem, then what's
an appropriate policy response—mandatory exams on "Personal
Journal" stories? But would the jump be included on the final? My
pet idea is to pipe *Squawk Box* into people's homes 24/7, with no
turning it off, à la North Korea. If we're nationalizing everything,
we might as well go all the way, right?

I'd say a better approach in the wake of this disaster is to reflect
on why all these "warnings" went "unheeded" and failed to pene-
trate the thick skulls of Pick-a-Pay Nation. Alas, the business press
does not appear to be in a reflective mood. But, business press, as
Jimmy Cayne might say, it's not about you. It's all about us. We

citizens, like it or not, rely on journalists to provide word of rampant wrongdoing, and now we find ourselves well beyond the worst of all worst-case scenarios, caused, by general consensus, to an overwhelming degree by this most central of business-press beats: finance. We need to learn the lessons of the past eight years or so, even if the press doesn't want to go along, and reexamine, from top to bottom, all the firewalls that we were supposedly designed to protect us from precisely the financial catastrophe that has just occurred. These firewalls start with risk managers, officers, directors, etc., within the financial institutions, then extend outward to accounting firms, rating agencies, regulators, and, yes, journalists.

The press's role is, as always, ambiguous. On the one hand, no one at *Forbes* sold a single collateralized debt obligation to any German pension fund, so the press certainly can't be blamed for causing the crisis. On the other hand, Bloomberg News employs 2,300 business journalists; the *Wall Street Journal*, 700-plus; the *New York Times*, 110; etc., and all business-news organizations purport to cover the financial system and imply, if not claim outright, mastery over a particular beat—the one that just melted down to China to the shock of one and all. So the press isn't exactly an innocent bystander, either. It's not 100 percent responsible, and it's not zero percent. It's somewhere in the middle, closer to zero than fifty, I'd say, but it had *something* to do with it.

Right now, the business press, which firmly believes it did all it could do, is in something of a standoff with those who believe that cannot be true. The discussion so far has been conducted largely at a schoolyard level: "You missed it!" "Did not." We also see a lot of defensiveness among business journalists, as though somehow individual reporters are to blame. This is preposterous. These are institutional questions. Senior editorial leaders and news executives are in the dock here, as is an entire media subculture. Leaders had the power; they set the tone, they set the frames, not this reporter or that one.

Major news outlets so far have not trained their resources on the question, a drive-by or two by Howard Kurtz notwithstanding. The *American Journalism Review*, quoted above, did take a look and found in the business press's favor. With all due respect to our cousins in Maryland, I find *AJR*'s approach—in effect, sticking a thumb into several years of coverage and pulling out some plums—inadequate. Of course *somebody* did *something*. And a few did a lot of things. But did the coverage even come close to reflecting the radical transformation of the mortgage industry and Wall Street in 2004, 2005, and 2006? Tellingly, "Unheeded Warnings" contains a disturbing number of examples from 2007, when warning were about as useful as a garden hose during the Tokyo fire bombings. It also dwelled on coverage of Fannie Mae and Freddie Mac, which odious as they were, *followed* the private sector into subprime.

In this debate, the business press has the advantage because the public cannot be sure whether in fact it did miss something. Being sure would require reading the entire record of what was printed on the topics of lending and Wall Street in several outlets over many years—hundreds and hundreds of stories. Who in his mind would do such a thing?

Well, somebody had to.

It struck us that it is impossible to avoid trying to assess the business press's performance in the run-up to the meltdown. The business press is the sole means by which normal citizens would know of goings-on in the lending industry and on Wall Street. It is the vital connection between the public on one side and regulators and financial institutions on the other. It is the only instrument capable of catalyzing the virtuous cycle of reform that emerges when dangers and abuses come under the public gaze. If readers screwed up, so be it. But if it is the business press, readers are going to have to insist on identifying weak points, cultural problems, skewed priorities, and areas in which the business press's institutional interests might be out of alignment with those of the broader public. If members of the public must go elsewhere for warnings, they need to know that, too.

It is true that few sectors of journalism, with the possible exception of the Washington press corps, are as infected with the extreme form of know-it-all-ism as the business press, which wields the complexities of its subject area like a cudgel against noncognoscenti. But readers should not shrink from asking relevant questions merely because they don't know the precise mechanics of a credit default swap and don't read *Fortune* as closely as they might, say, the Torah.

The fact is, you don't need to be a media critic or a quant to assess whether proper warning were provided. What's more, I suspect most rank-and-file reporters would welcome scrutiny, as long as it's fair. And so we undertook a project with a simple goal: to assess whether the business press, as it claims, provided the public with fair warning of looming dangers during the years when it could have made a difference.

I'm going to provide a sneak preview of our findings: the answer is no. The record shows that the press published its hardest-hitting investigations of lenders and Wall Street between 2000 and 2003, for reasons I will attempt to explain below, then lapsed into useful-but-not-sufficient consumer- and investor-oriented stories during the critical years of 2004–2006. Missing are investigative stories that confront directly powerful institutions about basic business practices while those institutions were still powerful. This is not a detail. This is the watchdog that didn't bark.

To the contrary, the record is clogged with feature stories about banks ("Countrywide Writes Mortgages for the Masses," *WSJ*, 12/21/04) and Wall Street firms ("Distinct Culture at Bear Stearns Helps It Surmount a Grim Market," *New York Times*, 3/28/03) that covered the central players in this drama but wrote about anything *but* abusive lending and how it was funded. Far from warnings, the message here was: "All clear."

Finally, the press scrambled in late 2006 and especially early 2007 as the consequences of the institutionalized corruption of the financial system became apparent to one and all.

So the idea that the press did all it could, and the public just missed it, is not just untenable. It is also untrue.

We went into the project with the working hunch that something was wrong. This stems from our belief in journalism itself. As journalists, we have to believe that what we do is not entirely ineffectual and that it has some impact on the outcome of events. Otherwise, why bother? Given that the system failure here is absolute, whatever journalism did do, as a matter of logic, was insufficient.

But a second idea going in was that this "debate" about business press performance is not really a matter of opinion at all. Either the work is there, or it isn't. Facts have a way of obliterating assumptions.

Our approach was fairly straightforward. We picked a date range of January 1, 2000, through June 30, 2007, with the idea that the early date would capture the entire housing bubble and the later date marked the period right after two Bear Stearns hedge funds collapsed very publicly and all warnings were moot.

We then came up with a common-sense list of the nine most influential business press outlets: the *Wall Street Journal*, the *New York Times*, the *Los Angeles Times*, the *Washington Post*, Bloomberg News, *Financial Times*, *Fortune*, *BusinessWeek*, and *Forbes*. CNBC and other television outlets were excluded both for practical and substantive reasons. With the help of some colleagues, we searched the Factiva database for the names of important institutions—Bear Stearns, Countrywide, etc.—and matched them with search terms that seemed appropriate, such as "predatory lending," "mortgage lending," "securitization," "collateralized debt obligations," and the like.

We then asked the news outlets themselves to volunteer their best work during this period. Some institutions were more diligent than others; so, on that score, the *New York Times* might tend to be overrepresented, while the *Washington Post*, which declined to participate, might get shorted. Similarly, Bloomberg, the *FT*, and the *Los Angeles Times* posed technical challenges. But, while we won't hesitate to differentiate between the relative performance of different outlets, (and reporters, for that matter), the goal was to assess institutional performance, not who "won." Nobody won.

The articles are in a spreadsheet, which can be found at www .cjr.org/the_audit/power_problem_spreadsheet.php. I was a staff writer at the *Journal* from 1996 through 2004, covering commercial real estate during the relevant period, and on contract at the *Washington Post* for 2005, covering white-collar crime; nothing of mine is on the list or deserves to be there. As of this writing the sheet contains 730 entries, but it remains open and we plan to add storied indefinitely as we come across them. Feel free to send your entry to editors@cjr.org. The database is meant to be used as a companion to this story. I hope it will be a reference for further research and that readers will use it to argue for or against *CJR*'s conclusions.

The list, then, was designed to capture all significant warning stories, not just some of them. And while 730 may seem like a lot of relevant stories, keep in mind the *Journal* alone published 220,000 stories during this period, so in a sense these were corks bobbing on a news Niagara. The list also includes as guideposts bits of context that we felt would give readers some sense of what was happening on the finance beat at the time (e.g., "Fed Assesses Citigroup Unit $70 Million in Loan Abuse," *NYT*, 5/28/04). Sprinkled throughout are some of those rah-rah stories ("Mortgage Slump? Bring It On; Countrywide Plans to Grab More of the Market as the Industry Consolidates," *BW*, 12/15/03), and a tiny fraction of the run-of-the-mill stories about important, and guilty, institutions that in retrospect were so far from the salient point that one wishes we could have the space and the reporters' time back ("Power Banking: Morgan Stanley Trades Energy Old-Fashion Way: In Barrels . . . ," *WSJ*, 3/2/05).

Let's get to it.

The most striking thing about the list for me is that the best work during the entire period—stories that hit hard at abusive practices and established the critical link between bucket shops and their Wall Street funders and bundlers—was done early, from 2000 to 2003. *BusinessWeek*'s Dean Foust, et al., explored Wall street's foray into the hard-money lending business, including subprime mortgages and payday lending ("Easy Money: Subprime Lenders Make a Killing Catering to Poorer Americans. Now Wall Street Is Getting in on the Act," 4/24/00). A handy chart at the bottom of the story ranks subprime securitization leaders: Lehman was number one. Citigroup's 2000 acquisition of Associates First Capital, a notoriously corrupt outfit (it employed a "designated forger," ABC's *Prime Time Live* reported in 1997), spurred the *New York Times* to publish "Along with a Lender, Is Citigroup Buying Trouble?" in October of that year. This fine 3,258-word story documented Associates' execrable practices fairly well (though it couldn't beat the anecdote from a 4/23/97 *Journal* story that described how an illiterate quarry worker, who owed $1,250 for—get this—*meat*, discovered that this loan had been sold to Associates, which convinced the quarry worker to refinance ten times in four years until he owed $45,000, more than half of it in fees, with payments that took more than 70 percent of his income. He had signed each note with an "X"). The *Times* duly noted Citi's promise to clean up its new acquisition by, among other things, holding upfront fees to a mere nine (!) points.

Business journalism during this period comes close to reaching the holy grail—the critical Wall Street/subprime connection—when the *New York Times*'s Diana Henriques, in a joint project with Lowell Bergman and ABC news (including, though he doesn't have a byline, the underappreciated Brian Ross), published "Mortgaged Lives: Profiting from Fine Print with Wall Street's Help" (3/15/00), linking another now forgotten but once powerful and rapacious subprime lender, First Alliance Corp., with Lehman Brothers and other Wall Street firms engaging in precisely the kind of practices that brought down the financial system. The story captures the

boiler-room culture that was then overrunning traditional mortgage underwriting, here with a quote from a twenty-seven-page
sales manual:

> "Establish a common bond," the loan officers were taught.
> "Find this early in the conversation to make the customer
> lower his guard." The script listed good bond-building topics
> (family, jobs, children, and pets) and emphasized, "It's really
> important to get them laughing."

The piece goes on to describe the Wall Street connection in
some detail: "No Wall Street investment bank had a bigger share of
that reviving 1999 [subprime] market than Lehman Brothers, Wall
Street's fourth-largest brokerage house."

This story and others were based on groundbreaking litigation in California that, importantly, would hold a Wall Street firm
responsible for the practices of its lender-clients. Had that principle stood up (an Orange County jury found for the borrowers in
2003 but the award against Lehman, $5 million, was small), there
would have been no mortgage crisis. The *Los Angeles Times*, led by
E. Scott Reckard, also dogged the litigation, recognizing the journalism opportunity for what it was.

John Hechinger of the *Wall Street Journal* also wrote fine
warning stories, including one about how brand-name lenders
were convincing the poor to refinance zero-percent loans from the
government and Habitat for Humanity (!?) with rates that reset to
the mid-teens and higher ("Best Interests: How Big Lenders Sell a
Pricier Refinancing to Poor Homeowners—People Give Up Low
Rates to Pay Off Other Debts . . . ," 12/7/01). The dishonor roll
is here:

> Some of the nation's biggest subprime lenders have refi-
> nanced zero-interest and low-interest loans from Habitat,
> including Countrywide, units of Citygroup Inc., Household
> International Inc., Ameriquest Mortgage Co. and a unit of
> tax giant H&R Block Inc.

Meanwhile, the *Journal*'s Jess Bravin and Paul Beckett painted
a devastating portrait of a compromised Comptroller of the
Currency ("Friendly Watchdog: Federal Regulator Often Helps
Banks Fighting Consumers—Dependent on Lenders' Fees, OCC

Takes Their Side Against Local, State Laws," 1/28/02). And *Forbes* did a beat-down on Household ("Home Wrecker," 9/2/02).

What is important to remember about the period around the turn of the decade—and this is not a knock on the press—is that predatory lending was high on the public's agenda, mostly in response to marauding behavior of old-line subprime lenders like Associates, First Alliance, Conseco Finance, Household, etc., who at the time were being joined by the new generation of subprimates— Ameriquest, New Century, et al. From the mid-nineties to the early '00s, foreclosures began to jump in urban areas around the country, rising half again in Chicago's Cook County; doubling in Detroit's Wayne County, Newark's Essex County, and Pittsburgh's Allegheny County; tripling in Cleveland's Cuyahoga County, according to *American Nightmare: Predatory Lending and the Foreclosure of the American Dream*, a muckraking book by Richard Lord published in 2005, based on his reporting in the *Pittsburgh City Paper* on this early subprime boomlet.

Between 1999 and 2004, more than half the states, both red (North Carolina, 1999; South Carolina, 2004) and blue (California, 2001; New York, 2003), passed antipredatory-lending laws. Georgia touched off a firestorm in 2002 when it sought to hold Wall Street bundlers and holders of mortgage-backed securities responsible for mortgages that were fraudulently conceived. Would that such a measure had survived. We forget now, but beginning in 2004 Michigan and forty-nine other states battled the U.S. Comptroller of the Currency and the banking industry (and the *Wall Street Journal*'s editorial page) for the right to examine the books of Wachovia's mortgage unit, a fight the Supreme Court decided in Wachovia's favor in 2007—about a year before it cratered. Iowa attorney general Tom Miller and Roy Cooper, his counterpart in North Carolina, made predatory lending the centerpiece of their tenures (see: "They Warned Us About the Mortgage Crisis," *BW*, 10/9/08) while in New York Eliot Spitzer gave grandstanding a good name in trying to bring attention to the issue ("Spitzer's Ghost," CJR.org, 10/14/08).

This isn't about identifying which journalist or economist was "prescient," the business-press parlor game du jour. What's important is that forthright press coverage and uncompromised regulation combined to create a virtuous cycle of reform.

Citigroup, remember, was forced to sign a $240 million settlement with the Federal Trade Commission covering two million customers. This is marketing deception on a mass scale, revealed and policed. A coalition of states forced an even bigger settlement, for $484 million, on Household. This was in 2002. It wasn't perfect, but it was working.

Alas, any fair reading of the record will show the business press subsequently lost its taste for predatory-lending investigations and developed a case of collective amnesia about Wall Street's connection to subprime, rediscovering it only after the fact.

There are a number of explanations (though no excuses) for this. First and foremost, was the abdication of regulatory responsibility at the federal level. Uncompromised regulation and great journalism go hand-in-hand. But when such regulation disappears, journalistic responsibilities only increase. What is important to understand first is that this press failure did occur. Readers needn't be bullied into believing they missed relevant independent press investigations of Countrywide, New Century, IndyMac, Citigroup, Bear Stearns, Lehman Brothers, or Merrill Lynch. Check the sheet; they aren't there.

What makes this development especially maddening is that subprime lending and Wall Street's CDO production at this point were only just getting started. Subprime mortgages in 2002 were $200 billion, 6.9 percent of all mortgages. By 2006 they were $600 billion and 20 percent of the market. Add poorly documented "Alt-A" mortgages and the 2006 figures rise to $958 billion and 32 percent. CDO production went from next to nothing in 2000 to half a trillion in 2006.

Behind those numbers were the boiler rooms, underwritten by the Wall Street masters of the universe depicted on business magazine covers. Yes, we must beware of hindsight-ism. But let us acknowledge that today, at least, we know that the lending industry from 2004 through 2006 was not just pushing it. It had become unhinged—institutionally corrupt, rotten, like a fish, from the head. I argued last fall ("Boiler Room," *Columbia Journalism Review*, September/October 2008) that post-crash reporting has given short shrift to the breathtaking corruption that overran the mortgage business—document tampering, forgery, verbal and written misrepresentations, changing of terms at closing, nondisclosure of fees, rates, and penalties, and a boiler-room culture reminiscent of the notorious small-stock swindles of the nineties.

Now the muck is finally bubbling to the surface as the Justice Department and several states gear up to prosecute "dozens" of leaders ("Financial Fraud Is Focus of Attack by Prosecutors," *NYT*, 3/12/09) and journalists latch onto the story in all its lurid glory. *BusinessWeek's* excellent Mara Der Hovanesian reports, for instance, that Wall Street demand for mortgages became so frenzied that female wholesale buyers were "expected" to trade sex for them with male retail brokers, according to "dozens" of brokers and wholesale buyers ("Sex, Lies, and Mortgage Deals," 11/13/08). But:

> The abuses went far beyond sexual dalliances. Court documents and interviews with scores of industry players suggest that wholesalers also offered bribes to fellow employees, fabricated documents, and coached brokers on how to break the rules. And they weren't alone. Brokers, who work directly with borrowers, altered and shredded documents. Underwriters, the bank employees who actually approve mortgage loans, also skirted boundaries, demanding secret payments from wholesalers to green-light loans they knew to be fraudulent. Some employees who reported misdeeds were harassed or fired. Federal and state prosecutors are picking through the industry's wreckage in search of criminal activity.

There's a Coen brothers movie in this. Yet sadly, as corruption heated up, business-news coverage generally downshifted into what I call service and consumer pieces: warning about the bubble and pointing to patently defective types of mortgage products. Indeed, business-news outlets, to their credit, seemed to fall over themselves to be first (bubble talk appears, surprisingly, as early as the fall of 2001) and/or loudest about calling the end of the bubble: "Is a Housing Bubble About to Burst . . . ?" (*BW*, 7/14/04), for example, or "Boom vs. Bust: The Housing-price Run-up Can't Last . . ." (*WSJ*, 6/14/04).

I don't mean to disparage bubble stories: these were real warnings. *Fortune* might well win the prize, if there were one, for bubble-bursting with "Is the Housing Boom Over?"—4,539 words by Shawn Tully, in September 2004; a year later, in October 2005, Tully answered himself with another five-thousand-plus words, "'I'm Tom Barrack* and I'm getting out,'" about a real estate investor. Meanwhile, the press was also warning consumers not to agree to a mortgage product containing terms that no well-regulated system would allow: "The Ever More Graspable, and Risky, American Dream" (*NYT,* 6/24/04); "ARMed and Dangerous? Adjustable-rate Mortgages Are Pulling in New Home Buyers—But the Risks Are High" (*BW,* 4/12/04).

Indeed, the *Journal* kept after the issue and essentially called these mortgages bad on their face: "For These Mortgages, Downside Comes Later," 10/5/04; "The Prepayment Trap: Lenders Put Penalties on Popular Mortgages," 3/10/05; "Mortgage Lenders Loosen Standards," 7/27/05.

It should be said these usually ran on D1, not A1, and so gave the impression of low-priority bleats from the back of the paper. Even so, there they were, and, so, yes, regulators and lawmakers did have information they could have used had they wanted to. So shame on them. These are valuable stories. But to get the public involved you need more. You need stories of institutionalized corruption. There's no way around it.

I would suggest that in approaching the mortgage story as a consumer or investment story, the business press was trying to fight the Battle of Tarawa with a Swiss Army Knife. What was missing—and needed—were more stories like the one that ran on February 4, 2005, in the *Los Angeles Times* by Mike Hudson and Scot Reckard: "Workers Say Lender Ran 'Boiler Rooms.'"

This was the real thing, a 3,220-word investigation that kicks in the door. It uses court documents and interviews with ex-employees and customers, nothing fancy, to expose Ameriquest, which at the time was one of the nation's leading lenders, "Proud Sponsor of the American Dream" and the 2005 Super Bowl half-time show, and owned by the politically well-connected Roland Arnall, soon to be named U.S. ambassador to the Netherlands:

> Slugging down Red Bull caffeine drinks, sales agents would work the phones hour after hour, he said, trying to turn cold calls into lucrative "sub-prime" mortgages—high-cost loans made to people with spotty credit. The demands were relentless: One manager prowled the aisles between desks like "a little Hitler," Bomchill said, hounding agents to make more calls and push more loans, bragging that he hired and fired people so fast that one worker would be cleaning out his desk as his replacement came through the door.

The *Los Angeles Times*, it's worth pointing out, also probed Ameriquest's attempts to co-opt critics ("Ameriquest's Ties to Watchdog Group Are Tested," 5/22/05), chronicled possible forgery at the lender ("Doubt Is Cast on Loan Papers," 3/28/05), and, crucially, explained how at least 20 percent of all subprime loans were going to prime borrowers, what I call the boiler-room effect ("More Homeowners with Good Credit Getting Stuck with Higher-Rate Loans," 10/24/05). It turns out that the number actually reached more than 50 percent, the *Wall Street Journal* found in December 2007. These all ran at over two thousand words on A1 and helped catalyze a multistate investigation that forced Ameriquest into an embarrassing $325 million settlement the next year.

Clearly, then, such reporting was gettable.

Two years later, the *Journal* published an Ameriquest story ("Lender Lobbying Blitz Abetted Mortgage Mess," 12/31/07), but by then, the lender was closed.

So let's be clear: stories like the *Los Angeles Times*'s Ameriquest probes are the exceptions that prove the rule. And while hand-wringing about the bubble and pointing out defective mortgage products is hard, muckraking about specific, powerful institutions is harder, more useful, and more fun to read:

> Lisa Taylor, a former loan agent at Ameriquest's customer-retention office in Sacramento, said she witnessed documents being altered when she walked in on co-workers using a brightly lighted Coke machine as a tracing board, copying borrowers' signatures on an unsigned piece of paper.

Great, right? If the muckraking story—a straight investigation aimed at the heart of the business model of an industry leader—was scarce in mortgage lending, it was rarer still on Wall Street's end of the mortgage machine. As far as I can tell it was the unicorn of business coverage.

One looks in vain for stories about Wall Street's ties to the subprime industry, even though the Lehman-First Alliance case had outlined it in detail and nearly all the major investment banks would, by the middle of the decade, go on actually to buy their own retail subprime operations (who remembers Bear Stearns Residential?). What was happening was a vast change, a paradigm shift. Citizens did not see it coming. Now we know why.

And a word about head-on investigations of powerful institutions: they're not optional. There is no substitute. The public
needed warnings that the Wall Street–backed lending industry was
running amok. It didn't get them. Remember Lippmann: no facts,
no democracy.

It is disingenuous, I believe, to suggest, as many financial journalists do, that they are unfairly expected to have been soothsayers
in the economic crisis (e.g., "Financial Journalism and Its Critics,"
Robert Teitelman, TheDeal.com, 3/6/09: "Why, among all other
journalists, are financial reporters expected to accurately predict
the future?"). Rather, the expectation is merely that financial outlets do their best to report on *what is happening now*, including, one
would hope, confronting powerful institutions directly about basic
business practices. This is not complicated.

Of course, anyone would applaud the astute and highly skilled
journalists who looked at brewing systemic problems, as did
Bloomberg's David Evans ("Credit Swaps, Some 'Toxic,' May Soar
to $4.8 Trillion," 6/26/03); *BusinessWeek*'s Der Hovanesian ("Taking
Risk to Extremes; Will Derivatives Cause a Major Blowup in the
World's Credit Markets?" 5/23/05); the *Journal*'s Mark Whitehouse
("Slices of Risk: How a Formula Ignited Market That Burned Some
Big Investors," 9/12/05; "Risk Management: As Home Owners Face
Strains, Market Bets on Loan Defaults," 10/31/06), and Gillian
Tett, John Plender, and others at the *Financial Times* (numerous
stories). But even these virtuoso efforts are still not the same as
confronting a Wall Street firm head-on for its role in underwriting
mortgage boiler rooms across the country.

A good place to start would have been Citigroup, apparently,
since Hudson—he of the Ameriquest stories—did it in his spare
time. Freelancing while working full-time for the *Roanoke Times*,
he pulled the cover back on Citigroup's huge subprime operation
in 2003 (!?) and won a Polk Award in the process ("Banking on
Misery: Citigroup, Wall Street and the Fleecing of the South,"
Southern Exposure, summer 2003). He mentions the mortgage af-
termarket only in passing, but that's where the national press can
take over for ground-level reporting. If only.

No reader, not even one really applying herself would have
found adequate warnings about the Wall Street/subprime nexus.
She would instead have found plenty of coverage focused on the
earnings horserace ("Putting the Muscle Back in the Bull; Stan
O'Neal May Be the Toughest—Some Say the Most Ruthless—

CEO in America. Merrill Lynch Couldn't Be Luckier to Have Him," *Fortune*, 4/5/04), personalities ("Rewiring Chuck Prince; Citi's Chief Hasn't Just Stepped Out of Sandy Weill's Shadow— He's Stepped Out of His Own as He Strives to Make Himself into a Leader with Vision," *BW*, 2/20/06), and situated comfortably within frames set by the industry itself ("Joining the Club— Inside Goldman's Secret Rite: The Race to Become Partner," *WSJ*, 10/13/06). I find Lehman and Citi coverage to have been especially poor, again, given what was known by 2003 ("Lehman's New Street Smarts; Under CEO Fuld, the Bond House Has Become a Dealmaking Power," *BW*, 1/19/04; "The Unlikely Revolutionary: Critics Are Sniping and the Stock Is Lagging, but Citigroup's Chuck Prince Keeps Charging Ahead, Blowing Up Business Practices Put in Place by His Famed Mentor, Sandy Weill," *Fortune*, 3/6/06).

Only after the crackup had already begun is Wall Street's role in subprime again laid bare ("Debt Bomb—Lending a Hand: How Wall Street Stoked the Mortgage Meltdown . . . ," *WSJ*, 6/27/07):

> Lehman's deep involvement in the business has also made the firm a target of criticism. In more than 15 lawsuits and in interviews, borrowers and former employees have claimed that the investment bank's in-house lending outlets used improper tactics during the recent mortgage boom to put borrowers into loans they couldn't afford. Twenty-five former employees said in interviews that front-line workers and managers exaggerated borrowers' creditworthiness by falsifying tax forms, pay stubs and other information, or by ignoring inaccurate data submitted by independent mortgage brokers. In some instances, several ex-employees said, brokers or in-house employees altered documents with the help of scissors, tape and Wite-Out.

Suddenly, the story—the one that counts—was gettable again. It referred, after all, to documents available for years. There is really no excuse.

The author of this *Journal* piece, by the way, was Hudson. He left the paper later that year and is writing a book about subprime.

It is true that Bush-era deregulation and the media's financial travails hampered investigative journalism (of course, the *Pittsburgh City Paper* could manage it, but never mind). But the business press also disarmed unilaterally. *CJR*'s study, I believe, provides strong support for the idea that sometime after 2003, as federal regulation folded like a cheap suitcase, the business press institutionally lost whatever taste it had for head-on investigations of core practices of powerful institutions.

Too bad that's precisely what was needed.

In light of this general system failure, what are the lessons for the general reader and the business press itself?

First, the public should be aware—warned, so to be speak—that its interests and those of the business press may not be in perfect alignment. The business press exists within the Wall Street and corporate subculture and understandably must adopt its idioms and customs, the better to translate them for the rest of us. Still, it relies on those institutions for its stories. Burning a bridge is hard. It is far easier for news bureaucracies to accept ever-narrowing frames of discourse, frames forcefully pushed by industry, even if those frames marginalize and eventually exclude the business press's own great investigative traditions.

Second, there's a difference between reporting from an investor's perspective and from a citizen's. The business press is better at the former than the latter, and the gap has only been growing. I would only caution that what's good for investors in the short and medium terms may not be good for anyone over the long haul.

Third, remember the nexus between uncompromised regulation and great journalism.

Fourth, lament the decline of the great business sections of general-circulation dailies, specifically those of the *Los Angeles Times* and the *Washington Post*.

Fifth, seek alternatives. Read *Mother Jones*, or something, once in a while.

Sixth, never, ever underestimate the importance of editorial leadership and news ownership, for in them rests the power to push back against structural conflicts and cultural taboos fostered by industry, to clear a space for business journalism to do the job it is clearly capable of, the one job that really needed doing.

4

THE FINANCIAL PRESS:
IT'S NOT AS BAD AS ITS REPUTATION

Chris Roush

Now is the time for all good journalists to come to the defense of the lowly business reporter, whose reputation continues to be unfairly maligned despite doing a yeoman's job during the first decade of the twenty-first century.

From the *Columbia Journalism Review*'s Dean Starkman, who reviewed thousands of articles to examine what was being written about leading up to the beginning of the economic crisis, to best-selling Swedish fiction writer Stieg Larsson, who wrote in *The Girl with the Dragon Tattoo* that business reporters "were thus either naive and gullible that they ought to be packed off to other assignments, or they were people who quite consciously betrayed their journalism function,"[1] the work of business journalists during the fiscal crisis that gripped the world beginning in 2008 has been picked apart and dissected, blamed for many of our troubles. Business writers should have forewarned us about the imminent bursting of the housing bubble, as well as Wall Street's insatiable appetite for risk, we're told. They should have sounded the alarm bells about derivatives and other speculative investments packaged as top-notch products, the critics add.

Such commentary gives omnipotent powers to the field of business journalism, making it sound as if reporters and editors have the ability to thwart corporate wrongdoing with one article and a couple of well-placed phone calls to regulators. The argument suggests that government agencies take their cues from the media in terms of regulatory enforcement at a time when society's trust of the media is at a record low. And the argument also requires that business reporters be able to predict the cause and extent of future economic calamities.

And the argument is also wrong—business journalism did warn its readers. In fact, the twenty-first century has produced more first-rate business journalism than any other decade since the creation of mass communication. In the years 2001 to 2010, there have been at least three business journalists who won Pulitzer Prizes and countless other stories—in print, online, and broadcast—that have given consumers enough information about what was going on that only those who turned a blind eye to the situation were surprised when housing prices started to fall and companies that invested in mortgage-backed securities began going under. We'll examine this stellar work in the second half of this chapter.

The problem has been that the average consumer has not wanted to understand what the business media were telling them or simply chose to ignore the warning signs. Here's the issue that financial journalism faces: no one likes a nattering nabob of negativism, especially when the stock market is climbing and all of our 401(k) plans are tied to it. So we, the business news consumers, shut out what we don't want to recognize because it conflicts with what we'd like to happen, which will fatten our wallets and our retirement packages.

To be sure, business journalism has not been so prescient that it forewarned loudly and consistently enough to override those who had tuned out. But to blame business journalists for failing to do their job in protecting society from the ills of big business is to set up an argument that turns reporters and editors into all-powerful government officials with unlimited abilities in terms of issuing subpoenas and seizing documents and blames the messenger without addressing what really went wrong. In January 2010, Federal Reserve Board Chairman Ben Bernanke blamed federal regulation, not lax business reporting, for the problems that led to the two-year-old recession.

"It's not we who are charged with taking away the punch bowl," said Marcus Brauchli, the executive editor of the *Washington Post* and a former top editor at the *Wall Street Journal* for much of the first decade of the millennium, in a phone conversation with me in late 2008. Brauchli was one of the editors during the decade who led hard-hitting coverage that asked tough questions about what was going on. "We pointed out the risks for a long period of time. And there were a lot of people in the financial world who knew what the risks were. But the history of manias is that people won't be stopped by the reality of the possibility that they may ultimately get wiped out because the prospect of riches is a powerful attraction."[2]

Reporter Erin Arvedlund's article in the May 7, 2001, issue of *Barron's* is a classic example of what Brauchli is talking about. Her story, "Don't Ask, Don't Tell," questioned the secrecy behind the hedge fund operations of Bernard Madoff. "Some on Wall Street remain skeptical about how Madoff achieves such stunning double-digit returns using options alone," Arvedlund wrote.[3] Her story should have touched off a round of investigations into Madoff's operations, but it failed to arouse the interest of regulators. It wasn't until 2008 that Madoff admitted he had been running nothing more than a scheme to defraud investors, who lost billions.

Unfortunately, the recent criticism of business journalism is nothing new. For most of the past one hundred years, business journalism has been blamed—and rightly so in some cases—for providing weak reporting and analysis that contributed to and caused many of the problems that have confronted the U.S. economy and business world.

In 1938, business journalist Howard Carswell, writing in *The Public Opinion Quarterly*, noted the preponderance of business news that focused on the stock market at a time—the Great Depression—when fewer than 10 percent of all households owned stock. "The New York Stock Exchange is treated as the fountainhead of all news of the business and financial world," he wrote. Carswell called for business news to expand itself to other areas of industry and finance. "Anything within the purview of business affairs should be eligible," he argued. "The editing should be reader-minded and not investor-minded."[4]

Writing in the *Harvard Business Review* in 1950, William Pinkerton noted the strain between business journalists and businessmen at a time when the economy was growing fast. The common complaints of businessmen who do not like the way they get into the news run like this: "The papers never get things right." "You can't trust reporters." "They didn't put in half of what I told them." "They missed the whole point of it." "I didn't say that at all."[5]

Famed investor Gerald M. Loeb, who in 1957 created a series of awards that today are considered the Pulitzer Prizes of the field and that honor the best of business and financial journalism, lamented the quality of business reporting compared to other fields, such as sports and politics, in a 1966 commentary in *Columbia Journalism Review*. Loeb wrote, "Many errors derive from superficial or erroneous reading of basic materials, like annual reports. The other day I saw the annual report of a company that showed earnings per share about the same as the year before. Examination of the footnotes, however, made it clear that had the same accounting been used in both years this company would have been several million in the red in the current reporting period. I rarely see this kind of explanation on the financial pages I read, and I read the best."[6]

Less than a decade later, business journalist Chris Welles, for whom this author worked at *BusinessWeek* in the 1990s, wrote in *Columbia Journalism Review* about the "bleak wasteland of financial journalism." Welles noted in 1973 that "too many business writers are mediocre rejects from other fields of journalism. The few ambitious and imaginative business editors struggle in vain against impassive superiors for more space, more money to hire better reporters. (Lacking any budget for financial news, radio station WCBS in New York recently recruited the editor of *Dun's Review* to give business commentaries in return for ads for his magazine.) Few senior editors willingly permit their careers to be sullied by a tour on the financial desk, which is widely regarded as a dead end."[7]

Two years later, Herbert Stein, former chairman of the President's Council of Economic Advisers, complained about how journalists wrote about the country's economy. "Not only do the media concentrate on the short-term aspects of the economy, they also dramatize them in ways that further exaggerate their performance," said Stein.[8]

In 1980, University of Missouri journalism professor William McPhatter, a former reporter for *BusinessWeek*, quoted an insurance company chairman as stating, "Most of us are fed up with the glib, shallow, inaccurate reporting and editing—tired of journalistic tastes which prefer sensationalism above the fundamentals that allow a Thespian to pose as a newsman. We've had enough crudity and rudeness."[9]

By the fall of 1991, Richard Cheney, chairman emeritus of the public relations firm Hill and Knowlton, changed the tone of criticism to one that took business journalists to task for being too soft on their subjects. "The business pages in the '80s particularly appeared to be written in one dimension, like *Citizen Kane* without Rosebud, sometimes even without last week," he wrote in *Nieman Reports*. "Scoundrels hoodwinked the public and the best of the media too rarely sounded the alarm until it was too late. Indeed, they rooted them on with puffery, detailing, day by day, tender offers and counter-tender offers, breathlessly following the bidding like hicks at Sotheby's. Hardly anybody stepped back to examine the consequences for the country."[10]

Merrill Goozner continued this theme in 2000, writing in *Columbia Journalism Review* that "coverage of the current prosperity can read like a sports page when the home team is on a roll: cheerleading can drown out the occasional story pointing out weaknesses in the squad or the challenges coming up in the schedule. Journalistic scorn is reserved for the players—or in this case stocks—that don't make their numbers."[11]

And by the beginning of the twenty-first century, business journalists were used as target practice, blamed for everything from the tech bubble to the dramatic rise in the stock market to the creation of companies such as Enron and WorldCom, which were allowed to grow into Fortune 500 companies using faulty accounting because reporters and editors were asleep at the wheel. *New York Times* financial writer Diana Henriques put it best when she stated, "I submit that there is no form of ignorance more widely tolerated in the American newsroom than ignorance about business and finance. For some inexplicable reason, it falls outside the category of common knowledge that any literate journalist is expected to possess."[12]

The paradox of increasing criticism of business journalism as the reporting and writing was getting better should be obvious. But it's also easy to understand. The job of business reporters became much more complex and sophisticated during the latter half of the twentieth century, as they were required to understand arcane accounting strategies and read income statements, cash flow statements, and balance sheets in order to fully explain what was going on. That's not an easy job, and some performed better than others. Business news consumers demanded more and more information as interest in the stock market and companies increased due to their growing influence in society, putting more pressure on business journalism to assess and analyze the big picture. But the error mentioned by Loeb—of failing to see the effect of an accounting change on a company's earnings—would not occur today in any respectable business publication.

Past criticism, however, is also not indicative of how journalists covered business and the economy in the twentieth century. It simply paints too broad a stroke. Some of the best journalism of the past one hundred years focused on business. In fact, three of the top six works of journalism in the twentieth century, as selected by New York University judges, focused on business and its negative effect on society—Rachel Carson's exposé of pesticide and chemical companies that were killing animals and plants, Ida Tarbell's exhaustive work in covering the Standard Oil Company, and Lincoln Steffens's examination of how businesses were bribing politicians to get what they wanted in major cities across the country. Other society-changing journalism was also included in the top one hundred, such as Ralph Nader's evisceration of the auto industry and Donald Barlett and James Steele's exhaustive reporting and analysis on the decline of American business for the *Philadelphia Inquirer.* And then there was other top-notch reporting, such as Jessica Mitford's stunning critique of the funeral industry.

Other examples of society-changing business journalism abound. Upton Sinclair's *The Jungle* forced the federal government to begin regulating the meat-packing and other food-related industries. Dozens of articles in the early twentieth century about the dangers facing children working in factories led to laws that put them back in the classroom. In 1952, *Reader's Digest* published stories that exposed the dangers of smoking and the tobacco industry in general. In the 1960s, the *Des Moines Register* printed articles that led Congress to close loopholes in plant inspections that led to diseased meat being packaged and sold in grocery stores. In the 1970s, *Mother Jones* warned consumers about the dangers of the Pinto automobile, which easily exploded if hit from behind. In the 1980s, *Atlanta Journal-Constitution* reporter Bill Dedman uncovered banks redlining, or ignoring, low-income neighborhoods when giving out loans. And in 2000, Houston television station KHOU uncovered the problems with the Firestone tires on Ford SUVs that were leading to dozens of deaths.

Many critics of business journalism would agree that the quality and depth of reporting about business and economics topics have improved dramatically in the past one hundred years—helped partly by the ability to see the tricks and games that companies played in the past before being caught. Despite the fact that many media outlets cut their reporting and editing staffs devoted to business and the economy, journalists in this field—particularly at the top media outlets—have shined in giving consumers the information they needed.

Unfortunately, the twenty-first century did not start well for business journalists. After playing cheerleader to companies, particularly those in the technology and Internet fields, that rode the stock market's rise in the late 1990s, business reporting had plenty of egg on its face after the market dropped and many of those same companies that had been media darlings closed their doors. There was a lot of hand-wringing among business journalists about this predicament, with the focus of the discussion being simply this: how can we improve ourselves and not get sucked in again by the crooks and shysters that sometimes invade the business world? "I was one of the ones that carried on endlessly during the stock bubble period that all of us had failed and that it was shameful," said Allan Sloan, who was the Wall Street editor at *Newsweek* during the first part of the twenty-first century and is now a senior editor at large at *Fortune*, in a phone conversation.[13]

Those lessons were learned. As in many cases where journalism coverage has been too soft before a crisis, the coverage swung to the opposite end of the spectrum. In December 2006—well before the housing bubble burst, leading to the exposure of other problems such as faulty mortgage-backed investments—Harvard Business School professor Gregory S. Miller published a story in the *Journal of Accounting Research* in which he studied 263 cases of accounting fraud. He discovered that the business press wrote about 75—or nearly a third—of these cases before the Securities and Exchange Commission or the company disclosed an investigation into potential impropriety. "Using a sample of firms sanctions by the SEC for accounting malfeasances, I find that the press is involved in early public identification of 29% of the cases," concluded Miller, who later added, "this paper provided evidence regarding the role of the press as a watchdog for accounting fraud."[14]

In fact, the business media appear to be a convenient scapegoat for those who simply want to ignore their own culpability in what went on during the first decade of the twenty-first century. Gone were the flattering CEO profiles and the touting of Internet companies with no revenue. The business media did yeoman work during the past decade-plus to expose the wrongdoings in corporate America. In fact, a review of the top business publications shows that these media blanketed the issues that caused the economic pain, from subprime loans to adjustable-rate mortgages to credit derivatives.

"I take umbrage at the notion that financial journalists have let us down," says Sarah Bartlett, a professor at the City University of New York's Graduate School of Journalism. Bartlett, a former assistant managing editor at *BusinessWeek* and business reporter at the *New York Times*, is emphatic: "I really feel confident that the major business publications have written extensively about the problem that was building up about domestic debt and the lack of savings, the excesses in the subprime markets, and derivatives as a risky venture."[15]

And the signs were there. *Fortune* magazine's Carol Loomis predicted derivatives could be "a villain, or even *the* villain, in some financial crisis that sweeps the world" in 1994. And yes, with some complicated investments, it does take that long to unravel. The *Wall Street Journal*'s aggressive coverage of government-based lenders Fannie Mae and Freddie Mac dates back nearly a decade. In 2004, one piece in the *Journal* compared Fannie Mae to Enron and WorldCom, two companies that crashed and burned the last time business journalists were blamed for an economic downturn. At one point in 2001, Fannie Mae CEO Franklin Raines complained to the paper about its negative coverage.

Back in 2007, under the headline "Mortgages May Be Messier Than You Think," Gretchen Morgenson of the *New York Times* wrote, "As is often the case, only after fiery markets burn out do we see the risks that buyers ignore and sellers play down."[16] Her colleagues Diana Henriques and Floyd Norris exposed shady lending to military personnel and shaky accounting, respectively, during earlier reporting. Steve Pearlstein, who won a Pulitzer Prize for commentary in 2009 for his business columns in the *Washington Post*, has been warning of financial trouble for years. On August 1, 2007, in a column titled "Credit Markets Weight Puts Economy on Shaky Ground," Pearlstein wrote, "This financial engineering has encouraged debt to be piled on debt, making the system more susceptible to a meltdown if credit suddenly becomes more expensive or unavailable."[17]

For those who don't read newspapers and magazines, investigative business journalist Gary Weiss exposed the seedy underbelly of Wall Street in his 2006 book *Wall Street Versus America: A Muckraking Look at the Thieves, Fakes and Charlatans Who Are Ripping You Off.* The title pretty much sums it up.

Although business news coverage often struggles to explain to readers the significance of what's going on, writers such as Morgenson and Pearlstein provided columns and articles that avoided the jargon found in some business journalism. Their work was written in language that is simple and clear enough for anyone to understand that trouble was brewing in the economy and on Wall Street. And these are just a few examples to show that regular readers of the business media were warned of the coming problems.

The current economic crisis and Wall Street turmoil have been caused by what's been going on in the housing market. In a bid to encourage continuing growth, lenders extended vast amounts of credit to home buyers, who might not have qualified for a loan previously. They then sold many of those loans to investors to get them off their books, allowing them to go out and push more questionable loans. The investments were called credit derivatives. The investors thought they were buying loans that had been properly vetted by the lenders, but they hadn't been.

Meanwhile, many home buyers were unaware of the terms of the contracts they were signing. Others were speculating in the real estate market, purchasing homes they simply wanted to flip to another buyer for a higher price.

A market based on rickety credit, fraud, and speculation can grow for only so long. Regulators from the Federal Reserve Board to the Securities and Exchange Commission kept it going for as long as possible by relaxing some of their regulations on lending and debt. When the real estate market started to fall, loans that had been sold to investors began to sour, and derivatives that lenders such as Fannie Mae had purchased as investments to protect themselves against higher interest rates led to more risk on their balance sheets than they could handle.

That led to the situation today, where the federal government has pumped $700 billion into the economy and billions more into these companies to avert another depression like the one in the 1930s.

If we examine the business media before spring 2007, when the first cracks began to appear in housing and investments, we find a mountain of coverage on these issues and topics. It would be easy to quote some of these articles and say the business press did its job, but that's too simple an analysis.

We need to examine the influential business media—the *Wall Street Journal*, the business sections of the *New York Times* and *Washington Post*, and business magazines such as *BusinessWeek* and *Fortune*. These are the media with the power to carry the conversation. Readers—from investors to regulators to company executives—who care about business and the economy read these publications.

Readers saying they weren't warned about risks in the housing and derivatives markets defies reality. The record shows that these media outlets, the business media influencers, were all over the story. Some, such as the *Journal* and *Fortune*, wrote and rewrote about the problems.

A fair number of smaller publications around the country, such as the *Charlotte Observer* in North Carolina, which ran a series about an unscrupulous lender in its market that caused the company to stop making loans and exit the area, were also on the story. In fact, eleven winners in the most recent Society of American Business Editors and Writers' annual Best in Business contest—for coverage from 2007—focused on the mortgage mess or credit problems.

Before we look at some examples of the coverage, it's important to note that those cited in this chapter are not the only articles written warning about the increased risk in the markets—both stock and real estate. The coverage was voluminous.

Let's start with the *Wall Street Journal*, considered the top business newspaper in the country, if not the world. Brauchli returned to the States after reporting in China and immediately began overseeing the paper's coverage of government-backed housing lenders Fannie Mae and Freddie Mac, two of the largest lenders. The first page-one story questioning the lenders' practices ran on July 14, 2000.[18] Brauchli was called to Fannie Mae's headquarters in 2001 to meet with CEO Franklin Raines, who was upset about the tone of the articles.

The *Journal* wrote repeatedly about the lenders, hammering away at the excesses it uncovered. And many of these stories appeared on the front page. On January 2, 2002, reporter Jathon Sapsford wrote about the dramatic increase in consumer lending.[19] On August 6 of the same year, reporter Patrick Barta followed up with a 2,400-word examination of Fannie and Freddie that asked, "With homeownership already so high, are Fannie and Freddie running out of room to grow?" In the fifth paragraph, he wrote, "The huge size and rapid growth, coupled with their concentration in a single industry, has brought concern about possible risk to the U.S. economy should one of them ever fail."[20]

A month later, on September 17, 2002, Barta was on the front page of the *Journal*'s Money & Investing section, noting the increased risk on Fannie's financial statements because of falling interest rates.[21] On August 19, 2003, Barta and fellow reporter Ruth Simon wrote a front-page story on the hidden closing costs behind mortgages.[22]

And a month later, a 3,000-word time bomb on Freddie appeared on the *Journal*'s front page, written by Barta, John D. McKinnon, and Gregory Zuckerman. They wrote: "Far from the sleepy mortgage company of its carefully cultivated reputation, Freddie Mac in recent years has evolved into a giant, sophisticated investment company, running a business laden with volatility and complexity. That change has sent risks soaring, not just for investors, but for U.S. taxpayers, who likely would be on the hook if the federally chartered company stumbled."[23]

Stories about the increasing risk in the real estate market appeared regularly in the *Journal* for the next four years until the market imploded. A May 2005 front-page story looked at home owners taking on too much debt to buy real estate.[24] An August 2005 front-page story examined the fact that lenders were selling more mortgages because investors wanted the securities that backed them.[25] James Hagerty wrote a front-page story on March 11, 2006, about dangers of adjustable-rate mortgages.[26] In December 2006, a front-page article about the increase of delinquent subprime mortgages appeared, noting: "If late payments and foreclosures continue to rise at a faster-than-expected pace, the pain could extend beyond homeowners and lenders to the investors who buy mortgage-backed securities."[27]

Another *Journal* reporter, Jesse Eisinger, was writing extensively about derivatives during this same time. And after switching over to work for Condé Nast *Portfolio*, Eisinger repeatedly wrote about how derivatives might cause turmoil on Wall Street, going as far as to predict in a cover story that Bear Stearns and Lehman Brothers would struggle to remain independent.[28] One went out of business, while the other was sold.

Nik Deogun, a former deputy managing editor of the *Journal* and now managing editor at CNBC, said the coverage intentionally repeated itself in an attempt to hammer home the point. "People may not have heard you, so you have to explore different angles to tell the same story a different way," he said to me in 2008. "I'm kind of curious as to . . . why [it is] that people were shocked, given the volume of coverage."[29]

The *Times* and the *Post* were offering similar warnings. In the *Times* on Sunday, October 3, 2004, a story by Morgenson was titled "A Coming Nightmare of Homeownership?" High up in the story, Morgenson wrote, "The most damaging legacy of Fannie Mae's years of unchecked growth may not be evident until the next significant economic slump."[30] When she wasn't writing about housing, Morgenson was also detailing the continued excesses of executive compensation and the credit markets. Alongside Morgenson's story was another one on Fannie Mae, by Timothy L. O'Brien and Jennifer 8. Lee, that said, "If the company encounters serious setbacks, the impact on homeowners and the world's financial markets could be unpleasant."[31]

Henriques of the *Times* followed at the end of the year with an exposé of lenders preying on military households, pushing high-cost loans with interest rates much higher than the norm. Three weeks later, on December 29, 2004, she had a story about how veterans were signing over their military pensions to receive a loan.[32] In this instance, there was a regulatory reaction to the business media coverage: congressional hearings were held, and laws were passed banning such practices.

Henriques believes she knows why regulators paid attention to her stories but ignored others about lending practices that were far worse because they were hurting investment portfolios. A friend who works for a big institutional investor was called to Washington, DC, to speak to lawmakers before the first bailout vote. The friend noticed that all of their offices had TVs tuned to what was happening in the House and the Senate, not to CNBC or Fox Business Network. "We wrote about the deregulation of the markets," she said. "We wrote about the risk of predatory lending. We wrote about the galloping Wall Street stampede into derivatives. We wrote about the lack of transparency in derivatives trading. What didn't happen was a reaction within the regulatory and legislative realm. We don't have handcuffs. We don't have subpoenas. We can't stop this stuff."[33]

And then there's Norris, whose coverage of accounting rules during this time now looks prescient. Time after time after time, he wrote about how companies, including Fannie Mae, were pushing regulators to relax standards or push the envelope as far as they could, just a few years after Enron manipulated accounting regulations all the way into bankruptcy court.

Pearlstein at the *Washington Post* was hammering away as well. As least someone noticed Pearlstein's work: he won a 2008 Pulitzer Prize in commentary—the first ever given to a business columnist—for a series of columns about the impending economic turmoil.

These reporters weren't alone. Their colleagues at the glossy business magazines were digging into these issues and coming up with some alarming stories as well.

Shawn Tully at *Fortune* raised serious questions about the housing market as far back as October 2002, when he wrote, "U.S. housing prices are stretching the outer limits of what's reasonable and sustainable. Instead of cooling down, prices keep hurtling upward, defying the laws of economic gravity just as grievously as those unmentionable dot-coms once did."[34]

In September 2004, Tully was back with a big story. The headline blared, "Is the Housing Boom Over?" The article stated, "Housing prices have gone up for so long that people think they'll never come down. But the fundamentals tell a different story—a scary one."[35] And in July 2005, Tully offered advice for how people near retirement could get the most from selling their house in the "overheated real estate market."[36] In May 2006, Tully wrote about the beginning of the decline of the housing market.[37]

Not to be outdone by her colleague, *Fortune*'s Bethany McLean—one of the first to expose Enron's problems—wrote two stories highly critical of Fannie Mae in early 2005.[38] And then there's Loomis's near-famous story—the magazine trotted it out in mid-2008 and put it back on its home page—about derivatives from 1994.[39]

At rival *BusinessWeek*, banking and finance editor Mara Der Hovanesian—now at the *Financial Times*—hammered away as well. Her September 22, 2006, cover story, "How Toxic Is Your Mortgage?" showed a snake slowly squeezing the life out of a home and covered the gamut from deceptive loan practices to investors willing to buy risky loan portfolios.[40] The previous year, Der

Hovanesian wrote about credit derivatives, essentially warning about a credit meltdown. "Surprises similar to Enron and WorldCom— large, investment-grade companies that fall from grace overnight— could roil markets," she said in a May 2005 story.[41]

An April 2006 Der Hovanesian piece titled "Mortgage Lenders: Who's Most at Risk?" exposed the subprime lending problems likely to face many finance companies.[42] A June 2006 *BusinessWeek* cover story by Emily Thornton raised general warnings about the crazy embrace of risk across Wall Street.[43] And smaller stories about the potential for problems were appearing in the magazine regularly.

A senior financial editor at Bloomberg told me to go back and look at a June 27, 2005, story in *BusinessWeek* written by Dean Foust and Peter Coy. The story, he said, read in retrospect as if the business journalists had traveled into the future and then back again to tell readers what to look out for. The story, titled "Housing: The Mortgage Trap," included such sentences as, "In the process, banks and mortgage companies appear to be taking on more risk than ever before—and if rates rise sharply or prices tumble, many of their customers could find themselves in deep trouble, too," and "at the same time, lenders are extending far more loans to borrowers who have had credit problems in the past."[44] In a sidebar, Coy pointed out that certain metro areas—San Diego, Atlanta, San Francisco, Denver, and Oakland—were prime candidates for the housing bubble to burst first because they were where interest-only mortgages, where payments could balloon as much as 50 percent, were most prevalent.[45]

This senior Bloomberg editor was apparently one of just a handful of people who remembered the story five years later. And some of the country's top business journalists worry about their craft because of the lack of attention paid to the voluminous coverage of problems in the housing market spilling over into Wall Street. (In the case of daily newspapers, many have cut their stand-alone business sections because advertising has declined.) If the general public and regulators didn't notice the warnings they were emitting regularly in the past five-plus years, then will they ever notice? "Like most people, I don't have a particular interest in sub-prime mortgages," said financial writer Gary Weiss. "You mention subprime to most people, and their eyes glaze over. But for beat reporters, if they were covering consumer affairs, they know there was predatory lending and they covered predatory lending. And if they covered banks, they wrote about subprime lending. But these articles are not popular."[46]

Andrew Leckey, director of the Donald W. Reynolds National Center for Business Journalism at Arizona State University, compares the coverage to a bad Christmas present that's wrapped up in shiny paper and a bow. Nobody wants to open the present to see what's inside. The reading public wants to read only what it wants to believe. Brauchli agrees: "The notion that the business press wasn't paying attention is wrong, and the assertion that we were asleep at the switch is wrong. We were attentive. We were aggressive. We were aware. We wrote abundantly. But it is very hard to get the public's attention for stories warning of complex financial risks in the middle of a roaring, populist bull market."[47]

In other words, it's time to stop blaming business journalism for its inability to tell us precisely when to get out of the stock market or when to sell our homes. If business journalists could predict such things, they wouldn't be reporters and editors. They'd be multimillionaires.

Of course, mistakes were made. There were just as many stories that spoke about the positive aspects of predatory lending and derivatives as the examples that warned of their dangers. But let's think about that for a moment. Isn't it the job of a journalist to present both sides of a story and to let the public—whether it's investors, regulators, or consumers—decide what they want to believe? Just as many reporters banged their fists in warning, claiming that the sky was falling, as those who saw nothing but sunshine.

Henriques, who grades the coverage from the print business media as a B+ to an A in providing ample warning about the housing and credit markets, believes that business journalists can do one thing to sound the alarm even louder: connect the dots more clearly between Washington policy—or the lack thereof—and how Wall Street operates.

The strong coverage, however, continued through the crisis. In 2009 alone, the Pulitzer Prize selection committee picked five finalists in various categories that produced coverage related to the economy. The *New York Times* was lauded in the public service category for "its comprehensive coverage of the economic meltdown of 2008, setting a standard for depth and sophistication while making the arcane world of finance and banking accessible to an often bewildered public." Robert O'Harrow Jr. and Brady Dennis of the

Washington Post were finalists in the explanatory reporting category, in which the judges noted "their vivid, richly documented explanation of why AIG, the insurance industry giant, nearly collapsed and what lessons the crisis holds for the nation's policymakers." In national reporting, the *Wall Street Journal* staff was praised for "its highly detailed coverage of the collapse of America's financial system, explicating key decisions, capturing the sense of calamity and charting the human toll," while columnist Paul Krugman of the *New York Times* was a finalist in the commentary category for "his prophetic columns on economic peril during a year of financial calamity, blending the scholarly knowledge of a distinguished economist with the skill of a wordsmith." In editorial writing, Charles Lane of the *Post* was a finalist for "his succinct and insightful editorials on the nation's economic collapse, zeroing in on problems and offering solutions with a steady voice of reason."[48] In no other year has one topic dominated the Pulitzer finalists.

Despite the strong reporting about business and the economy, I worry about future coverage. Most mainstream media outlets have reduced their coverage of business and the economy. Even some of the publications mentioned in this chapter, such as *Fortune*, have downsized and cut back on the number of issues they'll publish. The fear is that fewer stories—particularly investigative stories— will get published. Daily newspapers have virtually given up on aggressive, hard-hitting business journalism by eliminating their business sections and chunks of their business news desks.

Those fears are soothed by the growth of nontraditional business media such as blogs and Web sites, which seem to be taking up the slack. Matt Taibbi's 2009 writing in *Rolling Stone*, of all places, about Goldman Sachs shows that hard-hitting business journalism can appear anywhere.[49] In addition, wire services such as Reuters and Bloomberg have remained strong and have added staff. Reuters created in 2009 a team of reporters and editors to do investigative work, and the Associated Press produced an ambitious series of stories spanning five weeks examining how the economic meltdown and the Great Recession have changed everything from Wall Street to Main Street.

Let me end by noting that business journalism did its job well during the years leading up to the economic crisis because it forced one family—mine—to take a hard look at its savings and retirement plans well before the market crashed. And when the market fell, more than half of my family's savings was in cash and money market accounts, not stocks.

We'd read too many stories warning us that there was too much risk in the market and that something was going to have to change soon. Unlike a lot of other people, we reacted to the warnings that we'd read.

5

MISSING THE MOMENT

Ryan Chittum

The press, like so many of our institutions, fell short in the years leading up to the worst financial crisis in eighty years. Predatory lenders ran amok and were fed by a Wall Street machine that soaked up profits by soaking borrowers. And the press, with notable exceptions, looked the other way.

Media coverage after the crisis commenced was better than in the years before it, in part because of the reactive nature of the press: the stories were largely already out there. Millions of Americans were losing their homes. A breaking-news story like the collapse of Wall Street in September 2008 showed the press at its finest, covering the story aggressively while not furthering a panic, all while imparting to readers the historic import of what was unfolding.

But what's most important is not what happened in September 2008; it's what had happened in the years leading up to the collapse and what's being done about it. What were the conditions that caused it? Who did what to whom and why? On that crucial front, press coverage was less than successful, resulting in the ability of someone like CNBC's Rick Santelli to spark a popular uprising blaming neighbors rather than bankers. If the press had really told the story of the predatory lending and the machine behind it, such an argument would have gained far less traction.

As the *Columbia Journalism Review*'s Dean Starkman (my editor) put it in an essay pointedly titled "Boiler Room" in September 2008—the month Wall Street melted down—was this a natural disaster or was it a crime scene?[1]

> David Brooks, George Will, and other cultural conservatives—let's call them behavioralists—have felt free to blame the unraveling of the financial system on some sort of spontaneous mass deterioration of public morals. Structuralists like myself, meanwhile, argue that people didn't change, the marketplace did. Most journalists, I would argue, retreat to the mushy middle: the there-is-plenty-of-blame-to-go-around school, a theory of more generalized cultural decay that includes undisciplined lenders as well as irresponsible borrowers.

> The trouble with this debate is that all the evidence is on my side. All they have is lazy musings about Woodstock and tattoos. This argument should be over by now, and I honestly believe if these cultural commentators (and everyone else) had better information, it would be.

That a wide swath of public opinion could blame borrowers for defective mortgages—and it was hardly just conservatives making such arguments—points to serious press failures in digging out and explaining critical components of the crisis. For the media, coverage often implied or directly stated that the whole thing was beyond anyone's control.

The natural-phenomenon presentation was taken to its absurd epitome by one of the most widely praised journalistic accounts of the crisis, *Too Big to Fail*, a book by the *New York Times*'s Andrew Ross Sorkin.[2] A six-hundred-plus-page Great Men of History account of executives (and former executives like Treasury Secretary Henry Paulson) scrambling to save Wall Street in the dark days of 2008, it hardly pauses to point out that its stars, like Lehman Brothers CEO Dick Fuld, were instrumental in creating the very mess they were scrambling to clean up. It's a wholly Wall Street–centric view of the world, presented with hardly a nod toward placing these views in context—like talking to the criminals for a heist story and skipping the victims and police.

Too Big to Fail exemplified a critical issue in journalism: all beat reporting has an access problem. The pressure to deliver news and inside information is at odds with the imperative to cover powerful institutions and their leaders without fear or favor. Governments and businesses use the promise of access to prevent reporters from writing too negatively. To do so is to risk losing access to inside information, getting scooped, and being unable to fully perform one's job.

If anything, access is a bigger problem when covering business, which isn't subject to open-records laws or electoral pressure and has more money to create lobbying, marketing, and public relations campaigns that flood the system with its message.

Coverage is tilted toward how businesses' actions affect their stocks or other corporations' businesses. This is the financial version of the horse race predilection of the political press. Corporate impact on society, consumers, or the company's employees is primarily an afterthought. Of course, the business press is primarily read by businesspeople. It has to write for that audience. But the press shortchanges its business readers by not reporting well on the conditions affecting their customers—and how these businesses' decisions affect them. The run-up to the recent crisis is a perfect example of this, when the hollowness of the economic expansion wasn't fully explored. And while the press has upped its efforts in the wake of the crash, it's still missing some of the root causes.

Let me say upfront: examples of great work can be found in areas the press has covered poorly, just as bad work populates areas it has covered well. The criticism that follows here isn't to say that *all* coverage is one or the other. It's easier to find perfectly fine stories than demonstrably wrong ones, especially in the top tier of the financial press. But the hardest part of journalism is the picking of priorities. A news organization can only cover so much. What was left out or under-covered is as much a part of the story of how the press performed as what made the papers.

Moreover, the financial difficulties of the press itself should not be forgotten when assessing its coverage. At a time when it could least afford it, the press not only was hit by the plunging economy but also by a secular decline in the business itself—one that shows no signs of turning around and which poses an existential threat to its once-mighty institutions. It's impossible to tell what the coverage would have been like with a healthy fourth estate, but it surely would have been much better.

At the same time, the very idea of "the press," as understood at the time of the last stock market crash, which bottomed just five years before the current crisis began, had changed irrevocably in the interim. The Web, which pulled the plug on the old business models, and which was in its infancy during the tech bubble, gave rise to new sources of information that enabled readers to hear from and talk directly to expert sources, to become presenters of information themselves, challenging the fusty conventions of just-the-facts-ma'am journalism and injecting a new dynamism into the public conversation.

The story of how the press covered the crisis is still unfolding, as is the financial wreckage itself.

There's no precise start date for the credit crisis; you can take your pick. Housing started to decline in 2006. Spreads on soon-to-be-infamous credit default swaps were widening early in 2007. Hiccups in the credit markets started appearing in the spring. New Century Financial, a giant subprime lender, went bankrupt in April. But the collapse of two Bear Stearns hedge funds in the early summer signaled that the fallout from subprime would not be "contained," as Federal Reserve Chairman Ben Bernanke had predicted that March.

Reporter Matthew Goldstein's groundbreaking *BusinessWeek* story in May 2007 showed that Bear was trying to unload the funds' subprime securities onto an unsuspecting public via a stock IPO announced a few days earlier, a scandal that had gone unnoticed by the rest of the press, and a glimpse at the bucket-shop mentality that prevailed among the banks.[3] Three weeks later, the *Financial Times* finally picked up on the story,[4] and markets shuddered as the *Wall Street Journal* reported in mid-June that Bear Stearns was scrambling to sell its subprime securities as their prices collapsed.[5] The first Wall Street domino was set to fall.

Frustratingly, the press periodically did outstanding work but failed to follow up thoroughly enough to change the narrative.

The *Journal*'s "Debt Bomb" series, for instance, in the summer of 2007 still stands as some of the best reportage on the causes of the crisis. Michael Hudson wrote an all-too-rare story tying Lehman Brothers and Wall Street directly to the subprime mortgage industry, noting that "Wall Street firms helped create the mess by throwing so much money at the market that lenders had a growing incentive to push through shaky loans and mislead borrowers," which hit the core of what had gone wrong.[6] Ruth Simon and James R. Hagerty wrote about the broker boiler rooms that conned borrowers,[7] and Greg Ip and Jon E. Hilsenrath wrote the following in August, as part of a story examining the roots of the easy credit that fed the bubble:

> The financial system has absorbed the latest shock.
>
> So far. But credit problems once seen as isolated to a few subprime-mortgage lenders are beginning to propagate across markets and borders in unpredicted ways and degrees. A system designed to distribute and absorb risk might, instead, have bred it, by making it so easy for investors to buy complex securities they didn't fully understand. And the interconnectedness of markets could mean that a sudden change in sentiment by investors in all sorts of markets could destabilize the financial system and hurt economic growth.[8]

That December, a fourth story, by Carrick Mollenkamp and Serena Ng, told the tale of an especially toxic collateralized debt obligation (CDO) called "Norma" created by the hedge fund Magnetar.[9] The press would blow this story wide open—nearly two-and-a-half years later—when ProPublica's Jesse Eisinger and Jake Bernstein showed how Magnetar's bid to short housing perversely, and nearly single-handedly, kept the bubble inflating longer than it would have.[10]

If you happened to read these four *Journal* stories—which were printed months apart—in isolation, you would have a good start on understanding the root causes of the financial crisis. But amidst the wave of words written, how many truly remember such work? The press has done a decent job in the three years since explaining the Ip and Hilsenrath easy-credit story but a poor one of investigating the Wall Street–boiler room nexus that implemented what happened in the neighborhoods.

This was particularly evident when the press presented home owners as being just as culpable for the housing bubble and fraud as the financial institutions that aggressively lent to them.

*   *   *

Plenty of stories have focused on the huge amount of debt piled onto households in the last thirty years. But relatively few of them focus on why households took on so much debt in the first place. The conditions of the crisis were created by the decades-long struggles of the middle and working classes, which became especially acute in the Bush years. As Wall Street fired up its money-making machine in the middle part of the last decade, churning out subprime mortgages at a torrid pace in 2005 and 2006, real median incomes were stagnating, lower in 2006—which, remember, was supposedly a boom year—than they had been at the start of the decade. Americans were borrowing more in an attempt to stay afloat. In the backdrop, the incredible amounts of wealth flowing to the very top concentrated wealth and power in the hands of a few in ways not seen since the twenties.

Whether concerned about class warfare or liberal bias, the press all-too-infrequently made explicit the deteriorating financial condition of the average American family. The ideology of Wall Street—the deregulatory, business-knows-best mantras—had so infiltrated it that talk of an oligarchy still smacked of class warfare even while bankers, whose machinations had sent nearly 9 million Americans to the unemployment lines in two years, were back at the trough in 2009 paying themselves record or near-record bonuses, and three years into the crisis, Congress couldn't find the wherewithal to institute basic financial reform.

Occasionally the truth peeked through, and sometimes from nontraditional business-news sources, as it did when an establishment figure, the former chief economist of the International Monetary Fund, Simon Johnson, wrote a compelling piece for the *Atlantic* in May 2009 called "The Quiet Coup," in which he describes a finance industry with its hands around the throat of the country:

> Elite business interests—financiers, in the case of the U.S.—played a central role in creating the crisis, making ever-larger gambles, with the implicit backing of the government, until the inevitable collapse. More alarming, they are now using their influence to prevent precisely the sorts of reforms that are needed, and fast, to pull the economy out of its nosedive. The government seems helpless, or unwilling, to act against them.
>
> Top investment bankers and government officials like to

lay the blame for the current crisis on the lowering of U.S. interest rates after the dotcom bust or, even better—in a "buck stops somewhere else" sort of way—on the flow of savings out of China. Some on the right like to complain about Fannie Mae or Freddie Mac, or even about longer-standing efforts to promote broader homeownership. And, of course, it is axiomatic to everyone that the regulators responsible for "safety and soundness" were fast asleep at the wheel.

But these various policies—lightweight regulation, cheap money, the unwritten Chinese-American economic alliance, the promotion of homeownership—had something in common. Even though some are traditionally associated with Democrats and some with Republicans, they all benefited the financial sector.[11]

Johnson sounded like a radical for speaking the obvious truth.

Why don't you put up a website to have people vote on the Internet as a referendum to see if we really want to subsidize the losers' mortgages or would we like to at least buy cars and buy houses in foreclosure and give them to people that might have a chance to actually prosper down the road and reward people that can carry the water instead of drink the water?

—CNBC on-air editor Rick Santelli[12]

When CNBC on-air editor Rick Santelli exploded on television in February 2009, the housing bust was in its fourth year. At the time, stocks had crashed by half just since October 2007, and Americans were losing their jobs by the hundreds of thousands every month. The government had bailed out Citigroup, AIG, Bear Stearns, Goldman Sachs, and a host of other mega corporations. But what got Santelli going was a modest proposal to help struggling home owners.

Santelli and many others missed the whole epidemic of fraudulent inducement that overtook mortgage lending in the middle of the decade. The point is, if you have someone—a bank, no less—telling you that you are eligible for a $425,000 mortgage that will be your entrée into the middle class—and anyway, if you can't afford it, you can sell it in a few months and make $50,000—you're going to take that deal. You have less information than the other

side. All you know is they must know what they're doing. This
is the very definition of predatory lending: when one side has so
much more information than another that it tricks people into
making decisions contrary to their own interest.

This blame-the-home-owners anger hadn't come from no-
where. The press enabled it—and indeed, fed it, in many cases—by
not aggressively reporting on the predatory roots of the housing
crisis—one of the great press failures of the last few years. (There
were exceptions that prove the rule: Mara Der Hovanesian's
BusinessWeek story, for instance, on how the frenzy for subprime
loans to package and sell devolved into sexual favor trading, was
excellent).[13] Stories about home owners "trashing out" their homes
competed with those about banks and brokers trashing home owners. Borrower fraud got a disproportionate amount of column
inches compared to lender fraud.

In no small part this is because of the failures of regulators
and prosecutors to aggressively investigate the scandals. But that's
no excuse. How many faithful readers of the business press knew
that Citigroup was built from the ground up on a subprime foundation? How many had heard much about Ameriquest, settler of
two massive class action suits for its predatory lending to hundreds
of thousands of borrowers that included "hefty upfront charges,
interest rates that were higher than promised by nine-tenths of a
percentage point or more, and loans with variable rates when fixed
rates were promised," and who "deceived borrowers, falsified loan
documents and pressured appraisers to overstate home values"?[14]

How many knew that the Bush administration gutted protec-
tions from predatory lenders with rules that superseded tough state
laws? How many knew that the subprime boiler rooms were not
just financed by Wall Street, but in many cases *owned* by them?
The top fifteen subprime lenders included names like Citigroup,
Washington Mutual, JPMorgan Chase, Wells Fargo, General
Electric, Lehman Brothers, and HSBC. The Center of Public
Integrity reported that of the twenty-five biggest subprime lenders, twenty-one received bailout funds. How many knew that at
the peak of the bubble, some 55 percent of borrowers who got subprime loans were eligible for lower-interest prime ones?[15]

That last fact is particularly interesting—and disappointing—
because it came from an excellent enterprise story by Rick Brooks
and Ruth Simon in the *Wall Street Journal* in December 2007,
which spelled out what it meant:

The analysis also raises pointed questions about the practices of major mortgage lenders. Many borrowers whose credit scores might have qualified them for more conventional loans say they were pushed into risky subprime loans. They say lenders or brokers aggressively marketed the loans, offering easier and faster approvals—and playing down or hiding the onerous price paid over the long haul in higher interest rates or stricter repayment terms.[16]

It's the kind of story that could have been a turning point in coverage. But it wasn't. That core fact—prima facie evidence of the corruption that fueled the bubble and Wall Street profits—is barely known. The *Journal* itself explored the issue just one other time.

Even when excellent subsequent stories delved into related matters, that revealing *Journal* statistic rarely showed up, illustrating a larger problem with connecting the dots of this sprawling, complex story.

The *Seattle Times*, for instance, wrote about hometown predator Washington Mutual a year after its demise without taking into account the *Journal*'s previous reporting:

> The worse the terms were for borrowers, the more WaMu paid the brokers.
>
> A WaMu daily rate sheet obtained by the *Seattle Times* shows how lavish the rewards could be. On an option ARM, WaMu would reward brokers as much as 3 percent of the loan amount—more than triple the standard commission at the time.
>
> Brokers would get an additional point—1 percent of the loan—for roughly every half-point in higher interest the borrower paid. So the broker would get 3 percent of the loan if he could get the borrower to pay 1.5 percent above the market rate.[17]

The inability to connect dots—to tie, for example, high broker compensation for subprime loans to the fact that many potentially prime customers were put in them—is not a simple problem to fix. Reporters have always faced pressure to produce bylines, and with the industry in freefall, this pressure only increased. At the same time, the amount of information to sift through has become exponentially greater.

And there are other roadblocks. One institutional barrier that helps prevent broad overviews is beat reporting itself, which tends to "silo" reporters in a sliver of the world. The housing reporter can't encroach on the bank reporter's turf and vice versa. The SEC reporter can't step on the Fed reporter's territory or the bond reporter on the corporate reporter's beat. It takes wise, creative, and aggressive leadership management to overcome this, and editors must take the greater part of any blame for their reporters failing to connect the dots.

Even when it succeeds in doing so, the press's instinct is to dig up a story, run it, and move on to the next one. But one-off stories rarely leave a large impact. Real change usually takes a drumbeat of reporting that pounds critical information into the collective consciousness, forcing the powers that be to act.

The resistance to be seen taking a side, even when reporting leads to a conclusion on what is factual, shackles the power of the press to effect change. Here's the *Seattle Times*'s kicker on its Washington Mutual series:

> Meanwhile, the FBI is investigating whether Washington Mutual executives broke criminal laws by deceiving shareholders about the bank's health. As for now, there is no known federal investigation under way for deceiving borrowers.

And, sad to say, even after that story, there still isn't.

Gretchen Morgenson of the *New York Times* understands the drumbeat phenomenon better than just about any mainstream journalist and deployed the method long before the housing market imploded—hammering on issues like excessive executive compensation. Unsurprisingly, Morgenson put out some of the most important work of any journalist on the collapse of the financial system.

Just a week into the meltdown of September 2008—in one of the great journalistic coups of the crisis—Morgenson wrote about how the government's rescue of AIG had also bailed out its counterparties, including Goldman Sachs:

> Although it was not widely known, Goldman, a Wall Street stalwart that had seemed immune to its rivals' woes, was A.I.G.'s largest trading partner, according to six people close to the insurer who requested anonymity because of confidentiality agreements. A collapse of the insurer threatened

to leave a hole of as much as $20 billion in Goldman's side, several of these people said.

Days later, federal officials, who had let Lehman die and initially balked at tossing a lifeline to A.I.G., ended up bailing out the insurer for $85 billion.[18]

Another reporter, Mark Pittman of Bloomberg, was on the story as well, pushing it forward the next day:

> "It was the biggest crisis ever—if you're an investment bank," said Joshua Rosner, a managing director at investment research firm Graham Fisher & Co. in New York. "We didn't just save AIG. We saved the counterparties, the banks. It's true that it would have been a disaster, but it would have been a disaster for them."[19]

This would turn into one of the key stories of the bailouts—one that raised serious questions about the cozy relationship between Wall Street and Washington. It's unclear if it would have emerged without Morgenson's and Pittman's work.

Time and again, important stories emerged from a handful of great journalists who demonstrated the primacy of investigative journalism: Morgenson and Pittman, Kate Kelly, Matthew Goldstein, Jesse Eisinger, Mara Der Hovanesian. Reporter/commentators like Jonathan Weil of Bloomberg and Gillian Tett of the *Financial Times* were indispensable. What did they all have in common? Their writing, at least, conveyed a palpable sense of right and wrong—that enormous injustices had been committed and that it was possible to find out who did them, rather than shrug their shoulders and accept the "everybody screwed up equally" line favored in some precincts of the press.

For instance, Pittman had adroitly traced Henry Paulson's role in creating the very subprime mortgage securities he later condemned as treasury secretary, noting that on his watch Goldman had created $37 billion in subprime CDOs.[20] You only do that story if you're on the lookout for hypocrisy. It was *wrong* for Paulson to try to act like he was blameless. While the sophisticates rolled their eyes and said "everyone is to blame," Pittman went to work and wrote some accountability journalism.

The *Wall Street Journal*'s Kate Kelly, who had written a memorable 2007 ticktock on the Bear Stearns collapse that revealed its septuagenarian CEO to be a dope-smoking, bridge-playing

Neroesque figure as his firm imploded,[21] made a major contribution to the Goldman story line early on. She showed how the company profited by creating toxic securities, selling them to its customers, and then betting against them—what Phil Angelides, head of the namesake commission, later compared to "selling a car with faulty brakes and then buying an insurance policy on the buyer of those cars."[22] For a *Wall Street Journal* story, particularly, it fairly bristled with this-is-wrong.

Pittman, with whom I became friends in the months before he died in November 2009, spoke derisively about stories that didn't have "moral force" and used his background as both a former police reporter and a self-taught bond expert to sniff out groundbreaking stories, winning a couple of Loeb awards in the process. In June 2007, he exposed how the ratings agencies were covering up subprime losses on CDOs, helping force them a week later to finally begin the downgrades that commenced the crisis in earnest.[23] His Goldman stories were crucial.

And Bloomberg, spurred by a frustrated Pittman, sued the Federal Reserve to force it to disclose what assets it had accepted for collateral in exchange for loans to Wall Street, including those that were part of an obscure program called the Primary Dealer Credit Facility. That a 2-trillion-dollar bailout program could be considered obscure is as much a testament to press and government failure as anything else, but Bloomberg at least did its best to bring it into the open. Pittman suspected the program was a scandal, as he told me in February 2009 in an interview for the *Columbia Journalism Review* while the debate raged over whether to nationalize banks and create a so-called bad bank:

> The thing that people don't realize is that the Fed is now the "bad bank." That's just something that people don't understand. They've taken collateral, and they refuse to tell us how they valued it. . . . Hopefully, we will be able to inform the people enough to know how badly we're getting screwed. We need to know how to prevent it from happening again, and we need to know who did it.[24]

Bloomberg won its lawsuit, but while the Fed continued to appeal Bloomberg's victories through 2010, a court examiner's report on the Lehman collapse offered a peek into the toxic assets the Fed took on.

Released in March 2010, the Valukas Report broke news of a $50 billion accounting trick Lehman used in its last months to obscure the real health of its balance sheet. The press had done good work on the subject, led by the *Wall Street Journal*'s piece on "The Two Faces of Lehman's Fall" a month after its bankruptcy—one that all but accused it of fraud:

> In the weeks before it collapsed, Lehman Brothers Holdings Inc. went to great lengths to conceal how fast it was careening toward the financial precipice.
>
> The ailing securities firm quietly tapped the European Central Bank and the Federal Reserve as financial lifelines. On Sept. 10, one day after Lehman executives calculated the firm needed at least $3 billion in fresh capital, the firm assured investors on a conference call it needed no new capital at all. Lehman said its massive real-estate portfolio was valued properly, but Wall Street executives who have seen it say it was overvalued by more than $10 billion. As hedge-fund clients began yanking their money from Lehman, the firm assured them it was on solid financial footing.[25]

But since then no one had been able to nail down an actual crime.

The Valukas revelations of the Repo 105 maneuvers did just that—a year and a half after the company's collapse. In the 2,200-page report news of something Lehman called the Freedom Collateralized Loan Obligation, Eric Dash of the *New York Times* dug out precisely what Bloomberg's suit was intended to find.

> They were considered the dregs of Lehman Brothers— "bottom of the barrel," as one banker put it.
>
> But as Lehman executives tried to keep the floundering bank afloat in 2008, they used these troubled investments to raise quick cash that helped mask the extent of the firm's troubles. And they did it with the help of the Federal Reserve Bank of New York.[26]

The Freedom CLO wasn't something Lehman had sitting on its books. It created it specifically to unload onto the Fed, making Lehman appear healthier than it really was. A couple of days later, the Lehman scandal fell off the nation's front pages.

Elizabeth Warren's appearance on NPR's *Planet Money* in May 2009 became one of the most revealing press moments of the crisis.[27] The Harvard professor and advocate of the middle class had been picked by Congress to head the Congressional Oversight Panel on the TARP bailout. But initially, the press stayed clear of her, and reporter Adam Davidson's browbeating offered a glimpse at why. She had a "point of view" outside the savvy-source consensus. Davidson repeatedly tried to delegitimize Warren:

> The American families are not—These issues of crucial, the essential need for credit intermediation are as close to accepted principles among every serious thinker on this topic. The view that the American family, that you hold very powerfully, is fully under assault and that there is—and we can get into that—that is not accepted broad wisdom. I talk to a lot a lot a lot of left, right, center, neutral economists [and] you are the only person I've talked to in a year of covering this crisis who has a view that we have two equally acute crises: a financial crisis and a household debt crisis that is equally acute in the same kind of way. I literally don't know who else I can talk to support that view. I literally don't know anyone other than you who has that view, and you are the person [snicker] who went to Congress to oversee it and you are presenting a very, very narrow view to the American people.

What made the incident particularly dispiriting was that Davidson and *Planet Money*, in cooperation with public radio's *This American Life*, were responsible for one of the finest pieces of journalism of the entire crisis.

When "The Giant Pool of Money" aired in May 2008, Bear Stearns had collapsed, but Lehman Brothers was still alive, if barely.[28] The Dow Jones Industrial Average was eight months into a bear market. Credit markets were closing in on a year of turmoil, and the housing market was now nearing the third year of its collapse, but almost no one—including the nation's financial journalists—could really tell you what had caused the worsening credit crisis in the first place.

The barriers to entry to understanding the crisis were daunting. Instruments like credit default swaps and collateralized debt obligations. Mortgage-backed securities, structured-investment vehicles, NINA loans, mezzanine tranches, super-senior debt, and so on. All seemingly named and designed to put people to sleep. They were part of the "complexity machine," a concept put forth by Warren herself to explain how Wall Street maintains its priesthood by manipulating consumers, regulators, and politicians.

You can add journalists to that list, too. Indeed, the financial press institutionally has yet to adjust to the centrality of the debt markets and present them to the layman in understandable terms. Debt reporting has long been a backwater of the mainstream financial press, which focuses on the equity side of finance. Almost all business reporters cover equity beats or focus on that aspect of the companies they cover, despite the fact that debt markets dwarf the size of the stock markets. That's not purely a journalistic fault—readers' eyes tend to glaze over when reading debt stories. Most business-press readers actually own stocks, and they make for sexier stories than fixed income, which still smells vaguely of mothballs and Mentholatum. So when the crisis hit, financial journalists had a shallow bench unprepared to explain it to the public.

With "The Giant Pool of Money," Davidson and Alex Blumberg did what no one before (or since, really) had been able to do: explain the crisis in terms everyone could understand, with a narrative that captured listeners' attention for an hour. It's one of the rare pieces of journalism that succeeds as a primer for beginners while helping those already informed about the issue synthesize what they know. The program more clearly tied the wreckage of millions of lives in the housing crisis to machinations on Wall Street than just about any journalism before or since.

The program starts with Davidson sitting in on an awards dinner for financial securities, including CDO of the Year, and ties it to a borrower in Brooklyn who had lost his house. That simple act—connecting Wall Street and the borrowers it preyed upon—was all too rare in the press. Seeing it put so plainly was a revelation to listeners who may have had a vague sense of it but couldn't quite put the pieces together. It was probably the best, most influential piece of journalism of the crisis. That it came from a sort of start-up within NPR is revealing. Also revealing: the only other piece that vies for "The Giant Pool of Money" for seminal status. It came from a magazine, but one not normally thought of in the same breath as *Fortune* and *Forbes*.

Matt Taibbi's "Inside the Great American Bubble Machine," which exploded in *Rolling Stone* in July 2009, will be read fifty years from now, long after any *Wall Street Journal* or *Financial Times* effort.[29] A scathing and often over-the-top indictment of Wall Street, Taibbi's rampage put Goldman Sachs front and center in a way that no other journalist did. His opening paragraph, with its vivid imagery, did as much to stain Goldman's white shoes as anything written in more respectable outlets, whose journalists largely dismissed Taibbi as a conspiracist, an idiot, or—worse in business-press circles—naive.

> The first thing you need to know about Goldman Sachs is that it's everywhere. The world's most powerful investment bank is a great vampire squid wrapped around the face of humanity, relentlessly jamming its blood funnel into anything that smells like money.

Taibbi's polemic caused a sensation among the public and the press. Mainstream journalists like Heidi Moore,[30] Charles Gasparino,[31] and Megan McArdle pushed back unsuccessfully from within the respectable journalism priesthood, the latter calling Taibbi "the Sarah Palin of journalism."

> He seems to deliberately eschew understanding his subjects, because only corrupt, pointy-headed financial journalists who have been co-opted by the system do that. And Matt Taibbi is here to save you from those pointy headed elites.[32]

While it's certainly true that Taibbi's screed wouldn't (and shouldn't) have appeared in, say, the *Wall Street Journal*, the reaction of journalists to an entertaining piece of pure outrage—one that, even with its flaws and exaggerations, captured Wall Street (and Taibbi used Goldman not as a singular institution, but as a representative of an entire culture—a bit of license his critics missed) better than a thousand sober he-said, she-said pieces.

It's worth noting that "The Giant Pool of Money" and "Inside the Great American Bubble Machine" were produced by reporters on the outside—or at least the outskirts—of business journalism.

New York University journalism professor Jay Rosen has a helpful idea for thinking about why this may be, positing that journalism's (he's speaking of political journalism here, but it's a broader phenomenon) bias is toward an insiderism he calls the Church of the Savvy:

Savviness—that quality of being shrewd, practical, well-informed, perceptive, ironic, 'with it,' and unsentimental in all things political—is, in a sense, their professional religion. They make a cult of it.[33]

Goldman Sachs, in the business world, is the savviest of the savvy.

The limits of this worldview could be seen in the explosion of the word "populism" in the press during the crisis, a sort of look-down-your-nose word that implied that anything or anyone that put the vast majority of Americans before the tiny slice of the financial industry was an unsophisticated prole or a cynical pol. Elizabeth Warren, unsurprisingly, put it best:

Pundits talk about "populist rage" as a way to trivialize the anger and fear coursing through the middle class. But they have it wrong. Families understand with crystalline clarity that the rules they have played by are not the same rules that govern Wall Street. They understand that no American family is "too big to fail." They recognize that business models have shifted and that big banks are pulling out all the stops to squeeze families and boost revenues. They understand that their economic security is under assault and that leaving consumer debt effectively unregulated does not work.[34]

Through 2009, as it became clear that Warren was a go-to person in Washington—her idea of a consumer financial-protection agency was touted by the president—rather than an outside advocate, the press warmed up to her as a source. It's worth noting that the closer she got to power, the more acceptable her ideas got to the press. That's understandable to a certain extent, but it raises the point of how journalists tend to talk to sources along a narrow spectrum of "acceptable" ideas—and why someone like Warren was considered an outlier.

It is ironic—indeed, downright strange—that financial journal*ism* would view Warren with such suspicion, given that her economic message of an American middle class under attack was true in spades for financial journal*ists*, who increasingly found their once-solid jobs not so secure and their pay and benefits under assault. For while Wall Street reeled, the press was in the throes of its own depression, with no bailouts forthcoming.

The *New York Times* kept its layoffs far below most papers but saw its bonds ratings cut to junk status and was forced to take a usurious loan from a Mexican robber baron—the world's richest man—at a particularly perilous moment. Its stock at one point was off its peak by nearly 95 percent in real terms; its market capitalization about half a percent of Google's. While it did much outstanding work, it's hard to argue that it was operating from a position of strength.

At the *Wall Street Journal*, its hapless owner Dow Jones drove itself into the arms of Rupert Murdoch at a particularly infelicitous moment: 2007, at the onset of the crisis. Murdoch's journalistic priorities could hardly have been more antithetical to the values of the *Journal*, and he radically and rapidly changed it, mostly for the worse. The *Journal* wandered astray just when it was needed most.

Just as financial journalism called for lengthy, deep-dive analytical journalism into the causes of the crisis and the ongoing fallout, Murdoch diluted what had been a particular *Journal* strength in favor of straight news and quickly reported stories—topped off with a sensationalism foreign to the paper's culture. With an eye on taking out the hated *New York Times* (and off the ball), Murdoch shifted resources to general news in 2008, the most critical year for capitalism in eight decades. Ironically, it ceded the explanatory supremacy it had in business journalism to the *Times*, which bettered the *Journal* with its "Reckoning" series in 2008—a bright spot in crisis coverage—and the *Journal* moved toward more of a British model, a more slapdash, less rigorous journalism.[35]

The story isn't quite so simple, of course, and Murdoch was hardly wholly destructive in the case of the *Journal*, which lost a staggering $87 million in 2009, according to ex-*Journal* reporter Sarah Ellison in her 2010 book *War at the Wall Street Journal* on the News Corporation takeover of Dow Jones.[36] The paper avoided mass layoffs in part thanks to the largesse of Murdoch, whatever his flaws. That doesn't excuse his dilution of its business journalism—the paper and the public would have been better served by maintaining its standards—but it illustrates the perilous position the press found itself in from 2007 to 2010.

With the industry's business model upended by a million Web sites selling ads, the crisis further gutted revenues and forced mass layoffs. Once-mighty metropolitan newspapers now tried to get by with half or a third of the newsroom staff they'd had just a decade earlier. Many shuttered business sections altogether, stuffing what little business coverage remained inside the paper.

The *Washington Post* found that it couldn't support a business section. The *Los Angeles Times*, once a credible rival to the *New York Times*, was a shell of its former self, with its staff halved and its ambitions slashed, as well.

While there were prominent exceptions, the local newspapers were almost invisible in reporting on the crisis, which was primarily left to big institutions like the *Journal*, the *Times*, Bloomberg, and the *Financial Times*. Gutted by layoffs, the local papers radically dialed back their ambitions, including in business coverage, during the latter part of the decade.

But the McClatchy chain produced some excellent work, including a series on Goldman Sachs in late 2009 that connected the bank to predatory business practices that fueled the housing bubble.[37] McClatchy's *Charlotte Observer* produced some of the finest work of the crisis just as it was beginning, with March 2007's "Sold a Nightmare" series showing how home builder Beazer Homes ripped off home buyers.[38]

A *Miami Herald* investigation found that do-nothing state regulators approved mortgage licenses for thousands of convicted criminals during the bubble, showing how an entire industry devolved into fraud. But these kinds of investigations were few and far between from the metro papers.[39]

It wasn't all bleak for the financial press, though. The highlight of the crisis was the rise of Bloomberg News to the top tier of financial journalism outlets. Not long ago a sort of in-joke in financial journalism, Bloomberg flexed its muscles in the crisis, with the deepest stable of debt reporters and the most journalists by far of any financial newsroom. It's no coincidence that its newsroom is backed by a powerful profit center, is privately held and thus protected from market pressure, and is perhaps the most sophisticated information company in the world.

Those factors combined to produce a newsroom that actually expanded business coverage significantly during the crisis, and whose technical expertise, especially in the arcane, ill-covered debt markets, gave it a leg up on a story that originated in them. It bought the struggling but scrappy *BusinessWeek* in 2009.

Magazines like the *New Yorker*, the *Atlantic*, and, surprisingly, *Vanity Fair* filled in some of the need for long-form journalism. *BusinessWeek* put out some excellent work, but *Fortune* and *Forbes* were largely irrelevant. One promising and well-funded journalism venture, Condé Nast's *Portfolio*, was an editorial mess—a big missed opportunity, particularly because it had a large, talented staff of business writers. While it printed important pieces like Jesse Eisinger's "Wall Street Requiem," which showed in 2007, five months before the collapse of Bear Stearns, why the Street's days were numbered,[40] the magazine also put American Apparel CEO Dov Charney on its cover as Wall Street collapsed around it. Condé Nast shuttered the magazine six months later.[41]

With traditional journalism mostly retrenching, it was up to others, especially the blogs, to try to fill the void. And so they did, expanding the news and commentary ecosystem with sites that barely registered in the middle part of the decade but came to command hundreds of thousands of visitors. The blogs were critical players—analyzing stories, advancing them, and hammering on themes that cried out for more reporting, like too-big-to-fail banks, mark-to-market accounting, Goldman Sachs's role in the crisis, and many more.

Sites like Calculated Risk, The Big Picture, Baseline Scenario, and Naked Capitalism aggregated important news, offering analysis and, usually, a clear point of view—often moral outrage. The traditional media was slow to fully embrace blogging and had few breakout stars in the form, Felix Salmon of Reuters, Paul Krugman of the *New York Times*, and Justin Fox of *Time* being prominent exceptions.

While newspapers remained the primary gatherers and reporters of news, blogs helped a perplexed audience read between the lines, something that the press, especially newspapers, all too often forced its readers to do. And like a shark that has to keep moving forward to survive, the legacy media all too often moved on from a story before it was halfway picked clean. The blogs saw to that. As Arianna Huffington put it: print has ADD, blogs have OCD.[42]

At its best, this created a symbiosis that pushed stories further than one or the other alone could have done (though at its worst, the blogs just contributed to a cacophony of near-useless information). Coverage of the Valukas Report on the Lehman Brothers bankruptcy offers a case study.

As the report's blockbuster findings were being buried inside business sections just a few days after its release in March 2010, bloggers were just getting started. Zero Hedge, a blog that blasted into prominence in 2009 with a dark, frequently conspiratorial take on Wall Street, took Dash's excellent *Times* report on the Freedom CLO and connected it to earlier writings it had done on the Fed's Primary Dealer Credit Facility—the one Bloomberg had sued over.[43] With often-obscure subheads like "The Liquidity Conundrum and the PDCF" and running at more than four thousand words, Zero Hedge's post (like much of its output) was hardly for the layman. But it offered a deeper look at a critical issue than the mainstream press—whose mandate to inform a broad audience means it can't inform it as well on any specific topic as a specialist—and, critically, served as a source of ideas for mainstream reporters.

The Web also allowed experts to bypass the media filter and talk directly to readers, either through their own sites or via the exponentially expanded op-ed opportunities offered by sites like the Huffington Post. The importance of this should not be underestimated. The op-ed pages of the nation's newspapers recycled the same well-worn commentators, usually from inside the status quo consensus—whether five yards into home or away territory. The *Wall Street Journal*'s influential editorial pages were almost completely dominated by far-right, fundamentalist capitalist commentators—ones whose policies, ascendant for three decades, lay in ruins. The *Washington Post* was so consumed by Beltway conventional wisdom it was essentially a self-parody. The *Times* was better but, as a general interest paper, had other matters to attend to, as well. Indeed, far and away the best op-ed page of the major papers belonged to the *Financial Times*, a British paper with a small U.S. circulation but an outsize influence. In particular, its longtime columnist Martin Wolf became an indispensable voice on the economics of the crisis.

But economists like Brad DeLong, Greg Mankiw, and Mark Thoma took to their own blogs, allowing them to bypass the media. Simon Johnson, the former IMF chief economist co-wrote the insightful and influential Baseline Scenario. Nouriel Roubini, whom it must be said, didn't lack for a mainstream media platform once the crisis began, nevertheless had his own outlet on the Web.

Without doubt, the proliferation of outlets like these resulted in a better-informed public. Those who wanted to delve more deeply into a story than their local paper ran could pick up a *Wall Street Journal*. Those who wanted to get even deeper than the *Journal* could go read Salmon or Fox. Even more detail was available on specialist sites like Bonddad or Econbrowser.

* * *

The press could claim some real wins in reporting on how the crisis was affecting Americans off Wall Street and outside the Beltway. Michael Luo of the *New York Times,* for one, set about chronicling their woes full-time with often-excellent stories given front-page display. But it was a new aggressiveness on consumer reporting that was one of the biggest improvements in business journalism.

For years, banks had been reaping massive profits from over-draft "protection" and overlimit fees, a $59 billion-a-year—with huge profit margins—racket that used shady tactics to entrap their poorest, least financially literate customers, charging annualized interest rates of 4,000 percent. Investigations by *USA Today*'s Kathy Chu dug up consultant memos that showed how the industry preyed on its customers:

> Some consultants offered banks ways to boost overdraft and credit card revenue. A 2001 "checklist" from Profit Technologies—a firm that has worked with 19 of the USA's 20 largest banks—has more than 600 strategies . . .
>
> But most relate to income from fees. One strategy listed to boost overdrafts: "Allow consumers to overdraw their . . . accounts at the ATM up to the bank's internally set limit." To increase credit card fees, banks can "delay crediting of payments not received in bank provided envelop (sic) or for which payment coupon is not received for up to 5 days," and "remove bar coding from remittance envelopes," slowing the payment.[44]

The *New York Times*'s Andrew Martin and Ron Lieber also were excellent, with drumbeat reporting that repeatedly put the issue of card abuses on the front page of the country's most important paper.[45] The *Journal* and *Washington Post* weighed in, as did plenty of bloggers.

Critically, this coverage forced real change on a financial industry that up to then had seemed near untouchable. Congress passed a law, the Federal Reserve tightened regulations, and big institutions like Bank of America abandoned much of the business.

The press also forced the issue as best it could on compensation, pounding the issue throughout the crisis to make sure it never fell off the front burner. Louise Story's *New York Times* article at the end of 2008 is one of the most memorable, deftly showing how Wall Street's pay structure led it to push for risks that ended up toppling it and the economy.[46] The press, late to the issue, finally focused on the critical problem of too-big-to-fail banks.

Reporting on regulation, long a press backwater, reemerged as a serious although still under-covered beat, as the ideology of deregulation—one that the press had internalized—lay in tatters. As Wall Street quickly recovered its footing, with the generous assistance of Washington, the press did a decent job keeping an a eye on its rearguard lobbying efforts, exposing its push to keep the status quo, and making sure voters saw as best they could how the sausage was being made with their politicians (or not made: as of this writing, financial reform still had not passed). Less covered in 2009 and 2010, unfortunately, was the disappearance of the so-called shadow banking system—a driver of the easy credit that enabled the crisis—from the regulatory agenda.

While the crisis has eased, its impact will be felt for years—probably decades. While it is top of mind, it's not too late for the press to pick up on some of the stories it has left under-covered. With Wall Street up off its knees and again wielding enormous political influence, it is vital for the press to lead in gathering the facts that will help Americans form a coherent narrative of what happened and why. It is essential, for instance, to continue to dig into how Wall Street stoked the predatory lending that stoked the crisis, captured regulators and politicians with its hands-off agenda, how this played out throughout the system all the way down to the mortgage brokers, and how, near the end in 2007 and 2008, the great investment banks ramped up the machine just before it blew up.

These stories are sitting there waiting to be told.

6

THE QUIET CRISIS

Peter S. Goodman

Long before the world recoiled at the financial crisis that would draw comparisons to the 1930s, before the demands for taxpayer-financed Wall Street bailouts from Treasury Secretary Henry Paulson and Fed Chairman Ben Bernanke—previously staunch advocates for letting markets do as they will—before even Alan Greenspan acknowledged fundamental errors in his libertarian beliefs, and before prominent investment houses crumbled and disappeared, a much quieter crisis was playing out for millions of ordinary working Americans.

It was a gradual, slow-rolling event, one that had been underway for two decades; a crisis of diminishing job opportunities for millions of working people, declining wages and stagnating incomes, all of which spoiled the arithmetic of everyday finance in many households and challenged the traditional conception of ample rewards awaiting every American willing to labor. It was no less than a breakdown in the basic functioning of the real economy for people living paycheck to paycheck (and more recently unemployment check to unemployment check).

In my reportage of the financial crisis during much of 2008 and 2009, I felt a compulsion to broaden the frame beyond the daily barrage of huge news and keep the focus on this deeper, more amorphous current of reality, the ordinary people grappling with this quieter crisis, even as the headlines came to be dominated by exotic financial derivatives, the war room calculations at the Treasury and the Fed, and the collapse of seemingly impregnable pieces of the financial skyline such as Bear Stearns and Lehman Brothers.

This was neither an ideological crusade nor an attempt to encourage particular policy outcomes, but rather a simple exercise in explanatory journalism, one that aimed to describe what was really happening in the American economy in the broadest, truest sense. The veritable five-alarm fire that leapt from the business pages to the front pages in the fall of 2008 merely exacerbated a chronic crisis of inadequate paychecks and too much debt saturating millions of households. It seemed clear then (and even clearer now) that if we in the press focused too narrowly on the events playing out on Wall Street and in Washington—the global fears of bank runs, the dramatic bank takeovers engineered by Treasury and the Fed, the plunge into derivatives with impenetrable names—and if we failed to include the perspectives and travails of ordinary Americans struggling to pay bills, we would miss a major component of the story. We would mask the broader sources of distress that caused so many people to ultimately find it impossible to stay current on their burgeoning debts, triggering the dramatic crisis unfolding by the day.

We needed to keep ordinary people and smaller institutions near the center of our stories in part because this makes journalism more accessible to a broader readership. Readers generally relate to people more than data points. Narrative and voice tend to inject human interest and flavor into the sometimes dull prose of traditional economic coverage, while preventing stories from feeling like mere fodder for intellectual parlor games or another round of partisan bickering. But enlivening the copy was not the primary reason to concentrate on the day-to-day challenges of real people. We needed workers, home owners, and small business people in our coverage because their stories bridged the two crises—the one immediately bearing down on the economy as spiraling defaults roiled the credit markets; and the quiet crisis that had been eroding incomes in many households since the early 1980s.

This bridge was required to understand how we got here and the dynamics at play as policy makers first sought to restore order to markets suddenly governed by panic and then turned to the bigger project of generating fresh economic growth. It was ultimately necessary to grasp this connection in order to make sense of the confusing, high-stakes debate over the need for taxpayer-financed bailouts of the financial system and the fairness of such proposals—the questions that soon became the dominant thread of the story. Policy makers would soon sell the bailouts to a considerably angry public in the name of sparing the real economy from the ravages of a dysfunctional financial system. For readers to be able to make sense of this debate and the potential consequences of inaction, the coverage had to reflect the crisis playing out over the kitchen table as well as inside the corporate boardroom.

The steady drip of declining incomes and less-rewarding jobs had been building and building until it finally made the immediate crisis unavoidable. Strapped households had finally exhausted a once seemingly bottomless well of credit that had been extended by banks and by Fed Chairman Greenspan, who kept interest rates exceedingly low throughout the late 1990s and into the following decade. For years, as working people had seen their incomes outstripped by the rising cost of housing, health care, and education, they had resorted to complex new mortgages that beckoned with enticingly low initial payments before resetting higher, while also tapping low-interest credit cards. The crisis that began unfolding in the summer of 2007 in mortgage markets, and then spread throughout the financial system in 2008, was most immediately triggered when many people finally reached their ultimate credit limits, confronting bills they simply could not pay. As housing prices, once pumped up by the abundance of easy money, began plunging in value, many people could no longer refinance their debts, because their homes were worth less than they owed on their mortgages. A society that had long disregarded the fine print in mountains of loan documents, taking assurances from a cavalcade of lenders that old debts could always be rolled into new loans with more attractive terms, had exhausted those options. The fine print was suddenly worth reading in detail: it described what was happening in American commercial life, and its details were crippling.

Wall Street had long operated as if housing prices could rise permanently, creating myriad forms of investments linked to mortgages. Now, the banks were awakening to the reality that millions of mortgages were sliding into delinquency. This diminished the value of their holdings tied to mortgages, and it diminished the value of the mortgage-linked investments that other institutions had pledged as collateral for loans that now might never be repaid. In suddenly anxious corporate offices across the land, the uncomfortable sense was taking hold that enormous—worse, incalculable—sums that had been lent out in support of supposedly low-risk investments were about to get written off as worthless. People in control of money were picking up the phone in unison, demanding swift repayment of any debts that could be called in. A wave of fear and uncertainty was rolling across the financial system and the broader economy.

Ordinary working people were at the center of this story, both its victim and its cause. Those who had not earned enough at work to pay their bills and had resorted to credit were now losing their jobs, delivering them into delinquency. Consumers who had swiped credit cards and borrowed against homes with abandon were suddenly forced to pull back, amplifying the fear and the sense of diminishing business opportunities, and thus exacerbating the layoffs that were already underway. Layoffs meant still fewer wages to be spent in the economy, further eroding business, thus reinforcing a disinclination to lend by bankers.

Here was a classic downward spiral: the crisis was most immediately the result of too many households having tapped too much credit to compensate for declining wages, and then abruptly losing access to easy money. And now the crisis was itself exacerbating the root cause of the trouble. You simply could not understand one without the other.

In seeing this connection and exploring it at length in newspaper stories, I claim no great personal discovery. I sought merely to illustrate and elaborate what was already well established in the academic literature and in the pages of journalistic accounts. It just so happened that my tenure as a national economic correspondent for the *New York Times* began in the fall of 2007, just as the quiet crisis that had long been building metastasized into the financial crisis of the moment, suddenly raising the volume on the strains of working people while creating an imperative for digestible explanations of what had gone so terribly wrong.

I got my first look at the quiet crisis inside a job center in downtown Oakland, California, in February 2008, an experience

that more than any other colored how I came to see the weaknesses of the national economy. The unemployment rate was then
a modest 4.8 percent, less than half the double-digit disaster to
come. There was already more than a whiff of economic concern
spreading across the country. Housing prices were continuing to
plunge, eliminating spending power for people who had grown accustomed to borrowing against increased real estate values. The
job market was palpably weakening. Some economists then placed
the odds that the economy would slide into recession at greater
than 50 percent. Worries centered on trouble in the mortgage
market. The word "subprime" was by then fully insinuated into the
American vernacular, with mortgages written to borrowers with
patchy credit already going delinquent in alarming numbers. But
the people in positions of greatest authority offered assurances that
things would almost certainly work out fine.

In a speech the previous year, Bernanke—the then–relatively
new Fed chairman, whose soft-spoken mien and neatly groomed
beard somehow conveyed his credentials as a Princeton economist—reassuringly described how subprime mortgages supposedly
occupied an alternate universe from the rest of the American economy. "Fundamental factors—including solid growth in incomes
and relatively low mortgage rates—should ultimately support the
demand for housing," he told a group of finance experts. "At this
point, the troubles in the subprime sector seem unlikely to seriously spill over to the broader economy or the financial system."[1]
At about the same time, Paulson, the last treasury secretary in the
George W. Bush administration, whose longtime leadership of the
investment banking giant Goldman Sachs imbued his pronouncements with special weight, offered that "credit issues" resulting
from subprime mortgage troubles were now "largely contained."[2]

A week before my visit to the Oakland job center, I had spoken
with Robert Hall, a prominent Stanford economist who occupied a
seat on the National Bureau of Economic Research, the panel that
decides when to apply the recession label to challenging economic
times. Ultimately, the panel would determine that a recession had
begun in December 2007. But as we ate sandwiches at a pleasant
café on the well-groomed Stanford campus in what would later be
counted as the third month of the most punishing economic downturn since the Great Depression, Hall shrugged dismissively when
asked if a recession might be upon us. "There is no sign of that in
the data," he said, cautioning me not to react to momentary blips.

Things, of course, were not fine. Not by any stretch. The economy was already in the grip of a recession that would upend much of American life, destroying millions of jobs, throwing people out of homes, eviscerating life savings, and imposing a deep and potentially long-lasting anxiety. And as I began to discover for myself the following week inside the Oakland job center, things had not been fine for a long time for significant numbers of people who had been doing what was asked of them through the traditional bargain of American economic life: getting up early for work, gaining training, seeking out new opportunities and trying to stay positive even as they slid deeper into the weeds of disappointed aspiration.

On my first morning inside the offices in downtown Oakland, I walked past people lined up in the lobby, waiting for a chance to sit in front of a computer and scan meager job listings. I met a man in his early forties, Greg Bailey, who had spent his adult life in a series of blue-collar jobs, first delivering fiber optic cables during the Internet bubble, and then installing washing machines during the housing bubble. He had trained for a better career in biotechnology through a state-financed program. Yet, eight months later, he had found no jobs in that field. And as opportunities diminished by the month, he was being turned down for the sorts of jobs from which he had hoped to escape—stocking shelves at a warehouse, driving a truck, lifting boxes. Soon, he would move into a temporary bunk at a homeless shelter.

Through the leanest periods of his life, Bailey had been able to count on securing day-labor stints at a local office where contractors showed up to employ capable hands. By the spring of 2008, he had to get there by four in the morning to secure an early enough place in line to gain a daily assignment when the office opened an hour later. By early 2009, as the worst of the financial crisis washed through the economy, there were already twenty-five people in line ahead of him when he arrived at four in the morning. And they were all waiting for nothing. "You don't even get called," he told me.[3]

According to the guiding narrative of American economic life—one that draws on the frontier roots of a land supposedly stocked with unlimited opportunities—Bailey was precisely the sort of person who was supposed to be succeeding. He was able-bodied, bright, and personable, and he was strategically looking to better himself. He was setting his alarm clock and going out in search of work. Yet, he was sliding backward. And he was surrounded by no end of others in similar straits, people who were losing hope, and whose stories seemed essentially the same, even as the details varied: they were looking for work. They were willing to take jobs that seemed beneath their skills and their experiences; that offered little in the way of advancement possibilities; that were often dirty or unpleasant or damaging to their bodies. And they were coming up empty.

This had been true long before the acute financial crisis of 2008. For two decades, most working people had seen their wages stagnate or drop while the costs of middle-class staples like education, health care, and housing spiraled higher.[4] The economic expansion that had just ended was shaping up as one of the weakest on record. At the beginning of the decade, the median American family earned about $61,000 a year, in inflation-adjusted terms. By 2007, even before the recession, the median family had seen its earnings dip to $60,500. For the first time since the government began tracking such records in the middle of the last century, an economic expansion had come to an end with the typical American household worse off than at the beginning.[5]

For those near the bottom of the employment ranks, paychecks were so lean that working sometimes seemed like a cruel joke. By 2006, nearly one-fifth of those employed in the private sector were earning less than $10 an hour, at wages considered to be poverty level.[6] For those out of work, climbing back into a job had become significantly more difficult, for the simple reason that the economy was creating fewer jobs than in decades earlier.

Though we tend to think of layoffs when we consider the trauma of an economic downturn, the long-running crisis confronting working people had much more to do with a growing predilection against hiring among employers—what one economist, Ed McKelvey, termed a "hiring strike."[7]

This was a complicated story, to be sure, one that touched on the weakening power of labor unions and the rise of off-shoring, which has sent American jobs overseas, particularly in manufacturing. Automation has provided employers with myriad ways to boost production while hiring fewer people. The rise of Wall Street and the expansion of 401(k) retirement plans has turned more ordinary people into stockholders, while further concentrating the ownership of large companies in the control of institutional investors, such as mutual funds. This, say economists, has intensified pressure on publicly traded companies to maximize their profits by minimizing their costs, something accomplished most expeditiously by keeping the payrolls lean. The consequences of this complexity are starkly simple: people who have spent their lives accustomed to working have in recent years found it increasingly difficult to secure employment. Joblessness has become a condition that is particularly difficult to escape.

Many of us in my profession missed this story. We were too busy writing about the wonders of technology in the 1990s, the surge of home ownership and real estate wealth the following decade, and the enormous corporate profits that reinforced Wall Street's place as the locus of global finance, a place of considerable innovation and unprecedented lucre. Amid so much conspicuous American prosperity, stories like Bailey's had seemed marginal, pushed off to the side of the mainstream attention span as unfortunate examples of the losers in any dynamic economy, the flip side to the abundant winners, yet hardly a sign of systemic trouble. But as the financial crisis intensified during the course of 2008, stripping away the easy finance that had masked this long-term decline of paychecks, jobs were harder than ever to secure. The long-term dearth of work and stagnating wages emerged as an unmistakable component of any complete explanation of the daily barrage of momentous news. Systemic troubles had finally gotten so big, that they had grown conspicuous, helping give rise to a financial crisis now demanding hour-by-hour attention.

I was fixed on telling the story of the quiet crisis in part because it helped cut through some of the more widely heard, bogus explanations for the events of the day. As mortgages soured, bankruptcies soared, and Wall Street buckled, Americans heard a good deal of moralizing from the screaming heads on cable television that our economic troubles amounted to a societal comeuppance for years of extravagant spending. People had failed to live within their means and would now be forced to reacquaint themselves with seemingly antiquated concepts such as household budgeting. This sounded wholesome, like an obese person with terrible eating habits being forced to forgo the doughnut shop for a trip to the gym and a swing by the green grocer. Yet, this was a simple-minded, even cartoonish view of events that masked one of the root causes of the crisis: the scarcity of paychecks and the rising costs of middle-class life.

There was certainly some truth to the talk that reckless spending had contributed to the bust. Indeed, the first story I ever wrote

for the *Times*, in the fall of 2007, explored how the fall in housing prices was leading to a marked collapse in home-equity borrowing, and how this seemed certain to slow consumer spending,
which raised serious risk of triggering a recession. I wrote the
piece from Reno, Nevada, where the housing bubble had been
particularly potent and the accompanying bust especially severe.
There, I fell in with a crew of thirty-something guys who had
been working in the local mortgage and home-improvement industries, folding their earnings into speculative real estate ven-
tures and living large on the proceeds. My local guide to the
festivities had financed a sumptuous Napa Valley wedding followed by a honeymoon in Tahiti on his home-equity loan, while
filling his closet with dozens of pairs of shoes and adorning his
walls with giant flat-screen televisions. He boasted to me that he
had once traded in his car for a new one purely because he wanted
a different-color vehicle. They frequently met up to celebrate
their good fortune inside one of the VIP lounges at the local casinos, where a bottle of liquor ran into the hundreds of dollars. But
when I met these guys, they had turned their attention away from
seemingly magic variable-rate mortgages and construction loans
to the particulars of bankruptcy law and foreclosure. They were
learning to buy groceries at discount wholesalers, staying home
and watching television, and getting used to the idea that their
addresses were unlikely to be upgraded anytime soon. Austerity
reigned.[8]

Such tales often seemed the dominant explanation for what
had gone wrong: we had gluttonously spent ourselves into oblivion,
as if the only cure for our ills was a good calculator and more realistic expectations. Yet, this was far from the whole story. Often
lost in the depictions of the crisis as comeuppance was the reality
that many had lived beyond their means for the simple reason that
their means could not cover the costs of what most would consider
the trappings of ordinary middle-class American life. Many debts
had been amassed not through buying electronic gadgets and vaca-
tions but by paying for medical bills and keeping gas in the car to
get to work.

At the Oakland jobs center, I met a woman named Dorothy
Thomas whose story has stayed with me ever since, becoming something of a talisman. She had grown up poor, in rural
Oklahoma, an African American girl sent to a forcibly integrated
school district. She had not made it through college and she was in-

tent that her two daughters would. For two decades, she had worked a series of medical-billing jobs in northern California, earning as much as $22 an hour, but she had spent more than she brought home from work: she lived in better neighborhoods than she could afford in order to send her daughters to better school districts, recognizing that this would increase their odds of getting through college. Both girls made it, but Thomas was still effectively paying the bills. She had failed to pay for a required $10 registration sticker for her car, drawing the notice of a police officer who had her vehicle towed away. With no car, she could not get to work, and she lost her job. With no wages, she could no longer pay rent, and she moved into a beaten-down house in Oakland on a street she came to call Crack Avenue. Soon, the landlord stopped paying the utilities, resulting in the water and electricity being shut off. When I met her, she was trying to figure out whether she could even justify paying the bus fare required to get to the jobs center, knowing full well that openings were few. She was trying to understand how to make herself presentable for interviews in a house without a working shower, and with no money for makeup. She was trying to make sense of what had happened to her life, proffering her resume with its history of white-collar working experience as evidence of having somehow been shorn of her real identity.

For the first time in her adult life, Thomas had passed a year without working.

"If you had told me before that a person could look for a year and not find a job, I'd have said they were just lazy," she told me the day I met her. "Every day, I feel like I'm losing a piece of myself."[9]

If the financial crisis was a comeuppance, why were its consequences falling so heavily on the backs of people who had been forced to choose from an array of essentially lousy options? Thomas had confronted a choice that neatly encapsulated the sorts of trade-offs faced by millions of other people—those who had taken out terrible mortgages, or who lacked adequate health insurance and paid for prescription drugs with credit cards, people who now faced a terrible reckoning. She could live on what she earned and thereby consign her daughters to accepting lesser educations, raising the odds that they would struggle to maintain even her tenuous economic station; or she could breach the limits of her income in a strategic bid for upward mobility while hoping the bill collector would not catch her.

As the crisis became a platform for pundits admonishing Americans for their financial mistakes, I tried to keep one question at the center of my reporting: How did so many people find themselves staring at such unworkable options? What had happened to the economy such that owning a home or simply keeping groceries in the refrigerator too frequently came to involve some form of financial witchcraft?

And how had credit come to seem like savings in so many households? This mind-set stemmed partially from an abundance of optimistic narratives about a lucrative future, which seemingly justified debt. (When housing prices are only going to go up, why forgo a honeymoon in Tahiti? Why fail to feed one's family organic produce or steak on the grill?) But it was mostly about too many people not having had enough in the here and now and feeling a compulsion to use credit just to get by.

In any individual case of financial mishap, it is easy to identify poor decision making, choices that went awry. How had Dorothy Thomas managed to leave herself so vulnerable? Why didn't she just pay that $10 auto-registration fee? There was no good explanation for this, as she would be the first to tell you. She had made a terrible error and her world had come crashing down around her. But that begged the real question: How had so much of American society come to run its household finances in a less-extreme yet similar fashion, managing Thomas's conundrum by taking on spiraling debts? How had so many people come to live in such close proximity to disaster, where one bad decision, one piece of unexpected news—an illness, a lost job—could bring calamity? That could not be explained away by the poor decision making of the individuals involved—not unless huge segments of the American population had somehow lost their minds. It could only be explained by a lack of alternatives. To understand this, one needed to understand the quiet crisis, and the degree to which the economy had for years been downgrading American living standards, forcing growing numbers of people to choose from an assortment of altogether unsatisfactory (and unsustainable) options.

This was a story that required data to carry authority, but it needed real people and their real-life dilemmas to bring home to a general audience. You needed to absorb the individual cases in the sort of vivid detail that made them part of human experience to see just how and why trillions of dollars of debt had been distributed throughout the economy in ways that otherwise seemed impossibly absurd.

In our newsroom at the *Times*, many reporters had a more sophisticated grasp of Wall Street than I did. They were better versed in the workings of the investments at the center of the crisis, instruments with forbidding names like collateralized debt obligation and super-SIV. We had a deep bench of beat reporters able to peer behind the public relations walls at major banks and the Treasury to divine what was happening inside those institutions. What I tried to contribute was a broader context of the financial crisis by imbuing our coverage with the voices and dilemmas of ordinary people. I aimed to demystify the strange events of the period, strip them of jargon and break them down for a general audience. I had come to my job following five years in Asia, where I had specialized in going into the field, taking narrative approaches that sought to make sense of big questions—China's shift toward capitalism, the tension between the private sector and state-owned enterprises—by introducing readers to problems faced by working people, peasants, small businesses. My own journalistic values had been forged with a heavy bias toward spending time with people whose job descriptions did not include talking to journalists, while eschewing the specialized vernacular of experts. This was the sensibility that I tried to bring to our financial crisis coverage, in the hopes of linking the unraveling on Wall Street to the quiet crisis that had entrenched itself in American households.

Part of my motivation in attacking the comeuppance narrative was that it clearly failed to account for a perversity delivered by the financial crisis and the broader recession: their worst impacts fell hardest on people who had not even shared in the spoils of the easy money that had engendered the crisis. People who had for years been barely hanging on to tenuous stations in the middle class, failing to cash in on the surges in stock and real estate markets, were now suffering the effects of so many other people losing their spending power and their nerve.

Two debt-financed investment bonanzas had laid the groundwork for the downturn—the orgy of speculation in technology in the 1990s amid the magical notion that the Internet justified limitless prices for Web-related companies; then, the fantastical trading of real estate the following decade. As formerly free-spending households eschewed the shopping mall and deferred home renovations, people like Greg Bailey, who had installed the washing machines for $14 an hour, were now out of work. Most of the people I met at the Oakland job center, and later in unemployment offices across the country, had never cashed in on the investment bubbles, yet they were the ones paying the steepest price for their unhappy endings.

This was something I found myself thinking about constantly as the financial crisis gathered force and intensified pressures on the job market, and particularly as the debates began over the appropriateness and fairness of what would become a $700 billion taxpayer-financed bailout of financial institutions.

A loud chorus of dissent rapidly emerged, with critics arguing that taxpayers should not be put in the position of having to rescue investors from the consequences of their bad wagers, be they Wall Street financiers whose bets reached into the hundreds of billions, or small-time home owners who had borrowed irresponsibly on the assumption that their houses were inexhaustible reservoirs of cash. There was no easily dismissing such sentiments. Who could defend, in moral terms, the helping hand of the taxpayer for banks that had amassed multibillion profits for years, paying handsome bonuses to their executives along the way, while making the sorts of loans that triggered foreclosures and a financial crisis that essentially wrecked the economy? Why should someone who had bought a modest home and paid his mortgage on time for years now be forced to bail out his neighbor, who had bought at bubble prices and then borrowed extravagantly on the assumption that real estate prices would climb forever?

These were hard questions. Criticism of the bailouts emanated from across the political spectrum, in a fashion that scrambled traditional partisan divides and notions of right and left. Libertarians found bailouts anathema to the concept that the nation's economic fate should be placed in the hands of free markets. They argued that recovery would happen most quickly if the government simply stayed out of the way and let the markets impose their judgment, punishing the reckless and rewarding the prudent. In this view, bailouts would reward irresponsible behavior while interfering with the correction that the markets would administer. From the other side of the spectrum, liberals wound up in a similar place. They had long been critical of how free-market reverence had captured the levers of economic policy and were now inclined to watch bankers choke on some of their own potion, as markets went malevolent. Conservatives had long chiseled away at the social safety net, arguing that handouts interfered with the efficient functioning of American capitalism. In the flavor of market fundamentalism that captured policy making from the Reagan years forward, poor single mothers were supposed to go out and support themselves with paychecks in place of welfare checks. Now that huge banks and their wealthy executives were the ones crying out for relief, why should the principle be any different? The bailouts, from this perspective, made the American economy seem like a con game, with generous welfare benefits for the well-heeled and remorseless capitalism for everyone else. From both ends of the ideological spectrum, a deep revulsion against the bailouts emerged.

Yet, in covering the events of 2008 and 2009, as the labor market began to shed six hundred thousand and seven hundred thousand jobs a month and as the unemployment rate reached levels not seen in a quarter-century, tightening the vise on people like Greg Bailey and Dorothy Thomas, it was hard to imagine how policy makers could just sit back and leave it to the market to sort the winners from the losers. What about the people who had never cashed in, who had pursued the idea of working hard for eventual gain, and now suffered the collapse of the broader economy? What was the taxpayer's responsibility for these people? Where did fairness fit in for people like Thomas and Bailey, who had extracted few benefits from the boom-and-bust cycles delivered by Fed Chairmen Greenspan and Bernanke and a financial industry run on easy money, yet were now suffering an outsize share of the hurt? I felt an obligation to keep these people in the story, along with the home owners and the bankers and the rest of the characters caught up in the financial crisis.

The debate over the bailouts and whether they were needed was a challenging story to capture, one that came wrapped in more speculation than fact. Reporters are constantly seeking to get to the bottom of the story, to a place where readers can be told with some authority how questions shake out. But in the debate over the bailouts, we ran up against the complexities of mortgage-linked investments and the institutions that had traded in them, not to mention the basic limits of economics—the same complexities that vexed policy makers. Despite the earnest attempts by academic economists to assume the trappings of scientists, economics is not physics, where truth can be clearly validated in controlled experiments.

It is more like politics, a realm in which perceptions form their own kind of reality; where the effectiveness of a given policy can depend upon what markets and ordinary people think of the policy. As the markets fretted about the extent of the losses left to be tallied in the financial crisis, the people in control of real dollars were holding on to them for dear life, exacerbating the bite of that crisis. Many economists were clamoring for bailouts for no other reason than to soothe the market's fear of a freefall, which seemed to hold the danger of becoming a self-fulfilling prophecy. Indeed, serious economists who had been correct about much of what had happened were, by the middle of 2008, suggesting that if fear was allowed to spread unchecked in the financial system, we ran a real risk of suffering a repeat of the 1930s banking crisis. Then, the economy might slide into such a deep hole that it could take years to escape.

"The open question is whether we're in for a bad couple of years, or a bad decade," declared Kenneth S. Rogoff, a Harvard economist who had previously served as the chief economist at the International Monetary Fund when I asked him for his outlook in the summer of 2008.[10]

By then, the sense of crisis was nearly total. It had begun with the near-collapse of the investment bank Bear Stearns in March 2008 and gathered force through the summer, as the government effectively nationalized the mortgage finance giants, Fannie Mae and Freddie Mac, which together guaranteed more than $5 trillion worth of American home loans. Then came the full-out panic of the fall, as major financial institutions such as Lehman, Washington Mutual, and Merrill Lynch vanished as stand-alone entities. And then came the Bush administration's demand for the massive bailout program.

The financial crisis effectively lifted the quiet crisis to the fore for all to see. The same sorts of stories that had always interested me—those looking at the difficulties people were having paying their bills, hanging on to their homes, finding work—now had a sense of immediacy and urgency that they had previously lacked. Stories that had once struck readers and editors as merely sad and seemingly confined to the margins of American life—tales of foreclosure, diminished retirement prospects, austerity imposed through layoff—had become indicators of broader economic distress and portents of fresh losses yet to reach the balance sheets of major lenders. Such stories were now central to the debate in Washington about what to do, who ought to be bailed out, and how; how much taxpayer money to expend in the interest of engineering a revival.

Dorothy Thomas's experience could no longer be set aside as merely an isolated depiction of human suffering—sympathetic to some, and less so to others. Tales such as hers, then multiplying as the unemployment rate climbed, signified that something was seriously amiss in the economy. Large numbers of previously working people—people who had earned and spent money, distributing their wages at other businesses and thus creating jobs for others—were sidelined, removing their spending from the economy and spreading the forces of the downturn. As job losses spread, so did foreclosures, making more mortgage-linked securities go bad, and threatening the balance sheets of more banks. And as more red ink washed through the financial system, banks further tightened credit, which squeezed more vigor out of the economy.

This pernicious dynamic was at the center of the debate over the need for bailouts. By the middle of 2008, the overwhelming message from most economists was clear: like it or not, the interests of Wall Street and Main Street were indivisible. Liberals were already inclined toward government intervention in the marketplace in times of crisis. Soon, the Bush administration put aside its ideological predisposition against bailouts and publicly pleaded for taxpayer aid for Wall Street, arguing that this was required to protect all Americans—working people as well as investment bankers—from the wolf howling at the door. "I'm a strong believer in free enterprise, so my natural instinct is to oppose government intervention," President Bush declared during a nationally televised speech in late September 2008, beseeching Congress to deliver the largest bailout in American history. "I believe companies that make bad decisions should be allowed to go out of business. Under normal circumstances, I would have followed this course. But these are not normal circumstances. The market is not functioning properly. There has been a widespread loss of confidence, and major sectors of America's financial system are at risk of shutting down."[11]

In sounding the alarm so emphatically after many months of blithely dismissing warnings, President Bush sharply elevated public concern about the economy and the financial system, while also engendering suspicions about his administration's motives. Now, there seemed an insatiable appetite for analysis in our pages. Day after day, our beat reporters on Wall Street and in Washington were scrambling to keep up with the latest news as another financial institution was sucked into the maw of the crisis and the Treasury and Federal Reserve began to debate what to do about it. I was frequently asked to pen an essay on what these events meant in terms of the broader economy, drawing on large data points and the views of economists.

A moment of historical import was at hand, one fraught with risks. We had to capture what was happening in a story now changing by the hour while also helping make sense of these unsettling events for our readers. Newspaper people are perhaps overly inclined to drape the banner of history over whatever they happen to be covering. I tend to be suspicious and even disdainful of such talk, having had my fill of hot air claims of "unprecedented new developments" during the late 1990s as a telecommunications reporter, and then again in China the following decade, where the narrative of ascendant Sino-supremacy soon felt like a tired cliché. That said, the atmosphere in the fall of 2008 really did present one of those moments when it felt like the stakes could not be exaggerated. Fifty-cent words like "significant," "ominous," and "extraordinary" now seemed both gratuitous and inadequate. The facts alone were compelling enough—money freezing up in the economy as enormous institutions collapsed, threatening to take down broad swaths of the global financial system; layoffs accelerating; fear and uncertainty spreading. The events unfolding had enormous implications, and they contained obvious parallels to the 1930s. Economists who were not inclined toward alarmism openly feared the worst.

Inside our newsroom in midtown Manhattan—now crackling with special intensity as reporters and editors huddled at all hours—we understood that we were not merely passive chroniclers of external events. The sportswriter can describe what is happening on the field from a dispassionate distance, without imagining that the words he types may somehow influence the events he is witnessing. Not so for those of us writing about the financial crisis: we were effectively on the field while the game was still underway. Investors and markets and ordinary people would move their money in reaction to what we and other major media were reporting, and this would in turn affect the policy climate, the perception of need for emergency measures, the politics of the debate over those measures, and the public mood, which then reverberated back on everything else.

We were certainly cognizant that our words had impact in the midst of the crisis, and this amplified our sense of responsibility— one that we took most seriously—to make sure that our writing and reporting were motivated by the pursuit of clarity; to make sure we were reflecting the best available assessments of the situation at hand, as opposed to simply conveying emotion and partisan positioning. We were accountable to reality above all, even as we grasped that we were influencing the very reality we were reflecting. In such a situation, the primary responsibility of any journalist is to ensure that one's motivations are pure. You make sure that you are not steering toward one partisan view or another, listening too intently to the opinions of regular sources to the exclusion of other points of view. You dig deep to extricate what is really happening, and then you put aside concerns about how your stories may be influencing reality and hope that, through solid reporting clearly driven by a genuine pursuit of reality, better outcomes result.

In addition to the daily analysis of the macro picture, I was encouraged by editors to join a broader effort to dig into the bigger questions about how we got here. By this point, the subprime mortgage story was well understood, as was the role of credit ratings agencies in vouching for mortgage-backed securities that proved toxic, mortgage brokers who had netted huge commissions in arranging bad loans, and the contributions of the government-backed mortgage giants, Fannie Mae and Freddie Mac, who had lowered underwriting standards. But one assignment stands out for me from that period, one that added a layer of information to the explanation—a retrospective on the role that Alan Greenspan played in laying down conditions for the crisis. This was the brain-child of Tim O'Brien, the *Times*'s Sunday business editor, who had recognized that a key piece was thus far missing in terms of illustrating the roots of the crisis: derivatives, the exotic investments that were supposed to have spread risks within the financial system to minimize the risk of a crisis, yet wound up spreading them more like a virus.[12] As a reporter in the 1990s, O'Brien had covered emerging worries about derivatives trading and early efforts to regulate them—efforts that wound up being squashed by Greenspan, aided by a pair of Clinton administration treasury secretaries, Robert Rubin (who went on to a prime executive position at Citibank) and Larry Summers (now President Obama's primary economic adviser). By late 2008, Greenspan had already taken criticism for his role in the housing bubble through the low interest rates he supplied as Fed chairman and his minimal regulation of the banking system. But little had been written about the key role he had played in persuading Congress to allow derivatives trading to explode virtually without limit. This trading was at the center of the casino-like practices that came to shape Wall Street in the years before the crisis. Derivatives such as credit default swaps seemed to provide financial institutions with insurance on their burgeoning portfolios of mortgage-backed securities, emboldening them to pour more money into real estate.

I wish I could say that this line of reporting featured me skulking around in a trench coat, but it was not particularly glamorous. I sat in a windowless room at the *Times*, away from the telephone and the chatter of colleagues, and I read through thousands of pages of Greenspan's testimony over the years on Capitol Hill. There, I encountered a story that was just lying in plain view, waiting to be harvested. As the nation's most influential economic seer, Greenspan had persuaded Congress and successive presidential administrations to attach the nation's fortunes to his libertarian ideals. Much the same way we count on the local baker to sell decent bread or risk his standing in the community, we could count on Wall Street to regulate itself, he argued. The institutions that were buying and selling derivatives could be trusted to safeguard the financial system more than any regulator. Surely, the people running these institutions would be motivated to make sure that the people on the other sides of their trades had the money to cover their bets, far more motivated than any faceless bureaucrat.

In the annals of American thinking, this mind-set and the deregulation it fostered must surely go down as one of the more consequential mistakes. Indeed, less than two weeks after that story ran, Greenspan went up to Capitol Hill again, this time to acknowledge an error in his way of thinking.

"Those of us who have looked to the self-interest of lending institutions to protect shareholders' equity, myself included, are in a state of shocked disbelief," he told members of the House.[13]

Later that year, I joined with my colleague Gretchen Morgenson to exhume one failed mortgage lender, Washington Mututal, whose credo had been "The Power of Yes." WaMu, as the bank was known, had lived this credo to the limit, paying huge commissions to a national network of wholesale and retail mortgage brokers who had written up loans—often at poor and little understood terms— to seemingly all comers. Much of this sort of reporting tends to occur at the boardroom level, but it seemed clear that if we could get to the foot soldiers inside the branch offices, we could sidestep the public relations filters and duck under the sanitized histories sanctioned by the company. We could find out what had really happened and how, simply by talking to people who do not usually encounter the press. I used Facebook to find people who had recently worked at branches from Southern California to Illinois to Florida, and they introduced me to others. They described in vivid detail the pressures they faced to find reasons to say yes to deals, even as they knew that many of the loans would end badly.

The trail took me to a California penitentiary near the Mexican border outside San Diego, where a former WaMu manager who regularly snorted methamphetamine in the office—and who was by then serving time for theft—confirmed that the bank had been a place where the only real rule was that loans were made. He recalled how he had signed off on a large mortgage for a mariachi singer who had no verifiable income: he had the man stand in front of a home in his mariachi outfit, where he photographed him. The photo went into the file as supposed proof of income. Approved.

"It was the Wild West," a New York appraiser told me. "If you were alive, they would give you a loan. Actually, I think if you were dead, they would still give you a loan."[14]

This was the backdrop to the crisis, a story that had to be told to help the reader understand the context in which the debate over bailouts and other policy responses was occurring.

Given what we have subsequently learned about the government's crafting of the bailouts, the people who sold them, and the way they were ultimately administered (both by the Bush administration, and subsequently by the Obama administration), it is legitimate to ask how effectively we in the press protected the public interest in scrutinizing the motives and claims of those involved. Dorothy Thomas and Greg Bailey never got bailouts. Neither did millions of home owners soon threatened with foreclosure whose loans had once boosted the stock price of Washington Mutual and other large lenders. Neither had small businesses whose distress was—unlike that of General Motors—too small to threaten broad economic ramifications. But the insurance giant AIG, which—thanks to the deregulatory work of Greenspan, Summers, and Rubin—had been allowed to trade in derivatives such as credit default swaps without limit, got bailed out to the tune of $180 billion. The biggest banks that wrote the largest volumes of toxic mortgages were bailed out, too, even as their executives departed with their winnings in hand. Questions about the fairness and propriety of these arrangements will be picked at for years, no doubt, and these questions must be asked. The form and structure of the bailouts—issues that we in the press explored as best as we could in real time—will remain the subject of debate well into the future.

Critics at the time that the bailouts were being formulated argued then and more strongly since that we in the press helped facilitate a scare campaign conducted by the Bush administration, one that exaggerated the threat posed to the economy by the financial crisis to justify an enormous transfer of public wealth into private hands. Such perceptions took root early on, fueled by the imperious fashion in which Treasury Secretary Paulson first asked Congress for the money in the fall of 2008: with a three-page proposal for a $700 billion bailout, to be handled essentially however his Treasury saw fit, with a special clause that expressly forbade any review or challenge by a court.

In the months that followed, the sense of grievance only grew. Paulson asked for the money so he could use it to buy toxic assets from the banks that were stuck with them on their balance sheets. But as soon as Congress handed it over, the treasury secretary changed his mind about what to do with the money, using it to inject cash directly into financial institutions. Banks on the receiving end of bailout funds continued to tighten their lending, particularly to small businesses, depriving the economy of needed capital. Major institutions handed out eye-catching bonuses to their executives, bringing denunciations from politicians and pundits. Perhaps most galling of all to a broadening group of critics was the way in which the New York Fed (then headed by Timothy Geithner, who would become treasury secretary in the Obama administration) approved the AIG rescue: the companies that held insurance policies written by AIG against corporate default were paid 100¢ on the dollar for their investments out of the bailout funds taxpayers handed the company, even though some expressed willingness to take less, and though claims on such investments had been settled by other parties for fractional amounts. (Both Paulson and Geithner would later tell a congressional investigative panel that they had nothing to do with that decision.)[15]

In short, more than a year after the monumental bailout, it had worked out well for large banks, whose stocks had risen, and for bankers on the receiving end of bonuses. Both the Bush administration, which launched the bailout, and the Obama administration, which continued it, declared that the expenditure of public money had been hugely successful in one crucial regard: it had blunted talk of a replay of the Depression, restoring order to the financial system, even as a general tightness of finance remained. But in many communities, the verdict on the bailout was poor, particularly as the unemployment rate climbed into double digits. All of which underscores the validity of accounting for the role that we in the press played during the crisis; whether we asked enough questions, and the right sorts of questions, as gigantic amounts of taxpayer funds were given to the very institutions that played leading roles in generating the danger.

Our job was to try to figure out what the stakes were, to help the public sort through the competing claims that the bailouts were an unnecessary form of corporate welfare, as one camp had it, or rather a required if unpleasant form of medicine to keep the economy from sliding into the abyss. And if the bailouts were necessary, then came the myriad, messy questions about how they should be handled and what the taxpayers ought to get for their money—controlling stakes in the companies? New rules on the future financial system, such as limits on executive compensation?

Covering even the simplest part of the argument—bailouts or not—was by itself a difficult reporting assignment. Part of the difficulty in getting at the merits of the argument was the perception that the chief messengers of the warning came with substantial conflicts of interest. In essence, the press was being lobbied aggressively by the Bush administration, led by Hank Paulson, the former head of Goldman Sachs, to sound the alarm that hundreds of billions of taxpayer dollars had to be given immediately to giant Wall Street institutions (Goldman Sachs included) or we risked a financial catastrophe.

Newspaper reporters must not serve as stenographers for the views of the White House or Treasury any more than we ought to parrot the messages of the military in prosecuting a war. It is imperative for the healthy functioning of democracy that we scrutinize assertions made by those with control over the decision-making levers, squaring their claims against the facts as best we can while testing the assumptions that are built into their policy proposals. This accountability function is the most crucial role of the press, and it falls particularly heavily on the national print media, which is singularly endowed with the resources needed to make sense of events as complex as the financial crisis.

In my own experience, I can say without reservation that we were fully motivated to ask the questions that needed asking. We certainly did not pull punches in deference to sacred cows, fear of being seen to be in one camp or other, or concerns about offending the powers-that-be—a charge that often runs through critiques of the press. We tried to make sense as best we could of what was happening around us, critically scrutinizing policy proposals and public pronouncements amid a relentless blizzard of news. Looking back on the coverage many months later, it is clear that all of the perceptions that have dogged the bailouts in the months that followed, the arguments over fairness and effectiveness and taxpayer compensation, were aired in our paper right then at there, at inception, alongside our efforts to analyze the stakes hanging in the balance.

"This administration is asking for a $700 billion blank check to be put in the hands of Henry Paulson, a guy who totally missed this, and has been wrong about almost everything," fumed Dean Baker, co-director of the liberal Center for Economic and Policy Research in Washington, in the days after the treasury secretary first revealed his proposal—a comment that I included in an analysis piece that ran on the front page of the *Times*. "It's almost amazing they can do this with a straight face. There is clearly skepticism and anger at the idea that we'd give this money to these guys, no questions asked."[16]

The same story featured this snippet:

Some are suspicious of Mr. Paulson's characterizations, finding in his warnings and demands for extraordinary powers a parallel with the way the Bush administration gained authority for the war in Iraq. Then, the White House suggested that mushroom clouds could accompany Congress's failure to act. This time, it is financial Armageddon supposedly on the doorstep.

"This is scare tactics to try to do something that's in the private but not the public interest," said Allan Meltzer, a former economic adviser to President Reagan, and an expert on monetary policy at the Carnegie Mellon Tepper School of Business. "It's terrible."

For me personally, seeing Paulson cast as the chief lobbyist for the bailout was jarring. Only two years earlier, I had covered his first trip to Asia as the then-newly installed treasury secretary.[17] Impatient and blunt, he had carried himself as the proselytizer in chief for American-style commerce, which seemed synonymous with keeping the government out of the way of business. In Singapore, he had urged the International Monetary Fund to do a better job monitoring the market-interventionist modes of China, whose currency was supposedly maintained at an artificially low value against the dollar to make its goods unfairly cheap on world markets. In Beijing, he played the elder statesman from the citadel of capitalism, counseling an elite group of university students to embrace an opening up of the Chinese banking system—which was dominated by state institutions—as the best way to boost national fortunes.[18] Now, here he was only two years later, in the midst of a storm, and seemingly putting aside the philosophy that he had espoused throughout his career. Suddenly, the solution to the problem at hand was massive state intervention in the marketplace. And this was needed, he kept saying, not just to save banking, but to spare ordinary citizens—by inference, those like Dorothy Thomas, Greg Bailey, and other working people whose livelihoods were connected to a functioning financial system.

"I am convinced that this bold approach will cost American families far less than the alternative—a continuing series of financial institution failures and frozen credit markets unable to fund economic expansion," he said in delivering his bailout request to Congress. "The financial security of all Americans—their retirement savings, their home values, their ability to borrow for college, and the opportunities for more and higher-paying jobs—depends on our ability to restore our financial institutions to a sound footing."[19]

How ultimately could we assess such claims? It was more art than science, given the complex, mysterious nature of the investments at the center of the crisis and the uncertainties about who owned what and was exposed to whom. We in the press suffered from the same difficulties that plagued the markets: the pile of toxic assets at the center of the crisis was so enormous, complex, and interlinked that it was difficult to figure out the extent of the dangers. We were essentially required to make a snap judgment about the dangers, in real time, as the financial markets were roiled by abject fear and uncertainty, and as the people who presumably had the most detailed information—the Treasury, the Federal Reserve, giant Wall Street institutions—proclaimed loudly that any delay in producing bailouts risked a systemic meltdown.

What were the potential losses to the financial system if the reckoning continued unimpeded? The estimates ran the gamut, from hundreds of billions of dollars to multiple trillions of dollars. And these numbers depended upon estimates of the real worth of the sundry investments built of huge pools of mortgages, whose values fluctuated in the marketplace, moving in response to other variables such as interest rates, confidence in the housing market, and the depth of fear about the extent of the crisis itself. A bailout might restore confidence and thereby lift the values of mortgage-backed securities. That might reduce the need for some institutions to come up with extra collateral against their credit guarantees—cash they might otherwise be forced to obtain by selling assets, which would drive prices down further. That seemed to many economists a reasonable argument, a justification for expending taxpayer dollars. But it was speculative. It might work as planned, or it might work out some other way. Each potential policy outcome was dependent upon how the market construed the effectiveness of the policy, and that was anyone's best guess. Every question about how a proposed bailout scheme would work—nationalization of the banks, as some economists demanded; or capital injected into the banks—essentially involved fitting together a puzzle made of myriad moving pieces and guessing about its final composition; estimating what comfort the market would or would not take, with what resulting impacts on the financial system and the real economy.

Which takes me back to the persistent criticism that we in the press wound up participating in a fear-mongering campaign to the detriment of the taxpayer. This notion is predicated on two assumptions, one dubious and one wrong. The dubious assumption is that the economy would have been better served by no bailouts of the financial system, an argument one still encounters with regularity. Perhaps this is so (though it certainly did not look that way at the time to most economists). Perhaps it is otherwise. The point is, as we have already explored, there was simply no way to know. Such questions may be debated until the end of time by economists (who, after all, still do not fully agree what caused the Great Depression!). But in the moment, no one could have known with assurance, because such claims occupied not the province of facts but the realm of theorizing and conjecture.

The false assumption is this persistent idea that fear was man-
ufactured, when it was clearly embedded in much of commercial
American life. I could feel it as I spoke with people who had been
out of work for months and saw no evidence of anything but more
layoffs on the horizon. I could sense it as I interviewed managers
who were frantically laying off workers to cut costs out of anxiety
that they might get caught without adequate bank financing and
would be unable to get more. I could feel it as I spoke with economists who had been measured and careful in their descriptions of
the recession and who, by late 2008, were speaking of a one-in-
four probability of another Great Depression. The idea that fear
was the mere product of a political strategy may make sense to
conspiracy-minded analysts from afar, but it simply did not gibe
with the sense of events on the ground. With jobs disappearing
along with retirement savings and a deep panic spreading by the
day, it was not possible to write about the debate over the bailout
without conveying fear, even while noting the skepticism and unease with the process. Fear was palpable, real, and pervasive. Had
we in the press chosen to consciously not broadcast the fears out
of concern that we might be used as conduits for bad information
from the government, we would have been censoring ourselves and
depriving readers of a full sense of what was actually going on.

None of this is to dismiss the continuing and necessary debate over the shape of the bailouts, and whether they amounted to
overly generous gifts for Wall Street with not enough benefit for
taxpayers, home owners, and working people. Such debates were
present in our coverage at the time, and such arguments will and
should continue—a healthy process. But those who are critical of
the policies that arose from the deliberation may be unduly inclined to pin the deficiencies on journalism, as if cogent reporting
somehow guarantees thoughtful policy. If history has proven anything it is that warnings are never a guarantee that danger will be
avoided.

It is not possible to discuss accusations of press-enhanced
fear mongering without thinking of the run-up to the Iraq War,
when the American media (and the *New York Times* in particular)
were criticized by media writers, antiwar activists, and the public
in general for failing to adequately scrutinize claims made by the
Bush administration about what the intelligence-gathering appa-
ratus had learned about Saddam Hussein's military arsenal. Subsequently, major newspapers such as the *Times* and the *Washington*

Post acknowledged that they focused too much on capturing what the White House would do while fumbling the crucial role of asking whether the war was being planned and sold honestly. Some critics of the press and the bailouts have claimed similarities in the coverage of the financial crisis and the debate over the need for Wall Street rescues.

But there were crucial differences between the fear that pervaded the crafting of the bailouts and the way in which the United States entered Iraq in the spring of 2003. In the case of Saddam's threat, the claims lay squarely in the province of fact, verifiable or debunkable: either Saddam had chemical weapons or he didn't. This was a mystery that had a clear answer. What was the risk faced by the American economy without a taxpayer financed bailout of Wall Street? What would have happened had the bailout come with different obligations for the financial system? Well, it depends. The answer to these and a thousand related questions depends on a host of ultimately unanswerable questions, a rich stew of interlinked conjecture and assertion about multiple variables—from the reactions of foreign creditors holding trillions of dollars worth of dollar-denominated assets to the inclinations of American employers to fire more workers as the crisis built. It is very much a theoretical debate, one best reserved for taverns and academic conference halls, a debate that will no doubt fill out doctoral dissertations for generations. But for working people, business owners, policy makers, and journalists, these were questions that played out day by day, hour by hour, with potentially catastrophic consequences resulting from a failure to do enough.

The press does not have the benefits enjoyed by historians and academic economists who can spend decades parsing data and studying transcripts from subsequent congressional hearings. The press does not have subpoena power or access to all of the rooms in which the government deliberates. In the fall of 2008 and into 2009, when it looked to many reasonable people from across the ideological spectrum that the world was at grave risk of an economic calamity, with the quiet crisis by then fully blossomed into an outright financial panic, we had our hands full simply trying to make sense of the crush of events unfolding day after day.

It has been said that newspaper journalists write history's rough draft. In that vein, revisions are already underway on the key questions that must be debated in the interest of a full accounting of the public interest: Why did the Bush administration, followed by the

Obama administration, opt not to take greater control of banks in exchange for so much taxpayer money? Should the bailout funds have been conditioned on salary caps, and on limits for bonuses? Should the bailouts have been administered in parallel with a reform of the financial regulatory structure, to eradicate the incentives that encouraged banking executives to take so many risks?

These are all important and legitimate questions, questions that were debated at the time in the press, and questions that are still with us many months later, as fresh details trickle out about deliberations over the bailouts, and why the deals were cut as they were. Sharp differences of opinion exist over the quality of the decisions that were made, the fairness of the bailouts for taxpayers, and their efficacy in reducing the likelihood of fresh crises. Debate continues over whether Lehman Brothers should have been spared from collapse, and how events might have transpired differently had government stepped in with a bailout for that institution.

But as the events of 2008 and 2009 recede into history, it is imperative that we in the press not lose touch with the understanding that we gained about the root causes of the financial crisis—the quiet crisis that had been gnawing away at American economic security for much longer. Any complete assessment of the media's role in covering the financial crisis must ultimately take the long view. One enduring question is whether we manage to retain the knowledge that wages and incomes for working people are the crucial indicators of economic health, and not the wonders of some new technology or another investment fad. This is the real lesson we must recall again and again, lest we lose focus when and if the next investment bubble comes along, seemingly offering up an elixir of wealth that justifies an extended departure from financial common sense.

Everyday finances were strained and untenable in millions of American households long before the banks came tumbling down. How that story plays out over the years to come is a crucial thread every bit as consequential as the continued debate over the response to the financial crisis.

7

THE REAL HOUSING CRISIS
OF ORANGE COUNTY
Moe Tkacik

These guys disdained the medium. . . . They had open contempt for the medium. . . . I want to be in that pantheon. I keep thinking, God, I can disdain the medium, because those guys did, and they were great men. They were great men. . . . They really got it, and I think about them and I think [a lot] about . . . How do you go beyond the four walls? Picasso was plagued by the four walls, but then how do you have the hubris to even think you should be in the room with Picasso and Matisse? No! No—because those are great men. But you want to aspire to it—so rather than be constrained by the four walls of TV, why not try to be like these heroes, even if it's hubris to try. Why not try?

—Former hedge fund manager and popular CNBC host Jim Cramer, on his post-Impressionist role models, from a 2009 *Esquire* profile written in the aftermath of the most devastating financial crisis since the Great Depression

A television studio has four walls. A house, particularly one built, or appended with a home-equity-financed addition, during the period in which we were all encouraged to do such things, probably has a few more. A mortgage bond contains a few thousand

mortgages backed by houses with four walls, only the bond transformed into a structure that works something like a terraced rice
paddy on a hillside, where if a certain number of people can't make
their payments it's like a mild drought, and the bottom tiers of the
terrace will yield no rice; and if a slightly larger number of people
can't make their payments, it's like a more severe drought and the
middle tiers won't yield rice either. Only in an ingenious twist, the
thing actually looks like a rice paddy upside down, so the biggest
layer lies on top, because the odds are so slim that anyone won't be
able to pay their mortgages that only the tiniest tip of land really
stands to suffer. Maybe in a highly unlikely scenario the second-
tiniest slice gets parched as well, but really the likelihood of any
of that ever occurring is so totally remote and completely unprecedented that we've already knocked out all the lower layers of those
deals and rolled them into what we call a mezzanine collateralized
debt obligation, which yields in exactly the same way as the initial
reverse rice paddy we were talking about, except where before all
those bottom layers considered themselves first in line to get wiped
out, the probability of that even happening in more than a few
upside-down rice paddies is so unthinkably small that we can pretty
much guarantee you right now that no fewer than four-fifths will
absolutely, definitely promise to deliver beaucoup crops this year.
In fact, our authorities on the real estate market have such complete, unshakable faith in our innovative paddy structures' proven
ability to weather just about anything Mother Nature has got for
them that we have cloned about five to ten "synthetic" paddies to
track the *performance* of most of our mezzanine paddies, that are
literally mirror images of the paddies we were talking about before,
except no one has to go through the trouble of actually trying to
farm rice on the things.

The above is a somewhat lame attempt to illustrate some of
the major challenges of illustrating the roots of the financial crisis
within the confines of the "four walls" of two-dimensional television programming. Systems do not make the easiest television
characters to begin with, even those as familiar and photogenic
and intuitively understood as vital to the history of civilization
as the terraced rice paddy. The rise of the market in mortgage-
backed securities is of course none of those things, but the imagery of irrigation and "waterfall structures"—and also, PowerPoint
graphics depicting the complex structure of CDOs as something
slightly more sophisticated than a steam engine—was widely and

incessantly deployed to exploit the myth of American invincibility and obfuscate the holes it had been spackling with credit card debt. Ride out the metaphor, of course, and the inverse pyramid scheme analogy only stands if there is no gravity—but then, where will the rain fall if gravity is suspended!?—and in any case floods are out of the equation, no doubt thanks to all the musical chairs going on, what with all the tranching and flipping and refinancing. . . . It could maybe work as a video game, in which shooting and exploding and Ponzi scheming one's score to ever higher numerals is the whole idea, but not on TV for anything longer than a highly stylized Lady Gaga music video. It just doesn't make enough sense. The reality of it is simply not realistic enough.

And so the tidal forces of financial "innovation" directly responsible for propelling Wall Street earnings numbers and bonuses and housing prices into the stratosphere went mostly undocumented on literal-minded television—which is to say, outside the absurdist ghetto of so-called reality, which we'll get to later. The cable network most conspicuously positioned to prepare itself and its viewers for the unnatural disaster that would ensue, the business channel CNBC, was caught utterly unawares. Its most decorated reporter, David Faber, whom audience members will recognize by his nickname The Brain (a long-standing reference to his cerebral disposition), recounted in a passage of his 2009 crisis book *And Then the Roof Caved In* an alarming call he received in February 2007 from a Texas hedge fund manager named Kyle Bass:

> I still have my notes from the call. The page is filled with words and phrases that I was hearing for the first time: CDOs; $100 billion in subprime mezzanine tranches; ABX Index; 1100 is mid-06 BBB on the index; '06 CDO issuance—$200 billion. . . . In the months to come, I would slowly begin to make sense of the avalanche of information Bass unleashed on that February afternoon.

"CDO issuance" had in fact been much larger than Faber's notes even indicated, according to Securities Industry and Financial Markets Association statistics: $520.64 billion in 2006 was joined by another $481.6 billion in 2007, totaling more than a trillion dollars worth of the things—most of which contained at least some less-than-prime mortgage bonds or their "synthetic" clones—released out into the global capital markets *after* the housing market had officially topped out. And yet you wouldn't know that to watch CNBC; you wouldn't even know what a CDO *was* to watch CNBC, because no one at CNBC had probably heard of CDOs before if The Brain himself hadn't, and even The Brain could only very *slowly* make sense of this massive avalanche rapidly charging in his direction. But the thing about TV, cable news channels especially, is that everything has to happen very fast. And to deliver fast-paced news coverage all day long, although the folks at Fox might be loathe to admit it, cable news relies heavily on the American government, which has traditionally dispensed not only the steady stream of regular press briefings and photo-ops, camera-ready legislative hearings, and public officials ready to spout talking points on the debate of the day but also the funding and resources for police departments and medical examiners, attorneys general and governors, and even the odd city mayor or decorated military official to stand ready and willing to hold an emergency press briefing whenever the inevitable unscheduled terrorist attack or celebrity overdose or Missing White Girl demanded it.

The government had an obvious incentive to do these things, of course; because when it did not, as every American with a television was reminded in the aftermath of Hurricane Katrina, there were only so many places to point the television cameras, and none of them reflected so well on the American government. Interestingly, in 2006 the blonde financial analyst and media darling Meredith Whitney, a CNBC regular, credited cable news coverage of Katrina for inspiring the detailed research and economic analysis that led to her prescient warnings that the banking system was not equipped to weather what she correctly saw to be an imminent recession that would devastate the country's lower working class. (If the Ninth Ward was what life looked like at the modern American poverty level, her reasoning went, the tranche of society living just above it whom the innovations of subprime lending had made into home owners could not be much better.) But if any fault lay in Whitney's prognostications, it was that her analysis was at once too sensible and understandable, and too unbelievable. Sure, statistics seemed to indicate that somewhere between 10 and 30 million Americans who were deemed uncreditworthy in the twentieth century had somehow gotten mortgages in the twenty-first, but what blue-chip financial institution would have actually enabled such a thing? Well, to answer that you needed first to grasp some essential basics about CDOs. But since no such widely broadcast disaster existed as an incentive to monitor the CDOs and other arcane financial instruments—which have since been described in writing as "exotic" and "sophisticated" and even "elegant" but in no way complied with the television definition of any of those words—the government succumbed to the myriad other incentives, from lobbyists and campaign contributors and the surfeit of polling data that never ceased to indicate monstrous rates of disapproval among the public (despite all their efforts) for the involvement of the government in anything, and it did nothing.

It should be established here that CNBC has always differed in a few important ways from other cable news channels. Its studios are based in suburban New Jersey and its executives do not report to the NBC news division (which is headquartered along with most other things NBC in the storied GE Building at 30 Rockefeller Center). It relies far less on government activity to fuel the insatiable news hole, and the public officials to which it does regularly devote coverage—Fed governors and Labor Department analysts and the odd SEC enforcement attorney—are mostly ignored by the rest of television news, probably because they don't make great television. CNBC's programming format more closely resembles that of ESPN, whose flagship highlight show "Sports Center" its executives often cite as an inspiration, only in the absence of the awesome visual spectacles of touchdowns and slam dunks, the built-in suspense of free throws and at bats, and the grace and inspiring civic pride displayed by loyal lifetime fans, CNBC substituted a colorful array of constantly shifting real-time charts, graphs, and indices accompanied by futuristic sound effects to convey the constant motion of the markets, and supplied suspense with digital stopwatches in the corner of the screen that counted down, by the hundredths of a second, the moments before the open or close of the market or the release of some sort of economic indicator or some other potentially market-moving event.

But what made CNBC such eminently watchable TV was the strategic deployment of certain reporters to deliver regular market updates live from the middle-aged male mosh pits that were the trading floors of the New York Stock Exchange, the Chicago Board of Trade, and the New York and Chicago Mercantile Exchanges where beefy men in ugly jackets pushed one another around in a deafening Hobbsian struggle to hear and be heard hollering out the constant indecipherable stream of buy and sell orders that set the prices of stocks, options, commodities, and futures at any given moment of the trading day. If you first began watching CNBC during the fin de siècle technology stock bubble, when its ratings regularly trounced CNN's, you knew all the headline-making market movements and record-breaking fortunes would be announced over at the NASDAQ site, where some dork with the temperament of a sedated meteorologist read the latest in tech ticker news from a giant light-up wall which displayed stock prices beneath their corresponding (and generally corny) corporate logos. The action was downtown at the NYSE, where Maria Bartiromo, the network's franchise reporter, a comely brunette with very full lips and a melodic if heavily Brooklyn-accented voice, kept viewers abreast of the latest machinations of the "old economy" stocks from a bustling trading floor that appeared all the more chaotic for the fact that the specialists and junior staffers working there were said to often purposely bump into her on their way from one side of the room to the other. When the dot-com bubble collapsed and investors repaired to the safety of the venerable blue chips, Maria's legend only grew. It was almost as if she'd been vindicated; everyone else on the Street with the chance to jump into the utopian tech stock game had taken it, but she'd stayed at the Big Board. The tabloids called her the "Money Honey"; she later trademarked the phrase.

The other trading floors from which CNBC broadcast live always seemed slightly more esoteric than the NYSE. But they were useful in contextualizing some of the broader trends that could presumably help viewers figure out the direction of the stock market. If oil futures were on the rise, for instance, that was dangerous for airplane stocks. If soybeans fell, Nabisco might benefit. Interest rate changes seemed to be good either way; when they were low, viewers were often reminded that it was cheaper for both consumers and corporations to borrow money, and that this grew the economy. But if and when the Fed decided to raise rates, institutions would likely rotate their funds *out* of bonds and into stocks, and that was mostly good, too.

For the first fifty years since it achieved a mass audience, although few besides cranky academics and foreigners understood it, television offered a near-unalloyed celebration of American market capitalism. Belonging to that mass audience, of course, signified one's membership in the affluent society; televisions were expensive and large in those days, and owning one meant you probably owned a house. You were more valuable to advertisers than the audience of almost any other property in any other medium, and the medium of television was infinitely more effective than any other for engendering desire or searing something in the memory of the consumer. Movies had flourished during the Great Depression by peddling high-end voyeurism at a set price to struggling masses; television had a more complex array of potential functions. Like radio and newspapers, it informed viewers of the news; like the old screwball comedies, it entertained. By the 1960s variety shows were increasingly necessary to keep the public informed about new entertainment; television was its own best advertisement, and almost inextricable from the idea of America itself. As Richard Nixon told Nikita Khrushchev during the great Kitchen Debate of 1959, in which the then-vice president and the Soviet premier held a rare cross-Curtain chat filmed inside the kitchen of a model suburban home the Soviets has somehow allowed the Americans to erect in a park outside Moscow: "There are some instances where you may be ahead of us, for example, in the development of the thrust of your rockets for the investigation of outer space. And there may be some instances in which we are ahead of you—in color television, for instance."

Nixon's simultaneous exploitation and celebration of television was so masterful it seems almost a deliberate plot that American children are still learning to credit his defeat in the presidential election the next year to the triumph of a tan and telegenic American Idol over an overworked and underpigmented policy wonk. Nixon very deliberately sought to establish himself as the guy who appreciated being able to own a TV infinitely more than he did the being able to appear on it. A full five years before Marshall McLuhan would famously observe that the medium is the message, the Kitchen Debate became one of the first events ever recorded and broadcast on color television. In this debate ostensibly about technological progress occasioned mainly by the Sputnik launch, Nixon took the perhaps counterintuitive approach of giving Khrushchev an extensive tour of newfangled American kitchen appliances, explaining that the American consumer had chosen to pursue technological progress in more peaceful, practical realms than missile technology. "Don't you have a machine that puts food into the mouth and pushes it down?" was the Russian's incredulous reaction to his introduction to cake mix and electric mixers. "Many things you have shown us are interesting but they are not needed in life. They have no useful purpose." Viewers who owned them knew otherwise, of course; the electric mixer was much more provably, tangibly useful than anything in outer space. Nixon's appearance was broadcast late at night with no translation in Russia, where few people had a TV anyway. But his argument (inasmuch as he had one) would nevertheless eventually prevail, as manufacturing of cake mixers and television sets moved to Asia and drove television prices down, and word got around about the verisimilitude of American television's affluence.

There is a telling scene in the most recent season premiere of Bravo's hit reality show *The Real Housewives of Orange County*. Gretchen and Lynne have gathered in what looks to be mid-afternoon at a leafy outdoor cafe, and because it is the premiere, they are supposed to have some catching up to do. Lynne, a very thin, bronze middle-aged brunette wearing tight white pants, a light blue lace-trimmed bell-sleeved off-the-shoulder top and matching frilly light blue drop earrings, wants to tell Gretchen about her new jewelry line and invite her to an event she is hosting in its honor. Every aspect of this setup is highly typical of twenty-first century reality television in that it is entirely staged for the purpose of generating enough scenes to fuse into some sort of narrative about the meaningless lives of heroically shallow people while simultaneously giving said shallow people ostensible products to shill and by extension sustain buzz for *The Real Housewives* franchise during the off-season (Gretchen is starting a makeup line), except for the fact that we have just learned that Lynne's jewelry actually needs to somehow turn a profit. Like nearly all the Orange County housewives, Lynne's lifestyle was sustained by the real estate business, but her husband's construction firm has gotten no work since the collapse of the California real estate market. As she mentions the jewelry event to Gretchen, a thirty-one-year-old platinum blonde in the Playboy mansion mold wearing some sort of checkered corset, Lynne begins to stutter and spasm slightly in the face, causing the younger castmate to intuit that she has already invited Tamra, another housewife who accused Gretchen on the reunion show of dating another man during the filming of the previous season, during which she had supposedly been totally preoccupied caring for her terminally ill fiancé Jeff. Tamra's accusation was based on the assertion of a man who had called her claiming to have been Gretchen's actual boyfriend during the prior season and also, some lewd (though not that lewd, in the scheme of things) photos of Gretchen that appeared on the Internet at some inappropriately brief time after Jeff died from leukemia. Gretchen maintains—and I paraphrase, because her vocabulary is slightly more limited than this—that the guy is a delusional stalker and that Tamra's eagerness to believe scurrilous gossip about her fellow housewives renders her untrustworthy. She pleas with Lynne—who like Gretchen was a fellow newcomer to the show during the prior season—not to forget how viciously two-faced she had been toward both of them.

GRETCHEN (*widens eyes; she is the most likable housewife, because her eyes are so big that when she widens them incredulously this way the viewer senses she might share their sense of profound dismay that such people as her co-stars exist*) Don't you remember? When she wrote about how [in a previously addresed e-mail] you and I "make her skin crawl."

LYNNE (*shakes head despairingly*) I don't know what to believe . . .

GRETCHEN It's right there! I copied and pasted it for you!

LYNNE (*continues shaking head, gestures toward eyes and ears*) I don't know, I don't actually believe anything until I actually hear it and see it with my own two eyes and two ears . . .

GRETCHEN You've seen it, and you've heard it.

LYNNE Till I see it, I won't believe it.

What I think is so compelling about this scene is that, for the audience at least, the basis of the appeal of *The Real Housewives* franchise is the way it has managed over and over again to engender, from the O.C. to Atlanta to New York and New Jersey to the White House state dinner, complete disbelief at what we have just heard and seen with our own eyes and ears. For the most part the housewives are, as opposed to the casts of reality shows featuring younger people, not exactly in on the joke, nor are they universally vacuous or devoid of redeeming qualities. Few in Orange County or Atlanta seem even to fit a loose definition of "housewives"; a couple seem suspiciously like the breadwinners of their households, but it matters not, because they all share an ethos that derived from having achieved some sort of ill-defined but transcendent state of Fabulosity. And what makes them superlative in the reality-show universe is the sort of pathological consumption habits that seemed to have programmed all the women to respond to each victory and defeat with a colossal piece of jewelry or a lavish six-course dinner party held to display a newly commissioned wall-sized portrait of oneself. At the beginning of each show, a fabulous lifestyle montage flashes on the screen of each housewife in swimwear, evening gown, driving a luxury sport-utility vehicle, working out at the gym, as her voice in the background sassily intones a personal statement, such as, "Money is a girl's best friend . . . and I like to have a lot of friends," or "Am I high maintenance? Of course I am. Look at me!" or "In Atlanta, money and class *do* give you power," or "I don't keep up with the Joneses; I *am* the Joneses." City by city, region by region, the evidence kept mounting: there was a massive population of middle-aged women in the country who had taken *Sex and the City* very, very seriously. Appropriately, Lynne's personal credo is: "It's not how much money you have, it's how good you look spending it." But it costs money to look good, and Lynne feels bad about her neck, and to peddle a jewelry line in compliance with such a brand motto, she determines it must be smoothed with reconstructive surgery. The era during which a kindly plastic surgeon might provide such a service complementary for the publicity having long since passed in Orange County, she signs up for an installment plan.

All the cute tautologies collapse in on themselves a few weeks later in the episode titled "You Can Dish It, but You Can't Take It." In a serendipitous bit of symmetry, the twenty-two-year-old daughter of another housewife named Vicki also requires neck surgery, to remove numerous possibly malignant tumors that have emerged on her thyroid gland. "How did this happen?" the dazed Vicki asks her daughter, a nurse, who responds, "I don't know, Mom, you created this body!" (We then learn Vicki also has had, among other surgeries, neck tumors removed.) Over at Lynne's house, one of her two teenage daughters answers the door to a strange man who hands her an envelope he says contains an eviction notice. This is peculiar, given that they had just thrown a housewarming party at the place. "Did that really just happen, or am I so fucking hungover that I'm still dreaming?" she asks her sister groggily as she wanders into the den holding her hand over the nose her mother will later pay to have fixed in commemoration of her nineteenth birthday. Lynne is not in the house, but when she emerges somehow looking shell-shocked, she castigates her husband using a range of female self-empowerment platitudes about the offense of "doing this to our children" and how she refuses "to be a victim" before realizing his offense pretty much amounted to having lied to her. "The reality is that you lied to me, Frank. I just feel like you treated me like I'm stupid, like I can't handle the truth," she says. "I can handle the truth, Frank." At which point he cuts her off and says, "Bullshit, Lynne. You don't want to hear the truth. The reality is that I wouldn't have to lie to you if demands weren't made that we had to live in these high rent districts." His use of the passive voice here is beguiling; how had the maker of their "demands" become so omnipotent and mysterious? "We need to get real, we need to get on the same page, and we need to start saving our money," Frank continues. "You live in this, like, little microcosm and it's not even real!"

And then the girls take a (previously planned) luxury shopping trip to San Francisco to recover from all the trauma, financed by Virgin America, Hotel Vitale, and an assortment of seafood restaurants, where Lynne bought a $1,185 leather jacket with some unspecified source of funds at a boutique that had kindly furnished all the housewives with champagne flutes, reasoning that she was soon going to receive her check—presumably the regular one she gets for allowing her life to be documented, and not from her nascent line of designer, ahem, cuffs. She and her husband would be served with three more eviction notices at their next house, although each time they would find a way to pay.

The eviction notices, foreclosures, judgments, failed mortgage modifications that have beset thirty-odd cast members of *The Real Housewives* franchise alone since the onset of the financial crisis could sustain its own scornographic tabloid magazine, but there is a substantial financial history book to be written about the evolution of the Orange County gang, which was not curated via the usual casting sessions, but by a producer who lived nearby a Playboy-Playmate-turned-real-estate-agent whose household antics he thought would make for entertaining TV. Its eminently watchable ocean sunsets, palatial estates, glimmering pools, and tanned and toned denizens indulging endlessly in elaborate sushi dinners had recently made Orange County the main attraction of a popular movie, hit television series, and a liberally spun-off hit reality TV series, *Laguna Beach*, inspired by the hit scripted series. But while those shows all had their lenses firmly fixed on its beautiful teenage population—whose affluence was marketably unencumbered by the alienating culture, sophistication, and traditional class-based snobbery found in New York and Los Angeles adolescents—*Real Housewives* was focused on the moms, the tongue-in-cheek part of it being that none of the women were really housewives but mostly working mothers of teenagers who invested an enormous amount of money and time in the effort to look and act as pampered and well-preserved as the "real" housewives of the county. The housewives were all actual friends or "frenemies" from working in local real estate, and the first season was filmed at the absolute peak of the Southern California housing bubble in mid-2005, when the median sale price of a house in Orange County hit a record high of $710,000, up from $318,000 a mere five years earlier. As with the larger national housing bubble, this explosion in prices was accompanied by literally no underlying fundamental economic or demographic shift that justified it. But its bubble was particularly exaggerated by the self-perpetuating cycle of its newfound pop cultural cachet and a relatively rich population of gullible strivers, from those living beyond their means, like the Curtins and their community of realtors and car dealers and sundry other newly affluent beneficiaries of whatever invisible economy had gone from trickling down to downpouring upon them, to the Mexican immigrants comprising a third of the population who maybe cleaned pools or moved boxes but in every case had been more likely to lend money to people back home than borrow it themselves before a mortgage lender offered them the chance to own a house with the aid of some new innovation like NINJA Option ARM, which gave people who lacked the documentation to prove the existence of any sources of income, job history, or assets the "option" of making two years of payments so low, the balance would keep growing if they paid them every month. (Two years later when their payments tripled, they could refinance.)

Orange County was the undisputed capital of subprime-mortgage lending, a trillion-dollar pyramid scheme financed by the growing coffers and pension funds of all the cash-rich countries that export things to Americans, whose custodians were wary of stocks even before the NASDAQ collapse, and almost more so of bonds after the cash flow statements of Enron and Tyco, Global Crossing, and legions of other companies with seemingly solid reputations turned out to be wholly fraudulent. Bonds assembled from American mortgage loans, on the other hand, rarely defaulted, and those very tangible houses backed the bonds, and that seemed fairly solid ground to stand on, so to speak, until people began to read the shamelessly predatory arcana of the loans themselves and the complex collateralized debt obligations through which they were investing in them. Fraud ran rampant, too; in 2004 the FBI declared it a national "epidemic" with consequences that could rival the S&L crisis of the 1980s, and that was before the truly ghastly things happened. Nearly 60 percent of the subprime loans originated that year and after were taken on by borrowers with good credit who had been somehow convinced they weren't qualified for a prime one, and the remaining 40 percent were mostly diabolical. None of these scams could rival the derangement that enabled the worst of those mortgages to not only back hundreds of billions of dollars worth of Triple-A rated bonds but clone themselves five and ten times over in the form of "synthetics" created to track those bonds; the whole scam was really too surreal for even reality TV.

In his book about the crisis *I.O.U.: Why Everyone Owes Everyone and No One Can Pay*, the British novelist and literary critic John Lanchester visits Baltimore and wonders why his favorite television show, *The Wire*—the HBO series about that city's cops, druglords, political operatives, and newspaper reporters that is generally deified by critics for its transcendent verisimilitude—"missed" the subprime lending chicanery that would soon turn the town into one of the more unlikely epicenters of the foreclosure epidemic. Having worked (as *The Wire* creator David Simon did) as a newspaper reporter in the only slightly less dissipated East Coast industrial, once-great city of Philadelphia, I wondered if it was even possible that someone so fluent in the dynamics of the sort of American city whose salient characteristic is its having been utterly abandoned by anything resembling what we think of as a private sector or capitalistic market forces could believe before the current disaster actually struck that capitalism would have figured out a way to turn a profit handing out home loans in the country's most wretched ghettos. *The Wire* was itself a phenomenon mostly shielded from market forces; HBO executives nurtured it for five seasons as a principled art project, despite anemic ratings and the fact that they knew it would never, as per the standard business model, recoup its costs in foreign rights since, as one told the *New York Times* magazine recently, "Shows that feature African Americans don't sell foreign."

Esoteric securities featuring their adjustable-rate mortgage loans, however, most definitively did. As you have no doubt read, loans made to minorities were some of the most popular loans to securitize, because their stratospheric interest rates enabled mortgage bond managers to turn them into some of the highest-yielding securities around in an era of low rates. Few outside the subprime-mortgage broker community headquartered in the O.C. knew how insatiable demand for subprime loans had become, however, and few outside the specialized "structured finance" community on Wall Street understood how utterly divorced from reality the structure of the average CDO had become. There was no clearinghouse, no frenetic trading floor, and no familiar barometers of generally accepted market sentiment for the fixed-income markets in which they traded. In theory, this was because fixed-income securities, with their straightforward promises of a "fixed" income stream, were not as inherently speculative as stocks, commodities, futures, and option. In practice, because interest-rate arbitrage—borrowing low, lending high—is Wall Street's age-old method of generating guaranteed profits, the fixed-income markets are dominated by arbitrageurs drawn to a game that is quite literally "fixed." Those guys are the reason America's unbelievable amount of mortgage risk did not get entirely dumped offshore; the yields on subprime securities were simply too tantalizing to many hedge fund managers, who were able to amp the returns by borrowing twenty and thirty times their cash under management.

The first major signal to the world outside mortgage finance that the market was in serious trouble did not come until the summer of 2007, when two multibillion-dollar Bear Stearns hedge funds sent notice to their investors that their investments had lost all of their value. That is a lot to lose when the income stream is supposed to be fixed, and the news sent utter terror through the bond markets—or at least, I read this narrative of events enough times to believe it is true. But bonds and the credit cycle were much more abstract things to me and most laymen than investments that were traded centrally. The boilerplate prose of financial wire copy was incapable of transcending these abstractions or conveying the sense of urgency and fear. CNBC, which focused mainly on stocks, was covering the thing with its usual debate team "to buy or not to buy" approach.

Then one afternoon in early August, Jim Cramer blew the cover. The occasion was a disturbing Bear Stearns conference call that had sent the investment bank's stock down 5 or 6 percent. Cramer is a former hedge fund manager with a thick Philadelphia accent and a meth addict's manic energy and wiry build whose one-man madcap afternoon call-in show about stock picking is—aside from being unlike anything else on television—the network's most watched show and the source of his reputation as Wall Street's pre-eminent emissary to Main Street. He was enduring his daily chat with Erin Burnett, a younger reporter with an almost Southern nubile-and-yet-maternal femininity who is primarily famed as the favorite to displace Bartiromo as the network's preeminent Money Honey. It's a segment that often resembles a therapy session, with the sputtering, risable Cramer unloading a sort of interior mono-logue of market sentiment on the measured, hypnotically fresh-faced Burnett, who calmly helps him retrace his steps and walk her through what the market was thinking at whatever points during the trading day it had decided to unleash some of its pent-up nega-tive energy upon a particular stock whose investors in the audience might be owed an explanation.

He began calmly enough. Bear had fucked up, he maintained, looking downward and pacing. They were going about it all wrong. They'd shown their cards, and the cards were worse than anyone had anticipated. When you're in Bear's position:

> You gotta adopt a Henry Ford attitude, and you never do that. You keep your mouth shut because you're gonna say something if you don't. And then you start to speak softly and reassure everyone that everything's fine, and then you wait till the shorts have done what they're going to do to the stock and you do what Dick Fuld did in 1998, you pick up the phone and call guys like me and you say, '32 bid one million.' And then, whack! You pick it up again and you say, '31 bid for two million.' But they're not doing that and that inspires more fear. And I like Bear Stearns very much, but I think that at this stage, this is not a good call, they shoulda just said *you know what*, we're doing well! and don't say another thing. just don't say it. It does not inspire confidence to have ten head-

lines come over about 'what to do?' I don't like it. The Dow can rally all it wants, this isn't good . . .

But Jim! [Erin wants to know]. They can't keep it all bottled up *inside* that way! Investors are going to start whining for an explanation, and if you don't give them one, won't they get suspicious?

You know what, forget the investors. Investors are gonna do what investors are gonna do. This is about Bernanke, you know, *he* is the one who's gotta be in on that call. Bernanke needs to *focus* on this. Alan Greenspan told everyone to take a teaser rate and then raised the rates seventeen times, and Bernanke is being an academic. It is NO TIME to be an academic! It is time to be on the Bear Stearns call. Listen, *open the door*, Fed window! He has *NO IDEA* how bad it is out there, he has *NO IDEA! NO IDEA! No. I. Dea.*

(There is something Pentecostal about the performance at this point, although it's harder to say whether he's preaching divine revelation or undergoing an exorcism. His body language is uncharacteristically restrained for a man who made his name bounding around the *Mad Money* set and slamming into sound-effects buttons in a manner that calls to mind the *Sesame Street* character Elmo. He will stomp his fist once or twice, tentatively. More so even than most cable news personalities, Cramer is paid to peddle harmless urgency and benign hysteria. But there is nothing benign nor hysterical about this time, somehow. Watching at home, I remember instant-messaging a friend who is a financial blogger. *U watching CNBC?* He was not. *Cramer is like . . . BATSHIT right now.* "Haha and, water = still wet!" he joked. *DUDE, just turn it on I'm telling you, how hard is that.* A clip had been posted to his site within the hour.)

I have talked to the heads of almost every one of these firms in the last 72 hours and he has NO IDEA what it's like out there. NONE! And Bill Poole, he has *NO IDEA* what it's like out there. My people have been in this game for 25 years and they're LOSING THEIR JOBS and these firms are gonna GO OUT OF BUSINESS and it's *nuts*. They're *NUTS!* They know *NOTHING!* This is a different kinda market. And the Fed is ASLEEP. Bill Poole is a shame, he's SHAMEUL! He

oughta GO, and READ the Accredited Home document, at
least I READ the darn thing.

At this point anyone watching at home is hopelessly lost.
CNBC has yet to explain to viewers what a mortgage CDO actually
is, so the morning's long-delayed filing of a 2006 annual report by a
moribund San Diego subprime-mortgage lender called Accredited
Home Loans had probably not struck too many as a must-read. So
what if one analyst called it "a well-written obituary on the industry" when the freaking stock was down 80 percent on the year? But
Cramer isn't talking to investors anymore, even though that's the
whole mantra of CNBC. He's talking to the Fed. And although we
all thought we knew vaguely what the Federal Reserve did—and
maybe we were even aware that the St. Louis Fed governor William
Poole still favored raising rates to tame inflation, while Wall Street
was desperate for rates to be lower—you had to be an amateur his-
torian or a conspiracy theorist to know about the "discount window," an emergency facility through which the Fed is allowed
to lend money interest-free directly to banks to fund operations
through market panics. Investment banks like Bear Stearns weren't
even eligible for the discount window at this point, although there
was some talk of getting around that rule by converting them all to
bank "holding companies"—which would eventually happen after
Bear Stearns went under. But Erin Burnett has done some home-
work, and she's not convinced this is a good idea. Wouldn't opening
the discount window at all surely send a frightening signal? And
wouldn't the stock market punish whoever was first to line up for
such a handout? She has talked to people who claim that opening
the window would unleash "Armageddon." This is Cramer's cue:

> We *have* Armageddon! In the fixed income market, we have
> Armageddon. . . . It's Armageddon right now. And sure, let
> them be *calm*, and then have them call me every day like they
> do on the way home from work and ask me, *Cramer*, what are
> you gonna do about it? Are you gonna help us? Are you gonna
> help us? *Are you gonna stand on the sideline like everybody else
> and say that it's fine?* Will somebody please come on the TV
> and tell the TRUTH about how BAD it is? Fourteen million
> people took a mortgage in the last three years. Seven million
> of them took teaser rates or took piggyback rates. They will
> *lose their homes.* This is crazy! I'm sorry to be upset about it

but you have to understand what they're saying to me, off the record, before I come in here, every night and every day, and what I hear from these *blowhardmanagers* . . . I mean, *call* someone for God sakes! *CALL* someone! I worked in fixed income at Goldman Sachs, this is not the time to be complacent! Sometimes I wish I didn't know anyone, so I could just sit here calmly and say, you know what? Go buy Washington Mutual. *Take that yield.* . . . Unfortunately, I know too many people, and I'm Too. Darn. Old.

"They know NOTHING!!" is today synonymous with the Jim Cramer brand. Although he has for some reason not yet made it available as one of his personalized ringtones, you can listen to it and thirty-one other classic Cramer side effects on the virtual "soundboard" maintained on the official Mad Money Web site. Nearly three years on, it seems not a CNBC commercial break goes by without reference to his prescient outburst, and yet to revisit it today in its entirety—which I had to do, since the network transcribes almost none of its programming and no amateur transcript was immediately Googlable—is to be alarmed and awed and entertained and demoralized all over again many times over. He begins in the minds of the bad guys, chastising Bear Stearns for exposing even a small fraction of its self-inflicted wounds to the public, invoking almost by instinct Lehman Brothers CEO Dick Fuld's legendary staring contest with the market during the Russian crisis of the prior decade, only to immediately snap into reverse, concede the futility of all the tried-and-true Wall Street bluffs in the brave new world of twenty-first-century finance, and try appealing directly to Ben Bernanke, berating the Fed chairman in the great Wall Street tradition of getting their way with regulators, by yelling loud and long and accusing him of being stupid. But then, perhaps conceding that the fault for the current terror lies with Bernanke's great predecessor, the one man in Washington the Street never accused of stupidity, he wisely changes course again and entreats the man to do something rarely recommended by Wall Street types and consult a dry report on the rampant abuses in an unregulated market if they don't believe him. And then finally, summoned back into the medium by his junior colleague's gentle reminder of the "he said, she said" imperatives of the format and helpful invocation of End Times, he can no longer conceal his contempt for the medium.

THIS *IS* ARMAGEDDON . . . and everyone who says otherwise is lying to you, and lying to "investors", and the only reason they can get away with it is because we never bothered to tell them about that whole "fixed income" thing where all these rotten loans are on the verge of poisoning the entire country, but I've been in this business for twenty-five years and those fuckers are scared shitless about what they've done to the economy, and you should be scared too, but it's been our jobs to get up every morning and let them lie to us for so long that no one can even tell the difference between truth and fiction anymore. But as long as 7 million Americans are going to be losing their houses and tens of millions more are going to incur total financial ruin over this one, I might as well give the blogs something to gawk over.

It was a strikingly nuanced and subversive bit of improvisation, although unsurprisingly the nuance and subversiveness seem to have gone largely unrecognized by the critics and television producers who have capitalized on its spectacle. By contrast, the equally famous spontaneous eruption a year and a half later of Cramer's Chicago-based colleague Rick Santelli would touch off the most formidable American grassroots political movement in generations and breathe zealous new life into a Republican Party whose political "brand" a party strategist had only months earlier likened to defective dog food. The peg was a February 2009 mortgage relief bill proposed by the new administration. Still smarting from the spectacular meltdown Cramer had predicted and the subsequent multitrillion dollar bailout of the Wall Street banks the network had cheered along for years as they shamelessly profited sowing its seeds, most members of CNBC's New York reporting staff regarded the legislation as an inevitability, but Santelli, an expressive albeit often incomprehensible television personality with the cartoonish facial features of a ghoulish muppet or a used car salesman with a heart of gold, had spent his entire career in the Midwest. He had risen up the Darwinian ranks of the Chicago Mercantile Exchange trading floor making markets in futures and options linked to gold, lumber, livestock, interest rates, currencies, and so forth, before defecting to become a CNBC trading floor correspondent, where he delivered his missives over the din of bids and orders above which he was often barely able to hear the questions or comments of his colleagues back East. Santelli had opposed all of the bailouts, but never so vehemently as this one, whose $75 billion price tag was decidedly puny in the breathtaking scheme of the scam. To hearty whoops from the trading floor and a collective eyeroll from the Squawk Box studio, Rick Santelli addressed the new president as Cramer had Bernanke:

> How about this, President and new administration? Why don't you put up a Web site to have people vote on the Internet as a referendum to see if we really want to subsidize the losers' mortgages; or would we like to at least buy cars and buy houses in foreclosure and give them to people that might have a chance to actually prosper down the road, and reward people that could carry the water instead of drink the water? This is America! How many of you people want to pay for your neighbor's mortgage that has an extra bathroom and can't pay their bills? Raise their hand. President Obama, are you listening? You know, Cuba used to have mansions and a relatively decent economy. They moved from the individual to the collective. Now, they're driving '54 Chevys, maybe the last great car to come out of Detroit. We're thinking of having a Chicago Tea Party in July. All you capitalists that want to show up to Lake Michigan, I'm gonna start organizing. We're going to be dumping in some derivative securities. What do you think about that? Listen, all's I know is, is that there's only about 5 percent of the floor population here right now, and I talk loud enough they can all hear me. So if you want to ask 'em anything, let me know. These guys are pretty straight forward, and my guess is, a pretty good statistical cross-section of America, the silent majority. You know, they're pretty much of the notion that you can't buy your way into prosperity, and if the multiplier that all of these Washington economists are selling us is over . . . that we never have to worry about the economy again. The government should spend a trillion dollars an hour because we'll get 1.5 trillion back . . . I'll tell you what, if you read our Founding Fathers, people like Benjamin Franklin and Jefferson . . . What we're doing in this country now is making them roll over in their graves.

That afternoon, a Web site dedicated to championing Santelli's Tea Party movement would go live and by the powers of search engine optimization, immediately get barraged by viewers wanting to learn more about the emerging movement. Left-leaning bloggers would immediately turn up evidence suggesting the rant had been somehow staged by right-wing operatives; Santelli would post a lengthy (and somewhat poorly punctuated) rant on the CNBC Web site, cancel a scheduled appearance on the *Daily Show*, and cut his ties with the network; bloggers would accuse him of being silenced by the Powers That Be at CNBC's then-parent company General Electric, which had issued $340 billion in debt backed by a FDIC program to restore trust in the bond markets in the throes of the crisis; an anonymous network staffer would later tell the *New York Post* that GE CEO Jeffrey Immelt had instructed them to go easier on the Obama administration at a private staff meeting held for senior reporters; the Tea Party movement would in the meantime become a staggeringly potent clearinghouse of vague anti-Obama sentiment without any further nurture from its Paul Revere figure, and CNBC would come under new ownership in GE's sale of NBC to Comcast. The quest to expose some insidious Establishment power as the true identity of the puppet master on either side of Santelli's peculiar rant was an irrelevant sideshow; as Cramer had been trying to point out, everyone was just imprisoned by the four walls of their own simplistic television-addled perceptions of how the world worked. But a trillion dollars is a desperately impossible sum to comprehend, something Santelli himself would later attempt to rectify in a curious segment on the myopia of outrage over the $165 million in retention bonuses AIG employees made in 2008 next to the magnitude of its $183 billion bailout. A more coherent reaction would be expected if the crisis had played out more like an episode of *Law & Order*, but they really knew nothing other than what they knew.

Shortly after the rant, Santelli granted a rare interview to the director of a documentary called *Floored* about the demise of the physical floor traders among whom he had spent his career. As with the floor at the New York Stock Exchange, whose emptiness CNBC no longer makes much of an effort to conceal, the vocation is nearly extinct. In its 1980s heyday five hundred traders regularly showed up to heave and holler through the trading day on the floor of the Chicago Board of Trade; now there are about fifty. The rest have been displaced, inevitably, by computers and the geeks who excel at manipulating them. In the film Santelli waxes elegiac about the culture that's been lost and the friends and colleagues who have become broken men as a result. It's the reason he now works for CNBC; in the golden era, the idea of launching a spontaneous political rally on the trading floor would have been laughable. But the evolution of the commodities and futures markets couldn't have happened any other way; the volume—in every sense—was too overwhelming, and there were too many orders and too many variables.

The economic crisis was in some ways portended more vividly and viscerally on reality television than it ever was on CNBC. Anyone who had borne witness to the era of easy credit through the lens of reality television, whether on any regional branch of the *Housewives* or *My Super Sweet 16*, or *Flip This House* or *Flipping Out*, *Million-Dollar Listing* or *Millionaire Matchmaker*, or *The Apprentice* or *Kimora: Life in the Fab Lane* or *Sunset Tan* or *Extreme Makeover* or *Pimp My Ride* or *Keeping Up with the Kardashians* or any other of the 350 similarly titled reality shows, would assume that the great American growth industries of the twentieth century were, in no particular order: party planning, luxury real estate, luxury rehab, luxury casinos, luxury handbags, plastic surgery, makeup, artificial tanning, sororities, sex tapes, gentrification, dermatology, lifestyle branding, luxury auto customization, dramatic weight loss pursued via humiliating tactics under the close supervision of cameras, and so forth. And would that have been so off the mark? Never in history had so much programming been so concerned with reflecting economic trends, and never before either had Americans been forced to confront the real cultural legacy of an economy and a mass media that had never given much consideration to what it meant to be "American" other than membership in the biggest and most voracious population of consumers in the history of the world. Did a single challenge on *The Apprentice*—the Donald Trump–hosted (and much spun-off) reality-show franchise which drew its contestants from the nation's bona fide "best and brightest" brand affiliations such as Goldman Sachs, Harvard Business School, Wharton—not fundamentally revolve around marketing? (Hint: event planning is a form of marketing.)

With the days of the floor traders long since passed, incidentally, reality television was a much wiser stepping stone for a younger generation to get a gig on CNBC; Rebecca Jarvis, an ambitious young trader-turned-trade-journalist living in Chicago in the middle of the decade, landed her own gig covering commodities on CNBC in 2006 after almost winning the fourth season of *The Apprentice*. (She left the network in September 2009 to take an as-yet-unannounced job on another network.)

If the old courtroom / emergency room / interrogation room dramas still thrived for their so-far unmatched ability to explore moral and ethical dilemmas through the perspectives of complex characters, reality television offered unparalleled access to the cultural and moral bankruptcy that seemed to naturally accompany the accumulation of so much excess and waste. And access was crucial: in the award-winning documentary special *House of Cards* that CNBC reporter David Faber eventually produced on the causes of the crisis, the Texas hedge fund manager Kyle Bass, his original source of all those unfamiliar new terms like "CDO" he had heard for the first time in 2007, said his probe into the subprime-mortgage market had been partially inspired by a YouTube clip of a publicity stunt for a $33.5-million movie being produced by an Orange County subprime-mortgage broker with a seventh-grade education named Daniel Sadek. The movie, *Redline*, largely centered around Sadek's formidable fleet of luxury cars— it also starred his then-fiancé, a soap opera actress—one of which he had allowed the actor Eddie Griffin to deliberately total on a racetrack in a publicity stunt. (Griffin would later accidentally total another.) The sight of a Porsche and a Ferrari perishing in such a way reinforced the hedge fund manager's convictions in a way nothing else could. "It was such a senseless destruction of capital," Bass later told the *House of Cards* cameras. Sadek's company, Quick Loan Financial, had extended about $4 billion in almost universally fraudulent mortgages, all of which were securitized, many if not most of which were cloned into "synthetic" bonds when the country literally ran out of dupes to give mortgages to. But for less than $2 million, easily less than one-twentieth of a percentage point of the damage Wall Street financiers would enable Sadek's company alone to wreak upon the economy, Sadek had driven the message home on the small screen.

Television is a powerful medium that way. In the new anthology *Reality Matters*, the former *Daily Show* correspondent Stacey Grenrock Woods credits *The Real Housewives of New York* for buoying her flagging spirits throughout the many months she spent unemployed during the financial crisis. Its characters are so irredeemably repugnant—and so brilliantly edited to highlight this fact—that she felt like less of a failure. And there was something deeply satisfying in the outrage the Republican Party was burdened with manufacturing in response to the successful infiltration of the Obama White House's first state dinner by Tareq and Michaele Salahi, a northern Virgina couple competing for a spot in the Washington, DC, iteration of the *Real Housewives* franchise. The Salahis might have belonged to Al Qaeda; but it seemed somehow much more fitting that the evening's greatest national security threat was simply the latest bleached-blonde member of the newest chapter of America's leading brand of vacuous middle-aged TV famewhores. They may not be the worst fair-weather freeloaders to attempt to leech off the Obama administration, though; Jeana Keough, an original O.C. housewife who is underwater on numerous properties, recently praised the mortgage relief efforts of the president—who incidentally received a larger percentage of the Orange County vote since any Democratic presidential candidate since Franklin Roosevelt—in a blog post. Santelli's apocryphal neighbor with the extra bathroom was not so apocryphal; perhaps one day a more united America will recognize its true enemy not as socialism or capitalism but the irresponsible and unsustainable waste and excess it intuitively knows to be the scourge.

This will not happen overnight, of course. But the landscape of American television has been irrevocably altered by the dramatic boom and bust of its first decade in twenty-first-century capitalism. By far the most successful television show introduced so far in 2010 has been a reality series produced by one of the inventors of *Project Runway* called *Undercover Boss*, in which CEOs undergo makeovers and spend a week working undercover in the bowels of their companies, trailed by a production team purporting to be at work on a documentary series on the experiences (and genuine trend) of white-collar layoff victims attempting to reenter the workforce by taking blue-collar jobs. None of the companies in question can claim the fat profit margins or innovation-based growth stories that land a CEO on CNBC, but they do all actually employ American people, which makes for undeniably riveting viewing. For the most part, we watch the CEOs fail—at Roto-Rooter, to unclog sewer pipes; at Waste Management, to vacuum a lineup of Porta-Potties fast enough; at Hooters, to bus tables; at White Castle, to do pretty much anything. Their new co-workers also bombard the CEOs with stories of their typically depressing daily struggles—foreclosures, lack of health insurance, dead children, and so forth—that force them to confront the predicable litany of ethical and moral dilemmas.

Critics of *Undercover Boss* have voiced skepticism that so many struggling workers would so automatically bare souls and unload sorrows before a new colleague on the first day of work, and they most assuredly would act differently around a boss. But people often become slightly more vivid versions of themselves in the presence of cameras and the attendant understanding that there might be thousands or millions of viewers on the other side. What is different about the ordinary Americans talking about their lives to the *Undercover Boss* is that they have no persona to impress upon or accessories line to shill to the consumers in the audience; they're just opening up to anyone willing to listen. Life is hard, that is a big theme; that so many people in pretty rotten situations managed to be compassionate and genuine and admirable human beings in spite of it—that's the revelation the television bloggers generally confess to getting "misty" about. *Undercover Boss* has become the most popular show on Sunday, regularly drawing about 15 million viewers who skew heavily young, especially for CBS.

There is an irony in the reality of young viewers, following years of being so aggressively coveted and courted by advertisers and catered to with the attendant aspirational programming about modeling and shopping and fame, tuning into a show about people who clean toilets and flip burgers for a living. (*The Real Housewives of Orange County* appears to be more popular, too, as a result of the wives' financial struggles; ratings for that show's fifth season grew 40 percent from the fourth.) Older viewers have meanwhile increasingly satisfied their appetites for economic understanding by tuning into the volatile fearmonger and Fox News Tea Party darling Glenn Beck but also Jon Stewart, whose *Daily Show* audience aged five years to forty-nine between 2008 and 2009, no doubt in part because the comedian has devoted such dogged coverage to the financial crisis.

Stewart's financial coverage often misses the proverbial mark, but he's a creature of the four walls. When in 2009 in the wake of Santelli's rant Jim Cramer offered himself up to the *Daily Show* for a dress-down of his industry, many regular CNBC viewers rightly pointed out that Stewart was indicting the wrong guy, conflating apples and oranges. But Cramer was visibly chastened by the destruction his industry had wreaked on the country, and that was worthwhile television. If there is a major logical flaw that Stewart's economic critiques have exhibited in the dozens of segments he has devoted to the crisis, it's his persistent outrage that there were so many people who profited from a collapse that resulted in so much misfortune. He is one of them too, and if fraud and injustice are ultimately exposed in the process, sometimes that is a price society needs to pay. *The Wire*'s David Simon recently somewhat sheepishly boasted that Hurricane Katrina had given him the chance he'd always wanted to do a television series about New Orleans; he and a friend polished off a pitch and sent it around to television executives two or three weeks after the levies broke; that series, *Treme*, premiered in April 2010. Meanwhile financial engineering and corporate scams have been a recurring (and hilarious) gag on the screwball FX series *It's Always Sunny in Philadelphia*, whose producer and star Danny DeVito has been recently floated as a shoo-in to play Goldman Sachs CEO Lloyd Blankfein in an upcoming HBO series based on *New York Times* reporter Andrew Ross Sorkin's best-selling meltdown narrative *Too Big To Fail*. Meanwhile, over at MSNBC, the left-leaning cable news network has finally found a financially literate pundit in the CNBC defector Dylan Ratigan, who eschews most culture war fare in lieu of lengthy segments enumerating the arcana of the 2,200-page Lehman Brothers bankruptcy examiner's report—all in the effort, he reminds viewers, to prove what it means to be a "true conservative."

And so as politicians and pundits, regulators and economists, wring their hands anxiously about the encroaching case of "outrage fatigue" and worry whether the crisis has been, to quote Rahm Emanuel, "wasted," they might find some small comfort simply in turning on the TV, if only in solidarity with the tens of millions of Americans who are more likely fatigued from having nothing else to do.

8

THE FINANCIAL CRISIS AND THE UK MEDIA

Steve Schifferes

Introduction

The world financial crisis struck the UK with a speed and intensity unmatched in any other financial center outside of the United
States. The cost of bailing out its financial sector was even higher,
with the government spending more on a per capita basis on the
rescue than in any other major country.[1] The UK's financial press
shared and perpetuated many of what have now been revealed as
illusions: the ever-rising value of stock and especially property assets, the easy availability of low-cost credit, and the benefits of
deregulation.

UK journalists faced a particularly daunting task in understanding the nature and magnitude of the crisis. It was a challenge
for UK-based journalists to understand the scale of the crisis in the
United States, and the linkages between subprime lending, U.S.
financial institutions, and the wider economy. It was even more
difficult, given the lack of transparency in the UK banking sector,
to understand how vulnerable it would be to the problems in the
United States. However, when the UK media did expose the depth
of the crisis hitting the UK, it was attacked for having exacerbated

the very problems it was reporting, and spawning panic. Later, the UK media was excoriated for being complicit in failing to expose those same problems in the first place.

One of the reasons for that complicity was the existence of certain ideological blinkers. The UK, like the United States had experienced an era of deregulation, when the economy had seemed to grow smoothly without inflation, under the auspices of a New Labour government that had embraced modernization. In particular, the UK economic boom was led by the rapid expansion of the financial sector, with the City (London's equivalent of Wall Street) reasserting itself as the world's leading financial center under the auspices of "light touch regulation," which seemed to give it a competitive advantage over European rivals such as Paris or Frankfurt. UK journalists generally applauded these developments and agreed with the underlying philosophy.

As the financial crisis began to unfold, the UK media did not have the same tradition of investigative journalism that has been so important in the United States. However, it did possess several key strengths of its own. First, there was a highly competitive and large national press, with a depth of business coverage that had been expanded in size in many papers. Although readership has been slowly declining, a large proportion of the UK public still read a daily newspaper. Within the business press, there was a strong tradition of analysis and commentary, with an unrivalled depth in business columnists—especially at the *Financial Times*.

The UK had a long-standing tradition, dating back to the 1840s and Walter Bagehot, the founder of the *Economist*, of economic literacy and intelligent policy debate in the opinion columns of the press.[2]

In addition, the BBC—a public broadcaster generously funded by American standards—played a leading role in its sector, and had recently revamped its business coverage, creating a combined newsroom that brought together TV, radio, and online journalists. The BBC had also hired a leading investigative journalist, Robert Peston, who was to play a key role in the crisis, as its business editor, and his blog was to become particularly influential.[3]

This chapter looks at the role of the media in the UK financial crisis through the prism of several key events: the collapse of Northern Rock bank in August 2007; the debate over when the UK entered a recession, and how seriously it would be affected by developments in the United States; and the role of Britain in the

G20 London summit in April 2009. But first it examines the role of the media in the period before the crisis, when there was an obsession with the property boom and an unquestioning acceptance of financial deregulation.

The City and Financial Deregulation

The vulnerability of the UK economy to the global economic downturn was no accident; it was implicit in the strategy adopted by both Labour and Conservative governments over several decades in building up the City of London as a global financial center.[4]

London, had of course, been the world's leading financial center in the nineteenth century when Britain dominated the world economy. But after World War II, with the UK having been forced to liquidate most of its overseas investments amid tight controls on its economy, London's role appeared to have been eclipsed by New York.

However, the City of London still retained some competitive advantages, especially in its provision of a diversified bundle of business-related services, such as law, shipping, insurance, advertising, accounting, and consulting, which helped it maintain its international role.

But the real boom in the City was triggered by the 1986 decision to open it up to foreign competition; a decision made by the Thatcher government and known as "The Big Bang."

This triggered a rush of foreign banks into London, especially major American banks, where they set up European headquarters and acquired smaller UK merchant banks and stockbrokers. The creation of a single European market also encouraged European banks to move to London.

The boom ultimately led to the creation of a new financial district—Docklands—several miles east of the traditional City of London—where many of these U.S. banks had their headquarters.

When Labour came to power in 1997, rather than reverse the trend to deregulation, they accelerated it. One of the first acts of the new government was to take away responsibility for financial regulation from the Bank of England and give it to a new body, the Financial Services Authority (FSA).

The FSA was explicitly charged with delivering "light touch regulation," which would preserve the competitiveness of London as a financial center. The FSA concentrated on regulating the conduct of firms in relation to consumers and paid relatively little attention to systemic risk to the financial system as a whole.[5]

In seeking power, the new leadership of the Labour party had explicitly cultivated leading businessmen and bankers, and their promise of a new pro-business approach to the economy, abandoning old Labour ideologies such as a belief in nationalization, was a crucial part of their strategy to broaden their electoral appeal.[6]

The growing success of the City of London as a financial center seemed to be a win-win situation for Labour. The tax revenues generated by high corporate profits and bonuses made it easier for the Labour government to expand its spending on social services like health and education while keeping public spending in balance. High bank profits boosted share prices, and the financial sector soon grew to be the largest single component of the London stock market.

In addition, UK banks themselves became much more international and competitive. Retail banking in the UK had long been dominated by the "Big Four" clearing banks, Barclays, NatWest, Midland, and Lloyds. But by the mid-2000s, only two remained— Barclays and Lloyds. NatWest had been taken over by a smaller Scottish bank, Royal Bank of Scotland (RBS), and Midland by HSBC, the international bank originally based in Hong Kong. RBS and Barclays both then embarked on ambitious overseas expansion plans. In addition, the former building societies (savings and loan banks) had been allowed to float on the stock market in the 1990s, and some of them became aggressive competitors for retail business, including the Halifax, which merged with another Scottish bank to form a fifth major retail bank, HBOS.

The international character of the City also seemed to make it more resilient to economic ups and downs in individual countries. The UK financial sector seemed relatively unaffected by the Asian crisis in 1997–98 and the U.S. technology stock bubble in 2001.

The press generally celebrated the growing strength of the financial sector as the example of the UK's competitive advantage in the service sector of the global economy, in contrast to the continuing decline of the UK manufacturing base. The financial press was also inclined to support London's struggle to maintain its predominance against its European challengers such as Paris and Frankfurt, which were characterized as overregulated.[7]

Banking bosses were increasingly celebrated as the leading businessmen of the age—though there was always a touch of skepticism in UK attitudes to business leaders, at least compared to the United States.

If there was any debate in the press about the growing role of the financial sector, it centered on the decline of the manufacturing base, with commentators such as Will Hutton of the *Observer* arguing that more attention needed to be paid to the revival of manufacturing industry. There was also much discussion of the regional disparities in economic growth, with the boom in London and the Southeast not matched by the same level of prosperity in the North.[8]

However, some journalists were aware of the dangers of financial deregulation, particularly in the hitherto obscure field of derivatives.

The most notable was Gillian Tett, the capital markets editor of the *Financial Times*, who had been warning about the dangers for the world economy of the growth of securitized mortgage debt, which institutions had been packaging and selling around the world. These were the debt instruments based on subprime lending, which had been repackaged and rated as safe by many ratings agencies.

In early 2007, she wrote a famous article, "Unease Bubbling in Today's Brave New Financial Markets," where she warned that according to her industry sources "there has never been a time in history when such a large proportion of the riskiest credit assets have been owned by such financially weak institutions."[9]

However, the impact of Gillian Tett's revelations on broader perceptions in the media were limited—partly because she was writing in a specialist area, capital markets, which was not closely followed by many business journalists, and partly because the technical nature of the instruments she was describing were hard to understand.

Even Martin Wolf, the chief economics commentator for the *Financial Times*, has recently admitted that other journalists on the *FT* did not fully understand the implications of Gillian Tett's analysis for the wider economy.[10]

And for most newspaper readers, the overwhelming impression of the coverage was of a boom that showed no signs of ending, coupled with low inflation and low unemployment.

The Property Boom

It was even more difficult for the press to criticize the rising property market than the boom in the City, as the housing boom seemed to be enriching millions of individuals. Indeed, the press played a central role in promoting the UK property boom, which made the rising house prices the obsession of the personal finance pages of the newspapers and dinner party conversation alike.[11]

The property boom even spawned a series of television programs where eager home owners were advised on how to expand or sell their house in order to move somewhere more desirable, either in the UK or abroad. Among the programs were the Channel 4 hits *Relocation, Relocation* and *A Place in the Sun*, where families were advised by real estate agents how to sell their home at a profit in order to move to their dream home overseas or in another part of the UK. The programs encouraged the belief that finding the property of your dreams was the road to self-fulfilment, a path that was available to all through rising house prices.[12]

For the press, there were economic interests at play as well. Local newspapers were full of classified ads for real estate and thick supplements. The main focus for personal finance reporters was on the difficulties faced by young people and first-time buyers in getting on the property ladder, which was seen as a one-way escalator to wealth accumulation.

Many leading financial journalists who covered the crisis shared the view that general news coverage of the property boom had been far too uncritical. In a speech to the Society of Newspaper Editors, BBC business editor Robert Peston added his voice to this criticism: "The media in general, in news but also in features, were in a sense complicit in the canard that house prices can only rise; for years and years endless property programmes and supplements created the myth that houses were a one-way bet and debts never had to be repaid."[13]

As an economics reporter for the BBC News Web site, I can testify that few stories elicited such passionate reader response—both positively and negatively—as stories about the future direction of house prices, particularly those which suggested that prices might be headed down.

The property boom had several causes. The relative shortage of land for building, due in part to strict planning legislation, acted as a factor to raise house prices. The fall in unemployment and rising real incomes meant that more households were able to afford to own their own home. Consistent with historical experience, there was a strong preference among the UK public to see investment in housing as a safe haven.

But the banking sector itself played an important part in fuelling the property price boom. The increasingly competitive mortgage market led to shaving of profit margins as major banks sought to increase their market share. The number of special mortgage deals increased dramatically, with many people swapping the traditional variable mortgage common in the UK (which followed the Bank of England base rate) to fixed-term deals of two to three years duration. The general decline in interest rates also made housing more affordable.

In addition, banks began to reduce the size of deposits required before people could purchase a home, with mortgages typically offered on 95 percent of value (requiring a 5 percent deposit, compared to 10–15 percent in earlier years). Some banks began offering a combined mortgage and personal loan at 125 percent of the assessed value.

Underwriting standards were weakened, though not as much as in the United States. The ratio of income to loan rose from the traditional two-and-a-half to three times earnings to four to five times earnings, and included all household members. And for the self-employed, self-certification meant that it was left up to individuals to provide their own estimates of income.

Rising property prices had important economic effects on spending. When real incomes began to stagnate by the mid 2000s, many households boosted their income through equity withdrawal—taking out a larger mortgage against the rising value of their home, and using the cash to boost their spending on other items.

By the mid 2000s, it appeared that by traditional measures (such as the ratio of average earnings to average house prices) that house prices were significantly overvalued. However, while personal finance reporters were celebrating the boom, the overall level of household debt and risk of asset bubbles in the system were troubling some economic reporters. These concerns about how sustainable the boom might be were joined by a surprising voice—that of the governor of the Bank of England, Mervyn King.

In June 2007, King issued a warning to the banks about the risks they were running and said that they should not rely on the government to bail them out: "Be cautious about how much you lend, especially when you know rather little about the activities of the borrower," he told his City audience at the annual Mansion House speech in London. "Excessive leverage is the common theme of many financial crises of the past. Are we really so much cleverer than the financiers of the past?"[14]

But with both house prices and bank share prices still rising, relatively little attention was paid in the markets to the warnings of Governor King.

The Run on the Rock

Neither the media nor policy makers, however, anticipated the extraordinary events of August 2007, when credit markets seized up as banks and other financial institutions refused to purchase the risky mortgage assets that had been fueling the boom—and a $4 trillion market disappeared overnight. The disappearance of this behind-the-scenes market for mortgage-backed bonds was to have devastating effects on the banking system. Most observers found it hard to believe that because of the difficulties in valuing these complex securities, this market would simply dry up for good.[15]

It was also completely unexpected that the UK financial sector would be hit with such dramatic force by these developments—so much so that within a month of the wholesale markets seizing up, there was the first run on a UK bank in 140 years—a story that the UK press would break in September. But at first it proved remarkably difficult to convince front-page editors about the significance of the crisis, as this reporter found from personal experience on the BBC News Web site.

It was difficult to explain the significance of these credit markets, which worked at the wholesale level, behind the scenes of the banking system, and it was even more difficult to explain why they might matter to ordinary people. Editors shared the view of readers that while the stock markets were still strong, there was nothing to worry about. The fact that the UK officials, especially in the central bank, seemed unconcerned also made the story hard to sell. (Unlike the U.S. Federal Reserve and the European Central Bank, the Bank of England had not publicly increased its lending to try and help banks that might be in difficulty.) So for the first month, the story stayed on the financial pages and in the specialist press, and when it was reported more prominently, it was more likely to be reported out of Washington because of the comments by the Fed chairman, Ben Bernanke.

But meanwhile, a huge crisis was unfolding, particularly for one of the UK's biggest mortgage lenders, Northern Rock, involving secret negotiations at the Bank of England.[16]

Northern Rock was in trouble because it was highly reliant on wholesale funding for its mortgage business—the very markets which had now seized up. Unlike many other UK banks, it was unable to fund its operations from savings from depositors. It had borrowed on these markets in order to expand rapidly under its aggressive chief executive, Andrew Applegarth.

Northern Rock also tried to get a bigger share of mortgage business through more generous lending terms. It specialized in 125 percent mortgages, which allowed customers to borrow more than the value of their house on the grounds that house prices would always go up, and also led the way in lending a higher ratio of income to mortgage, allowing individuals with smaller incomes to qualify for a mortgage.

The bank had been in negotiations for weeks to sell itself to Lloyds Bank, a major clearing bank with a relatively small mortgage business which it was eager to expand. The deal collapsed when Lloyds demanded guarantees from the UK government to underwrite Northern Rock's obligations up to £30 billion ($50 billion), something both the Bank of England and the Treasury refused to do. This essentially represented the money that Northern Rock could no longer raise by borrowing from other banks—and the government was worried about the size of such a commitment, which could grow even bigger if markets remained frozen.

The Bank of England had been determined to keep news of these negotiations quiet, and indeed little news of the Lloyds deal leaked out. Even when the Bank governor gave coded warnings about the potential need for intervention during testimony to a House of Commons committee, there was little public inkling that a crisis was brewing.

But on the evening of Thursday, September 13, 2007, viewers of BBC News were told the dramatic news that Northern Rock was in deep trouble. Robert Peston, the BBC's business editor, had learned that the Bank of England had agreed to provide emergency support to Northern Rock—and indeed were meeting that very night to approve a rescue package. Mr. Peston was careful to reassure the public that there was no need to panic: "There was no reason for people with Northern Rock savings accounts to panic," he wrote on the BBC News Web site. "This does not mean that the bank is in danger of going bust."[17]

However, the news did not reassure the public. By the next morning, long lines were forming outside Northern Rock branches, as individuals struggled to withdraw their savings; and the bank's Internet site had crashed. The small number of branches (only fifty for 1.3 million savers) also contributed to the difficulties of the bank's customers who were seeking reassurance about their deposits.

It was the first public run on a UK bank since the nineteenth century, and it was only brought to a halt the following week when the government stepped in to give a full guarantee to all depositors that their savings were safe and would be covered by the UK government—something that had not been available under existing legislation (which only guaranteed 90 percent of deposits up to £35,000 [$50,000]. By implication, that meant that the UK government was guaranteeing all retail deposits in the UK banking system, which amounted to some £850 billion ($1.3 trillion).[18]

Robert Peston's actions were therefore highly controversial.

The Bank of England was particularly furious when the news of the Northern Rock rescue broke in advance, although the Bank's governor, Mervyn King, later admitted that the response of its savers in rushing to withdraw their money was rational, given the weakness of the government's deposit insurance scheme. The governor and his staff had themselves come under fire from politicians for their slow response to the crisis.[19]

In previous banking crises, the Bank of England had been able to keep the crisis out of the media before arranging a rescue. For example, in the so-called secondary banking crisis in 1974, the Bank secretly arranged a "lifeboat" of support from other banks before any news of the crisis reached the public.

The run on Northern Rock highlighted several characteristics of the UK economy and the role of the press. First, it demonstrated the extreme vulnerability of the UK financial system to disturbances in international financial markets. Mortgage lending by other UK banks soon started to dry up as access to wholesale credit markets shrank.

Second, it illustrated the tendency of the UK government and media to blame the crisis on problems in the United States—with the implication that there was little that the UK could or should do to ameliorate the problem. In his first interview after the news about Northern Rock broke, the chancellor of the exchequer, Alistair Darling, said that this crisis was "made in America." This however, was a poor excuse for the slow response when the crisis hit the UK.

Thirdly, it showed the inadequacy of the UK government's regulatory approach, the so-called tripartite system. This system involved a cumbersome degree of coordination between three separate authorities, the Bank of England, the UK Treasury, and the Financial Services Authority, which was one of main explanations for the slow response to the looming crisis.

But above all, what the crisis showed was the larger role that the UK media was to play as the financial crisis developed and the controversy that role engendered. The search for scapegoats had already begun, with both the media and policy makers being measured for the role.

The Bank of England saw the exposure of its rescue plan before it was ready to be revealed as unforgivable—and the Bank sought, successfully, to include a clause in future legislation that would allow them to prohibit the publication of such information.

Nor was the UK government pleased that it had been forced into guaranteeing the entire system of UK retail deposits in order to end the panic by Northern Rock savers.

The whole way the Northern Rock crisis had developed and been resolved was in sharp contrast to the quiet, behind-the-scenes approach that had previously characterized the British response to a financial crisis; and it was therefore a sign that the cozy world of financial journalists as cheerleaders for the City, and as mouthpieces for the government, was coming to an end.

It was also no accident that it was Robert Peston who broke the story. He had been following the rise of Northern Rock for a number of years and viewed its business model as flawed even as it had doubled its share of mortgage business by aggressive marketing fuelled by borrowing on the wholesale markets.

But even Mr. Peston admitted that it had been difficult to get his story across before the crisis began because the soaring share price of Northern Rock had deflected any criticism of the bank's approach: "In 2003 I first identified Northern Rock as a bank whose business model I was a little bit concerned about; it seemed to me it was growing far too fast. I wrote about it in the *Sunday Telegraph*, and for years I looked like a bit of a plonker because the share price went up and up and up, and the fact I said I thought this may be heading towards some kind of an accident looked wrong; I looked like an idiot."[20]

However, the Northern Rock story also cast its spell over the UK coverage of the developing crisis, with much of the journalistic coverage over the next six months focused on political consequences of the fall of Northern Rock, which was the first big crisis to hit the new administration under Prime Minister Gordon Brown.

Mr. Brown had become prime minister just a few months before the crisis, replacing his long-standing rival Tony Blair in June 2007. Mr. Brown had been actively weighing the possibility of a snap election in October 2007, and the last thing he wanted was for the government to take over the failing bank—it smacked too much of nationalization, which the Labour Party had pledged to abandon in 1996 when it positioned itself to regain power.

So for five months the government sought private buyers, until it became clear that no one would be in a position to buy Northern Rock without massive government guarantees, which only grew larger as economic conditions worsened. Eventually the government nationalized the bank, and it was split into two parts, with the bad loans separated out. The potential losses were estimated at £100 billion ($150 billion)—enough to break the government's own spending rules designed to limit the size of government debt.

However, the attention paid in the political system to Northern Rock may have distracted attention from the more systemic crisis that was brewing for the banking system as a whole and for the UK economy. There was also little discussion in the press about which other UK financial institutions might also be vulnerable to the collapse of credit markets. Many journalists were reluctant to panic markets by discussing the potential next victims, although it was relatively clear from market and analyst reaction which banks were likely to be the most vulnerable if credit markets remained closed.

Indeed, even as revelations of the huge losses and write-downs faced by U.S. banks grew in the autumn, attention in the City—and the financial press—was still focused on one of the biggest takeover battles in banking history—the rival bids for the Dutch bank ABN AMRO by two UK banking giants, RBS and Barclays.

In a moment that revealed how little the systemic nature of the crisis was understood, the victory of RBS in the autumn of 2007 was celebrated as a great triumph, and a vindication of the leadership of RBS boss Fred Goodwin, who would soon be excoriated in the press when his bank came to the brink of collapse less than a year later.[21]

Further inhibiting any investigation of the state of the UK financial sector were the flat denials by major UK banks that they had any exposure to subprime loans of the kind that were causing huge losses to large U.S. banks and financial institutions, with ever-worsening figures emerging in each quarterly announcement. The UK banks were quick to protest about any stories that included them in a list of financial institutions vulnerable to such problems, as this reporter can attest from personal experience.

Talking Ourselves into Recession: The Role of the Commentariat

The UK financial press, with its strength in interpretation rather than investigation, came into its own during the next period of the crisis. This was the interval between September 2007, when Northern Rock collapsed, and March 2008, when U.S. investment bank Bear Stearns had to be rescued by the U.S. government. There was still a high degree of uncertainty about the state of the economy as well as the state of financial markets. During this stage, a key role was played by the editorial page writers and opinion page essayists, the so-called Commentariat, who helped shape public opinion as they tried to understand the full impact of the crisis.

For this they were often criticized by the government, which took the view that the UK was strongly placed to ride out events with relatively minimal financial damage, and that any further discussion of the potentially gloomy scenarios ahead would just reduce consumer and business confidence, thus "talking Britain into a recession."

It is true that at this time the economic signals were mixed. Despite the crisis in the wholesale money markets, the stock market continued to perform strongly, and other asset prices like house prices continued to rise. There was a great deal of uncertainty both in policy circles and in the financial press about the severity of what was still being called the credit crunch on the UK economy. It was also unclear how seriously the UK was going to be affected by the weakness in the U.S. banking system, which was forced by U.S. accounting rules to disclose some (although not all) of its losses much earlier than in the UK.

There was therefore a degree of skepticism among my colleagues when, as the BBC News Web site's economics correspondent, I proposed a trip to the United States to look at the economic consequences of the subprime crisis in October 2007.[22]

What that trip revealed to me was that there was a tremendous amount of unease in U.S. financial circles about the growing scale of the crisis, that the housing market was already reeling from the problems in subprime lending, and that policy makers did not have a clear idea of how to deal with the mess.

Covering the subprime crisis on the ground in Cleveland, Ohio, I realized that I had underestimated the scale of the crisis as I was driving through street after street of boarded-up homes foreclosed and abandoned in the Slavic Village district. And talking to some of those still struggling to keep their homes, like single parent Marion Gardner, I saw just how difficult it was for borrowers to keep afloat, when the mortgage companies kept changing the rules to make it difficult for people to repay once they got into arrears. I was also struck by the maps produced by sociologists at Case Western Reserve University, which showed the clear overlap between the location of subprime lending, foreclosures, and concentrations of African Americans in the Cleveland metro area.

It was even more revealing to observe the mood of international bankers on the sidelines of the International Monetary Fund annual meeting in Washington, where I had been just before arriving in Cleveland. Normally the meetings of the International Institute of Finance are upbeat, with bankers meeting finance ministers to discuss impending deals. This time the mood was very different: there was a clear sense of shock among European bankers about the scale of the U.S. problems and the unregulated nature of U.S. mortgage markets.

Just as worrying was the gloom surrounding a meeting of house builders and lenders that I also attended. It was convened to forecast the state of the housing market, but a lunchtime conversation revealed the real worry of the builders was that their banks were pulling back their lending to them as well to their customers who wanted mortgages, leaving them in a fairly desperate situation.

Policy makers in Washington, it seemed clear, were not yet ready to grasp the nettle of federal intervention. At the Treasury, undersecretary for domestic policy Bob Steel told me he was trying to fashion a private-sector solution to buying out the bad mortgage debts, while on the Hill the House Democrats, newly in power after the midterm elections, were not sure whether they wanted to save the banks or punish them.

This series on the subprime crisis that ran on the BBC News Web site had some of the highest numbers of page views in the business press that year. But there was still vigorous debate in the BBC newsroom over how seriously the U.S. crisis would affect the UK.

A similar debate was taking place in the press. This has been tracked by commissioned research undertaken by the PR and marketing firm Editorial Intelligence (EI).[23] Using its database of opinion and editorial pieces about the financial crisis that were written between August 2007 and March 2009 (a set of over 2,000 articles), it was able to analyze the changing balance of opinion among columnists and editorial writers, and it produced a report on how commentators did—or did not—predict the scale of the credit crunch and the recession. The report also examined the views, reactions, and opinions toward other aspects of the credit crunch by influential commentators, and it evaluated to what extent these views shaped public opinion.

There are two particularly interesting findings in the report. First is the reluctance, until March 2008, of many commentators to label the crisis a recession rather than a credit crunch. This question of labeling was crucial for the public perception of how serious the crisis was; a credit crunch implied a much milder, more manageable event which might not need massive government intervention. Using such terminology also kept the event in the sphere of the financial sector, rather than implying that it would have wider significance for the economy as a whole.

It was highly significant that the turning point in this perception occurred in March 2008 not because of any developments in the UK, but because of the collapse of one of the major U.S. investment banks, Bear Stearns, which had to be rescued by J.P. Morgan with financial guarantees provided by the U.S. Treasury and Federal Reserve. This suggests that even at this stage, the view was that this was a crisis originating in, and driven by, events in the United States.

The sensitivity of the label being applied to the crisis was particularly acute for the broadcast media. For example, the BBC had prepared a series of graphics, with a downward pointing arrow, to use as an introduction to all news items about the economic crisis. But the difficulty of determining the state of the economy had the effect of delaying the deployment of these graphics and changing the text. So until the official GDP figures showed two quarters of negative growth (an event that happened some time later), the BBC graphics used the words "credit crunch" and then "downturn" to characterize the crisis.

The other significant finding of the report was that throughout the period, it was the editorials that generally were more reassuring about the state of the UK economy. This may be because editorial writers were more attuned to the general political mood in the country, just like front-page editors at the earlier stage of the crisis, and they paid less attention to the analysis of their own specialist financial columnists. Editorial writers found it particularly hard not to blame the United States for the crisis, with a certain smug satisfaction that the UK was able to run its financial system more effectively.

Thus while commentators such as Martin Wolf and Gillian Tett were warning about the dangers of the credit crisis, on October 10, 2007, an editorial in their own paper, the *Financial Times*, asserted that "the fact that loans are changing hands at all is reassuring and it is crucial to ensure that the summer's credit squeeze does not turn into a fully-fledged US credit crunch."

However, some very well-known columnists also shared this view. Writing in the *Guardian*, the former *Economist* editor Bill Emmott, in a column entitled "What Pray Is All the Fuss About?" took the press to task and said, "we risk talking ourselves into recession through media scaremongering" (*Guardian*, January 3, 2008). One of the *Financial Times*'s most well-known columnists, Samuel Brittan, wrote, "I feel like saying Buck Up. . . . There is no need to talk ourselves into a recession" (*Financial Times*, February 1, 2008). Another distinguished economics commentator, Anatole Kaletsky of the *Times*, also downplayed the possibility of a recession in the UK. In a column entitled "Slowdown, but Not Crash and Burn" (*Times*, January 10, 2008), he wrote: "My hunch is that Britain will avoid a recession." He added that "the global credit crisis, far from taking a turn for the worse, is almost over."

Mr. Kaletsky is a well-known contrarian, so perhaps it is not surprising that he expressed such views—for which he apologized one year later. Mr. Kaletsky later argued that much of the blame must be attached to the economics profession and its inability to see the nature of the crisis. He wrote: "In general how many academic

economists have had something useful to say about the greatest
upheaval in 70 years? The truth is even worse than this rhetori-
cal question suggests: not only have economists, as a profession,
failed to guide the world out of the crisis, they were also primarily
responsible for leading us into it."[24]

There was certainly an argument to be made about the failure of academic theory to understand the nature of the crisis—and
the need to apply the insights of behavioral economics to the risky
decision making of key actors. But at this stage, it was certainly
possible to draw on a range of more critical independent sources,
such as Willem Buiter, Nouriel Roubini, and George Soros, whose
views had been given more credibility by the developing crisis.

However, although a number of distinguished commentators were lulled into a false sense of security, there were more like
Martin Wolf who were sharply critical from the beginning of the
"foolish investors, foolish creditors, and clever intermediaries . . .
who created the conditions for the current credit crisis" (*Financial
Times*, September 5, 2007). Mr. Wolf was admirably early in drawing attention to the problematic role that the "clever intermediaries" (the banks and investment houses) played in packaging up
risky debt and selling it to gullible investors. The development of
this critique of the crisis by such commentators as Alex Brummer
(*Daily Mail*), Jeff Randall (*Telegraph*), and Larry Elliott (*Guardian*)
was one of the major differences between the U.S. and UK coverage during this period.

Mr. Wolf was particularly influential in the policy community, both in the United States and the UK, and one of the striking
things about the UK press debate is how it paralleled a similar but
private debate among policy makers within the central banks and
regulatory agencies about just how serious and prolonged the crisis
was going to be. The Editorial Intelligence report argues, I think
correctly, that the UK commentariat was ahead of the policy community in their assessment of the seriousness of the crisis. Unlike
the U.S. Federal Reserve, which had concluded by January 2008
that dramatic action was necessary to restore the financial system
to health, the Bank of England was a reluctant participant in bank
rescue plans even at this stage of the crisis.

The Moment of Truth

The debate over how to characterize the crisis was brought to
an end in the UK in a most surprising way—by the intervention

of the chancellor of the exchequer, the normally dour and loyal Alistair Darling. When he agreed to be profiled in the *Guardian* newspaper's Saturday magazine section, even the journalist who was writing the story did not expect any great revelations from the normally very cautious chancellor. Yet, Mr. Darling made head-lines when he told Decca Aitkenhead on August 30, 2008—two weeks before the collapse of Lehman—that "the UK was facing its deepest recession in 60 years."[25]

Mr. Darling later said that it had become obvious to him in his discussions with key banking executives during the summer of 2008 that they were still having considerable difficulty in raising money and that as the impact of the financial crisis spread to the wider economy there was going to be serious trouble. The political circumstances of the interview were revealing. Mr. Darling was speaking to the journalist from his remote island holiday home in Scotland, with only the presence of his own personal adviser—away from the press pack at Westminster. And the interview did indeed cause a political storm. As he admitted later in a 2010 Sky News interview, "the forces of hell were unleashed against me."[26] The attacks on Mr. Darling did not come only from his opponents. Rather, they came from within the Labour Party—with anony-mous briefings from the office of the prime minister suggesting that Mr. Darling was not up to the job and would be removed from office in the next reshuffle.[27]

The subsequent controversy demonstrated how fraught with political meaning this question was in the UK. The crisis had come at a particularly sensitive time for the new Labour government of Prime Minister Gordon Brown. Brown was still reluctant to ad-mit the severity of the economic crisis—after all, he had staked his reputation on his management of the UK economy—and he had proclaimed "the end of boom and bust" when he had been the chancellor of the exchequer for ten years prior to becoming prime minister. The tensions between the two most senior officials in the UK government were to endure during the period in which the UK economy would be tested to the limits.[28]

The Lehman Crash

Less than two weeks after Mr. Darling's interview, it became clear that the UK was engulfed in a global financial crisis that would re-quire unprecedented intervention by the Treasury and the Bank of England to save the UK banking system.

The bankruptcy of Lehman Brothers on 15 September after attempts to rescue it failed sent shock waves throughout the global financial system—with Lehman's $687 billion of losses affecting banks around the world and pictures of Lehman employees leaving their office in London's Docklands flashing across TV screens.

Although not fully reported at the time, Mr. Darling had also played a crucial role in the evolution of the crisis by refusing during the weekend of September 13–14 to waive the regulatory hurdles that might have allowed Barclays to take over Lehman. Mr. Darling later said that, given his concerns about the state of the UK banking system, he was not prepared to expose it to further risk of losses in the United States.[29]

Instead, the UK government sought to protect its vulnerable banks by engineering a shotgun marriage between two of the UK's largest financial institutions—HBOS, the UK's largest mortgage lender, and Lloyds, the bank that had been prepared to buy Northern Rock one year earlier. The government agreed to waive its normal antitrust provisions to allow the merger to go through quickly, through the direct intervention of the prime minister, and the news was again broken by the BBC's Robert Peston.[30]

But within two weeks, as markets continued to tumble and the U.S. bailout package was rejected in Congress, the UK government was forced to come to the assistance not just of the newly merged Lloyds group but also of two of the other major UK banks, RBS and Barclays, eventually taking a majority stake in RBS and a minority stake in Lloyds. As with the previous crisis, the news of this rescue plan was leaked to the BBC's Robert Peston, causing a dramatic fall in the value of banking shares on the London stock market.[31]

During this critical period in early October, when, as Chancellor Alistair Darling later described it, the financial system was on the edge of destruction, the government was closely monitoring the availability of cash in ATMs in the stricken banks, and the Bank of England—it later emerged—offered tens of billions in overnight loans in secret to ensure that the banks did not run out of cash. None of this leaked out to the press, and there was no retail run on the banking system the way there had been during the Northern Rock crisis.[32]

By the middle of October, the scale of the government rescue of the UK banking sector became clear. Two of the UK's biggest banks were virtually in public ownership—Lloyds and RBS—with direct capital injections amounting to £50 billion ($75 billion), an additional £260 billion of bad assets guaranteed against loss at RBS alone, and further injections of liquidity in money markets.[33]

By February, the Bank of England, having cut interest rates to 0.5 percent, was forced to turn to unconventional measures of "quantitative easing"—that is, purchasing government bonds to inject additional money into the system to prevent a further decline in the economy as the squeeze on the banks reduced the amount of money in circulation. It was a belated recognition of just how serious the crisis had become.

The Media on Trial

In the most acute stage of the crisis, it was the media that came under fire for stoking up the flames of the financial collapse. The intensity and suddenness of the crisis led to a search for a scapegoat, and at first the press seemed a convenient target.

At the height of the crisis, a series of attacks was launched investigating the role of the BBC's Robert Peston as the harbinger of doom. The attacks were led in the press by the *Daily Mail*, which asked in a headline "Does This BBC Man Have Too Much Power?" In the story, the *Mail* wrote that "city traders were angered by his report which unleashed renewed market turmoil, and there was astonishment at the Treasury and fury in the government that news of the secret meeting had been given to Mr. Peston."[34]

Mr. Peston's scoops also became the target of criticism in Parliament, with Conservative MPs, especially those with City connections, asking if he had gone too far. Conservative MP Greg Hands, a former stockbroker, called for the Serious Fraud Office to investigate his role in causing the financial panic. Another MP, David Gauke, asked plaintively during a debate on banking reform: "The most striking thing about the last 13 months or so, about the various developments in this crisis, has been that practically every interesting bit of information has been revealed by Robert Peston on the BBC News. To what extent has that been a major difficulty for the FSA and the Bank of England—that control of the story appears to be in the hands of Robert Peston rather than the authorities? Is there anything in this regime that will prevent that happening again?"[35]

Leading figures in the world of banking and industry also joined in the criticism and broadened it to include the media as a whole. The head of the British Bankers Association, Angela Knight, said that the media should be investigated for spreading unfounded rumors that caused sharp falls in the value of banking shares. Richard Lambert, the former editor of the *Financial Times*, who heads the Confederation of British Industry, said in a speech in December 2008 that the press had spread rumors as facts, contributing to sound banks being put at risk—and called for the industry's self-regulatory body, the Press Complaints Commission, to investigate whether there should be some self-restraint by the media: "At a time when careless headlines or injudicious reporting risk becoming self fulfilling prophecies of a very serious nature, you might have thought that the industry's self regulatory body, the Press Complaints Commission, would have had some guidance to offer about the special responsibilities of business journalists as they pick their way through the dangerous minefields of the credit crunch."[36]

The controversy over the role of the media in the financial crisis was so great that a few months later, in February 2009, leading financial journalists were summoned by the House of Commons Treasury Committee to justify their role and explain their behavior during the crisis. This unprecedented action sent alarm bells ringing among advocates of press freedom who were concerned that without the U.S.-style protection of the First Amendment, pressure would grow on politicians to introduce laws or codes to limit disclosure during a crisis.

Some commentators, such as the former editor of the *Mirror* and journalism professor Roy Greenslade, argued that the politicians were aiming to blame the media for the global crisis:

> When the BBC's admirable Robert Peston first reported on the troubles at Northern Rock, he was traduced for inducing a run on the bank. Yet he was merely disclosing the truth: a bank was being covertly bailed out because it was in deep trouble. It was his job as a journalist to reveal to those out of the loop what those inside it were up to. That is not to say journalists should act irresponsibly. But it was significant that throughout the Commons hearing the MPs were hoist with their own petard. They wanted to blame Peston for revealing too much, and then tried the opposite tack of castigating journalists for failing to inform their readers, viewers and listeners of the coming crisis.[37]

The journalists offered a vigorous defense of their performance during the credit crisis and argued that it was in the public interest for people to know if banks were in trouble. They also argued that the problems in the system were so deep-seated that it was not the disclosure that caused the collapse.

In a key part of his testimony, Robert Peston defended his role and denied that it was the press that caused the demise of Northern Rock: "What led to the collapse of Northern Rock was not the retail run, it was the wholesale run: it was the institutions refusing to fund this bank. Northern Rock, frankly, would have collapsed, it would be where it is today, irrespective of whether there had been that retail run. It was plainly a big story at the time that the money was being withdrawn by retail investors, but that was not what did for Northern Rock."[38]

Mr. Peston was understating his role in the crisis. But for the most part, the journalists were successful in defending themselves from the accusation that they had acted irresponsibly in pointing out the severity of the crisis. And a number emphasized the fact that they did use their judgment in deciding whether or not to print or broadcast a story.

For example, the editor of the *Financial Times*, Lionel Barber, pointed out that it was wrong to see the press as publishing rumors: there were many stories that they didn't publish for fear of disrupting markets, and they required two sources for any story. His comments were echoed by Simon Jenkins of the *Guardian* and Alex Brummer of the *Daily Mail*.[39]

The hearings also revealed the direct pressure that had been applied against newspaper proprietors to try and stop unfavorable stories appearing in the press during the crisis period. A senior columnist at the *Daily Telegraph* newspaper, Jeff Randall, revealed that a leading bank, RBS, had demanded a front-page apology and called the owners of his paper when they went ahead with a story (which turned out to be true) that its chief executive was to be replaced as part of the bailout plan when the bank was effectively nationalized.[40]

While the press vigorously defended its role of watchdog during the financial crisis, the discussion before the parliamentary committee on the role of the press before the crisis broke was more nuanced. Although many of the figures called to testify had been among those who had been aware of the risks of the crisis at an early stage, they acknowledged that overall the press record was less than perfect in this area. The discussion focused on why the press had not anticipated the crisis, and whether it could play a better watchdog role in the future.

Why had the press missed the warning signs? One view expressed by the panel was that financial journalists had become too close to their sources, and therefore unable to think skeptically. According to the *Guardian*'s Simon Jenkins: "I think there is extraordinary closeness between British business journalism in the City in the same way that there is extraordinary closeness between British political journalism in Westminster, and these are essentially unhealthy relationships which tend to lead to the sort of mishaps that you have described."[41] This was a common view of critics of the media, and pointed to the problem of shared, unexamined assumptions about the functioning of markets.

Interestingly, such an explanation was rejected by Richard Lambert, the former *Financial Times* editor, in his critique of journalists' role in the crisis. He argued that it was precisely the opposite situation—that journalists had changed from cozy insiders to highly competitive outsiders, and this in turn had changed the nature of the coverage. Mr. Lambert argued that the world of cozy financial journalism, of long lunches when exclusive stories would be leaked to leading newspapers, had been undermined on both sides. He pointed out that the change in the culture of the City after the Big Bang had led to fundamental changes in their relationship to the press, with a bigger role for PR firms and analysts, which made it far more difficult to keep information secret for long. He argued, too, that the changes in the media, with the rise of twenty-four-hour news channels and the Internet, forced the media to compete more vigorously for stories and seek out more and more angles, no matter how soundly based they were. Mr. Lambert made an important point which has been given relatively less attention in most UK discussions of the crisis: the change in news culture. With continuous news, it is hard to imagine a return to the British style of closed-door management of financial crises in the future. Further, the Internet can be a source of damaging rumors as well as devastating facts.

But it is interesting to note that at the height of the crisis the public turned largely to trusted brands for its information. There were huge increases in the page views of both the BBC News Web site and the *Financial Times*. It was also to these trusted sources that the main leaks were made.[42]

When the Treasury Committee eventually published its report on the hearings, it exonerated the journalists and rejected calls for prior restraints to be put on press coverage at times of financial crisis. By that time the attention of the press and the public had swung to an even more attractive scapegoat: the bankers.

The Media's Moral Compass: Greedy Bankers

In contrast to its earlier admiration for wealth creation, and the praise for the financial system which had allowed people to get rich in the property market, in the autumn of 2008 the UK popular press swung to the other extreme in relation to bankers. As the crisis broke, "greedy bankers" became the watchword of the press as the public struggled to understand how the much-praised UK financial system started tumbling like a house of cards.[43]

The attack on the bankers personalized the crisis, always an attractive approach for the mass-market press, and also allowed nonspecialist journalists to weigh in with their comments. The leader of the Anglican Church, the archbishop of Canterbury, even became a much-quoted critic of the overly materialistic society that had led to the crisis.[44] The moralizing of the crisis also allowed popular anger to become focused on individuals, rather than on the system as a whole or on the politicians and regulators who had created the structures that had permitted such abuse.

Even before the crisis fully broke, bankers' greed was being highlighted in the popular press. In September 2008, the *Daily Express* thundered in an editorial, "In any other walk of life the negligence displayed by the greediest bankers would be classed as criminal." And in August 2008 the *Daily Mail* had commented, "Bankers are either oblivious to the depth of anger against those whose greed and recklessness crippled the global economy or they simply don't care." As the crisis reached its peak, the mass circulation *Sun* newspaper wrote, "We have been failed by the politicians and the fat cats in the City."

In the aftermath of the crisis that engulfed the UK banking system, there was one figure that stood out in popular opprobrium: Sir Fred Goodwin, the chief executive of RBS. Under Sir Fred, RBS, a medium-sized Scottish bank, had embarked on an aggressive expansion plan, first buying one of the largest UK clearing banks, NatWest, before embarking on an ill-timed takeover of the Dutch bank ABN AMRO in October 2007. Mr. Goodwin's reputation for ruthlessness and a propensity for firing workers at companies he acquired gave him the nickname "Fred the Shred" in the press. At one time, RBS's assets were larger than the UK economy, but in the collapse of the British banking system in October 2008, it was the biggest loser, with the government ending up taking a majority ownership stake in the bank—and firing Sir Fred.

It was the news that Fred Goodwin would still be hanging on to his generous pension of over £700,000 ($1.5 million) per year that precipitated the biggest wave of popular anger during the crisis. After making an abject public apology to Parliament's Treasury committee, Sir Fred fled to his holiday home in the south of France after vandals attacked his car and broke windows in his house in Scotland. The popular press had a field day. "Where lies the moral compass of this greedy little man?" wrote Carole Malone in the *News of the World* (March 1, 2009). And the *Sun*, writing after the vandalism incident, editorialized, "The yobs who vandalised Sir Fred's home and Mercedes have no excuse," but "Greedy Goodwin and his £700,000 pension is simply the focal point of a groundswell of fury . . . if Britain is angry, we all know why" (March 26, 2009). This time the quality press joined in as well, with political columnist Andrew Rawnsley writing in the *Observer*, "Bankers like Sir Fred Goodwin are lucky not to be in jail" (March 1, 2009).

The politicians also joined in with their criticism. Harriet Harman, MP, the leader of the House of Commons, called for the government to try and revise the terms of Sir Fred's payoff, which had been negotiated when the bank was nationalized. This was too much for some commentators, who reminded the public of how much Labour politicians had cultivated and praised leading bankers like Sir Fred as part of their drive to modernize their image.

The demonization of bankers served several purposes. It gave the public a ready set of villains, whose extravagant lifestyles and greedy selfishness contrasted with the circumstances of the ordinary reader. In that sense, it was in the same tradition of the tabloid press exposing the wrongdoings of the royal family or football stars, in that it coupled moral outrage with envy for the lifestyle of the rich and famous—and in some sense it also glamorized that lifestyle. The popular obsession with the bankers' bonuses did serve to distract attention from the debate about what to do about banks—especially whether they had grown too large to fail.

If the crisis had been caused by the moral failings of bankers, what was needed was a return to "old school," more moral bankers, not structural changes to the system as a whole. Talking about bankers' greed also distracted from discussions about the role of politicians in encouraging the development of the City as a free-wheeling financial center—and the dependence of the government on the huge profits and bonuses to fund its social programs. Greedy bankers were a far more exciting topic for the popular press than the equally scandalous role of the regulators, whose light-touch regulation they themselves now admitted had been a contributory factor to the crisis.

Nevertheless, it was not until more than one year later, in December 2009, that the government decided—despite owning two of the four major banks—to tackle the issue of bankers' pay and bonuses, slapping a 50 percent tax on institutions who gave out bonuses of £25,000 or more (but thus allowing the big financial institutions to pay the tax and still reward their staff). The delay in tackling bankers' bonuses, and indeed the delay in further taxation of the banks, was explained by the government as a result of the need to get international agreement with other major countries—something which was taking a good deal of time and difficulty to secure.

It was characteristic of the Labour government during this period to look for international solutions to the crisis. That reached its high point in the spring of 2009 when the UK hosted the G20 summit in London.

The G20 Summit: The Media as Cheerleader

The UK government invested considerable human and political capital in playing up the importance of the April 2009 London summit meeting, the first with President Obama since he took office in January 2009. The summit itself became another sort of turning point in the media examination of the crisis, when doom and gloom were replaced for the first time with some glimmer of optimism that the worst was over.[45]

This was certainly the intention of the UK government, which hoped that the sight of international leaders working together would calm the market as well as reassure the public.

The softening up of the press started early, with both the Foreign Office and Treasury teams deployed in full from January—three months before the summit—to explain its importance to both foreign and domestic media outlets.

For UK prime minister Brown, it was a chance to project himself on the international stage and perhaps regain some of his lost political luster—although he also attracted domestic criticism for trying to save the world while neglecting the problems that still existed back home.

Like many such events, the summit eventually took place in physical isolation in London Docklands, amid security so tight that several buses of journalists were initially refused admission to the center despite having press passes. It was far away from protest demonstrations.

What was interesting was the extraordinary amount of briefing offered by UK government officials on the activities of the summit as it progressed, providing the news to feed the live updates sent by the media out of the conference center.

For the BBC, which deployed a large number of reporters to the conference, there was also a degree of competition between the various news teams about who was to take the lead on the story—between the economics and business team, the politics team that was covering the UK prime minister, and the BBC Washington correspondent traveling with President Obama.

As Gordon Brown's team emerged with the news of a $1 trillion global rescue plan, it soon became the story—eclipsing any more complex analysis of who would actually have access to these funds (most of which were allocated to the International Monetary Fund and would only be available on a conditional basis). Meanwhile, the politics team, led by BBC political editor Nick Robinson, also won the right to lead the news on this item, thus also ensuring that there would be less examination of the complexities of the deal and its effect on developing countries than its effect on Mr. Brown's career.

Despite the broader makeup of the G20 group, it proved difficult to add a developing-country perspective to the coverage on the day, although considerable effort went into case studies from these countries on the BBC's world news outlets on radio and TV, and on the BBC news Web site. The news conferences were dominated by the rich nations such as the United States, the UK, France, and Germany. There was also far less coverage of the attempts to create a global regulatory framework for reforming the banking system—perhaps because here progress was much slower.[46]

Much of the optimism about the G20 process did prove to be something of a false dawn. The promise of international cooperation was always tenuous in relation to economic stimulus plans, and the subsequent Pittsburgh summit did not live up to expectations. It soon emerged—when the UK government came to revise its public-sector borrowing forecasts—that the scale of the problems facing the UK was among the biggest in the world. And subsequent summits have shown that disunity rather than coordinated action is more characteristic of these meetings.

But for a brief period, the vision of Britain once again leading the world in solving the economic crisis had proved seductive, even for a press jaded by the disasters of the previous few months.

Conclusions

In retrospect, the global economic crisis may be seen as a turning point in the relationship between the financial sector and the press in the UK, from a cozy codependency to a more critical stance.

After the events of 2007–2009, it will be impossible for the UK press ever to go back to an earlier role of bystander while financial crises are resolved behind closed doors in the tradition once so cherished by the Bank of England.

On the whole, this is a positive development. The public has a right to know if an institution is in trouble, and government deals concluded behind closed doors may look differently in the oxygen of publicity. And it has also served to reduce the gap between the information available to insiders and outsiders that has also historically been part of the British financial scene.

Of course, the enhanced role of the press in such crises does give it more responsibilities—to be sure of its facts and sources, not to inflame public fears, and even (in rare cases) to withhold information that could cause unnecessary damage.

One element of the UK media that proved extremely useful in this crisis was its long-standing tradition of informed commentary and analysis, based on a degree of economic literacy in the press and reading public that is less common on the other side of the Atlantic.

The complex nature of the financial crisis meant that it required a good deal of analysis to make the connections between different sectors clear to the public. Operating at a slight distance from the U.S. heart of the crisis, paradoxically, may have ultimately made it easier for the UK commentariat to see the crisis in its fully global dimensions.

Two aspects of the UK media coverage, however, raise troubling questions about its role in affecting the public mood. There is little doubt that overall the press was a co-conspirator in inspiring one of the biggest property booms ever in the UK, ignoring the lessons of history and the logic of economics about whether that boom was sustainable.

The financial press was also too often in the years before the crash the cheerleader for the financial sector as a whole, endorsing deregulation in the patriotic hope of preserving London's dominance in Europe.

The UK press never quite went as far as the U.S. media in building up chief executives as superstars; and indeed what is extraordinary is how rapidly the mood, particularly in the popular press, changed to vitriol. The tendency to blame the crash on the moral failings of bankers—however justified in the popular anger over the losses suffered by individuals—may have been a distraction from a serious analysis of the causes of the crash and possible remedies. Even the focus on excess bonuses can sometimes serve as a diversion from looking at the distributional effects of the crisis on those lower down the income scale.

Once the crisis had broken, there was a sharper debate in the policy community than the press, with central bankers and regulators proposing radical options such as breaking up the big banks or taxing their transactions more heavily. The media, led by political journalists, too often uncritically acceded to the government's more modest proposals such as, for example, those presented during the G20 summit in London.

A difficulty continually facing financial journalists covering the crisis has been the interaction of politics and economics. In the United States, the coverage of the crisis was hugely influenced by the fact that it occurred in the middle of the presidential election campaign, with events interpreted through the prism of their effect on the fortunes of the candidates. In the UK, the government had placed so much of its credibility on its economic competence that it found it difficult at many stages to acknowledge the scale of the crisis—a conflict exacerbated by the differing views of the prime minister and the chancellor of the exchequer on how to approach this problem.

Then there is the broader question of whether the UK media could have warned of the looming crisis ahead of everyone else.

As the distinguished student of financial markets Professor Charles Goodhart points out, crises by their nature are unexpected events, and it is the policy makers and regulators who are charged with designing systems to deal with the unexpected.[47]

Many journalists would argue that it is impossible for either journalists or policy makers to predict the future with perfect accuracy.

Larry Elliott, the economics editor of the *Guardian* newspaper, who was an early critic of the excesses of the credit crunch, agrees that "journalists cannot predict the future. Sometimes we have to say that we just don't know."[48]

In addition, there were particular complexities in telling the story of this crisis that made it difficult for any individual journalist to grasp, from the problems on the ground with subprime lending, to the methods by which the banks were securitizing these assets, to the credit default swap markets, to the regulatory systems in Washington that were dysfunctional. It was particularly hard for journalists from outside the United States to connect all these dots into a coherent story.[49]

Nevertheless, without expecting the media to predict the exact nature or timing of the crisis, it could have done a better job by looking more skeptically at the financial and regulatory system and questioning more thoroughly the prevailing wisdom about the allocation of risk.

A key lesson that should be taken from the failure of analysis to identify the major risks in the system is the danger of groupthink, which affected journalists, politicians, policy makers, and economists alike. Viewing the world through rose-tinted spectacles is easier when everyone is wearing the same color, and it was far too easy to fall into the belief that the world had entered an era of permanent low inflation and steady growth.

There were skeptics, both in the media and in the policy community, who identified some of the key pressure points in the system, and one lesson for the future would be to pay more attention to such views. But the assumption that the dispersal of risk through securitizing of assets made the world a safer place was not rigorously examined. Nor were the implications of information asymmetry in the creation of complex financial instruments fully spelled out, until fund managers themselves decided to avoid such instruments which they could not understand.

Little use was made of the history of previous financial crises, despite the recurring nature of bubbles and financial instability. The UK journalist Alex Brummer is right to point out that few of his contemporaries had personal experience of covering previous financial crises in the UK and few were prepared to learn the lessons of crises in other countries. It was less a case of "this time it's different" than "it can happen in Asia but it can't happen here."[50]

The severity of the crisis has shattered the paradigm that the markets are always right and that the U.S. model of capitalism is the most successful version—at least for many journalists outside the United States. But what is still unclear is what new models of economic and policy analysis will emerge from the crisis. There is still a debate in the profession between neo-Keynesians who believe that the crisis has showed how imperfect markets need more government intervention and those who still argue that government is part of the problem not the solution.

That debate is now playing out in the policy discussion over how quickly to reduce the huge deficits that governments incurred as part of their rescue plans. As the consequences of the crisis play out in terms of debt and deficit crises across Europe and the United States, the political battle has intensified. And with the economic recovery still uncertain and unemployment high, it still remains to be seen how long the consequences of the crisis will endure for millions of ordinary citizens.

WHAT WOULD GOOD REPORTING
LOOK LIKE?

Robert H. Giles and Barry Sussman

In March 2001, *Fortune* magazine published a story reporting that "for all the attention that's lavished on Enron, the company remains largely impenetrable to outsiders."[1] The story was written by Bethany McLean, a thirty-one-year-old reporter, who started with a basic question: how exactly does Enron make its money? "Details are hard to come by," she wrote, "because Enron keeps many of the specifics confidential for what it terms 'competitive reasons.' And the numbers Enron does present are often extremely complicated. Even quantitatively minded Wall Streeters who scrutinize the company for a living think so." McLean's story identified other concerns with Enron's operations, such as a substantial increase in the company's debt during the first nine months of 2000, and its use of derivatives to create contracts for third parties and to hedge its exposure to credit risks and other variables. "Actually," she wrote, "analysts don't seem to have a clue what's in Assets and Investments or, more to the point, what sort of earnings it will generate." She quoted skeptics who said that the lack of clarity raises a red flag about Enron's pricey stock: "The inability to get behind the numbers combined with ever higher expectations for the company may increase the chance of a nasty surprise."

The mainstream press largely ignored McLean's story. Coverage of the company continued to be positive, influenced by its rising stock price. But the "nasty surprise" wasn't far off. In December 2001, ten months after the *Fortune* story was published, Enron filed for bankruptcy under Chapter 11. At the time, it was the biggest, fastest corporate collapse in American history (since surpassed by the collapse of Lehman Brothers). Enron shares plummeted from more than $90 to just pennies, wiping out retirement funds of its employees and the investments of its shareholders.

Bethany McLean's story is what good business reporting looks like. It was grounded in a reporter's question that yielded no clear answer: how exactly does Enron make its money? The story should have intrigued other editors and business reporters, but instead of probing for an answer to the questions her story raised, their coverage of Enron continued along a familiar track, focusing on events after the fact. The company's collapse forced the business press to consider how they got the story so wrong. "What we clearly did not understand was that it was heading for a disaster," explained Alan Murray, Washington bureau chief of the *Wall Street Journal*, in an interview with media critic Howard Kurtz in the *Washington Post*.[2] The problem, Murray explained, is that such stories often turn on "arcane and technical" practices. "The press doesn't pay as much attention to some of these regulatory issues that have more impact on the world than the political issues we do pay attention to." Another explanation is that the business press relies too heavily on what the analysts are saying instead of being more independent, more searching in its reporting. Good reporting is shaped by a skeptical frame of mind, rigorous questioning of what the analysts are saying, and the recognition that critical information is hard to get. Equally important is the willingness to turn to a network of experts with counterintuitive points of view that might offer cautionary perspectives on the conventional wisdom that drives stories about the performance of markets and companies.

There's no secret to good reporting on the economic collapse or any other financial story. Journalists have broken major business stories for a long time. They sounded an alarm about the savings and loan scandal of the 1980s, the unsupportable rise in dot-com stocks in the late 1990s, and the recent housing bubble as well. In each instance, reporters recognized characteristics influencing the upward thrust of markets that were simply too good to be true and reported them. Each time, the most revealing stories were grounded in strong, independent work. But then, each time, the critical disclosures failed to grab the attention of policy makers and the public; nothing happened until the weight of these unsupportable undertakings brought them crashing down. The failure of hard-nosed reporting to influence a correction in the business world is not very different from what occurred on another issue of national urgency, the run-up to the war in Iraq, where the Washington bureau of a single news organization, Knight Ridder, wrote and distributed dozens of authoritative stories challenging the rationale for invading Iraq. The stories were prominently displayed in Knight Ridder newspapers across the country, but the leading national papers did not run them or refer to them and, thus, they got no traction in Washington or in the capitals of America's allies.

Even when editors and reporters follow the essential guidelines for covering the economy by being skeptical, thinking counterintuitively, and fighting a tendency to follow the pack, stories don't always make a difference. News isn't proprietary; it doesn't belong to the organization that is first to report it. But sometimes it looks that way. If the *Wall Street Journal* publishes a major investigative piece on the economy, it is not likely to get much, if any, attention in the *New York Times*, the *Washington Post*, the Associated Press, or the weekly news magazines. And so the impact of the *Journal*'s reporting is often limited to the audience that reads the paper.

In October 2009, the Nieman Foundation, in an effort to encourage improvement in the coverage of business and economics, posted on its Watchdog Project, www.niemanwatchdog.org, a series of interviews with independent experts or articles by them that sought to help editors and reporters understand basic economic issues. Each article suggested questions the press should ask about the economy and the economic collapse. The questions were intended to go the heart of economic issues in the stories; typically, they were questions that are not being asked and may not interest the mainstream press as much as those that explore possible political outcomes.

News organizations too often are content to rely on he-said, she-said stories, quoting company handouts and accepting without challenge the analysts' daily rationale for why the Dow is up or down. Intelligent financial reporting emphasizes original, independent work, pressing for answers and placing leaders' views in context.

The concept of journalism as a "fourth estate" envisions a respected, independent press. The reporter in this concept is viewed as an agenda setter, honest broker, and unbiased interpreter of events. The embodiment of a fourth-estate figure was Walter Cronkite, the much-revered anchor of CBS Evening News. When Cronkite said something, the country listened. Early in 1968, Cronkite returned from Vietnam after the Tet offensive and broadcast his opinion that it was time to negotiate an end to a war he felt America could not win. "If I've lost Cronkite," lamented President Lyndon Johnson, "I've lost middle America."

In reality, the role of the press as a fourth estate, with power and prestige, is greatly exaggerated. There were few if any journalists before Cronkite, and none since, who could command the respect he did from citizens and leaders alike. The closest journalists have come since Vietnam to matching Cronkite's public image was in the coverage of the Watergate scandal. Even then, only a few news organizations—the *Washington Post*, *New York Times*, *Los Angeles Times*, *Time* magazine, and the now defunct *Washington Star*—did original, continuing reporting. And that was almost forty years ago.

The decades since have been ones of decline for the press in terms of power, respect, and accomplishment. In recent years, the decline has been hastened as news staffs and news holes get smaller and smaller. Especially critical has been the shrinkage of local business news staffs and the disappearance in many papers of stand-alone business sections.

Stories still have the capacity to rouse slumbering public opinion into a powerful force that compels the government to act. The *Washington Post*'s reporting on the treatment of badly injured soldiers at Walter Reed Army Medical Center in Washington, DC, was such a story. This tragic event had a strong human element and is the kind of story that gets attention and action. It is the kind of story the press does best, an obvious, rectifiable injustice where good reporting quickly prompted military leaders to act decisively, firing the people in charge, detoxifying and painting the hospital, and firmly addressing the problem.

The Pulitzer Prizes each year are testimony to the excellence of watchdog reporting in U.S. newspapers. Nevertheless, there is a letdown in the coverage of systemic problems of which the recent great recession is a prime example. It's not that the press can't do such stories; it's that they hardly ever do. The difference between a Walter Reed story and good financial coverage is the difference between a four-month project and an effort at continuing hard work with no end point. That's a substantial difference.

Intelligent coverage of the economy requires independent reporting that might be little noticed by most citizens but that resonates with powerful groups, national leaders, and policy makers. Such reporting, for example, would explain that for almost thirty years those making decisions about the American economy have been guided by a flawed theory. We are referring to "efficient market theory," the doctrine in force since the presidency of Ronald Reagan, holding that the market will always correctly value capital assets in a timely and efficient manner, and that government's role is to stay out of the way. Efficient market theory enabled financial institutions to take on far too much risk as regulators looked aside. Government leaders, being among the efficient market faithful, encouraged the process, and the press, by and large, accepted the conventional wisdom that efficient market theory precluded the notion of systemic market collapse.

The role of the press as a public service is to dig out the details documenting what went wrong and to carefully explain the consequences of the failed theory of efficient markets, both in news stories and editorials. The story needs to be told, not just once or twice, but as part of the running account of the economy so that readers and viewers can understand and policy makers will find it more difficult to ignore. The failure to tell this story adequately is a great failure of the press, and it has had serious, unfortunate consequences.

While efficient market theory has exploded and crashed, some of its main proponents, Republicans in Congress and some Democrats, act as if it still applies. They are outspokenly opposed to government spending, without which there could have been no recovery, and they are clamoring loudly for spending reductions at a time when large, new infusions could protect and create jobs. The hypocrisy here is that few if any in Congress attacked President George W. Bush for his unrestrained spending and his reduction of taxes on the wealthy, both of which contributed to huge increases in the national debt. He never was pressed to explain how to pay for these fiscal excesses that played out over the eight years of his presidency, which came to an end with the onset of the great crash.

The deficits and the national debt are overwhelming, and the call to reduce them resonates with the citizenry. The outcry over deficits comes on top of understandable, widespread public resentment that financial institutions were made whole at taxpayer expense while millions of Americans lost their homes or their jobs and any financial security they may have had. Compounding the anger were the immense bonuses handed out by executives to themselves—they didn't waste any time—once the bailouts stabilized the big financial institutions.

One result of the antideficit clamor was to box in President Obama so that he took only halfway measures toward job creation. As we write this, Obama has announced a spending freeze that seems aimed more at placating critics and the public than improving the economy. It is clear that Obama could have done better explaining the need for massive spending and the rationale for putting deficit reduction on hold. So could the people around him. And the press could have pressed the president for more clarity on his proposal. It could have done a better job explaining what caused the collapse. It could have, and should have, explained the failings of efficient market theory as a major contributor to the collapse.

In its coverage of the continuing story of how to get the economy stabilized and on the way to recovery, the press has given abundant, mostly uncritical voice to Republicans and others who continue to promote efficient market theory. Reporters fail to challenge statements from major political sources that they know to be questionable or false. The admirable press ethic of giving both sides of a story does not extend to presenting equal weight to arguments that aren't equal in merit. Television, especially cable TV, is a major contributor to this problem. In December 2009, Senator James Inhofe, a Republican from Oklahoma, reacting to the Environmental Protection Agency's announcement that it will now consider carbon dioxide a pollutant, a move that clears the way for stricter regulations of the greenhouse gas, said on CNN's *The Situation Room*, that the science behind the announcement "has been pretty well debunked." These kinds of comments, no matter how silly, are held to be serious, worthy of airing in discussions of global warming, Obama's country of birth and his religion, evolution, or, more to the point of this chapter, deficit spending.

News stories that hold leaders accountable would serve a dual purpose of informing readers and viewers and influencing a change in the political debate. Defenders of efficient market theory might be forced to give more regard to facts if stories continually explained why their public statements were questionable or false. News organizations and individual journalists seldom hold politicians' feet to the fire. To the extent that they don't, it's fair to say that the press at large is partly to blame for shortcomings in the economic recovery. By not repudiating a failed system and by continuing to give generous space and time to its promoters, the press has, unwittingly perhaps, taken sides in the political debate and weakened the level of public discourse by failing to point out repeatedly in stories that facts are skewed or are spun from an ideological perspective. There is good reason why our citizens can't distinguish between cynical posturing and serious economic argument—and plenty of blame for the press.

The case of Social Security is an example. Politicians in both parties routinely sound alarms that it is heading for insolvency when, in fact, it is actuarially sound. By failing to spell out the facts and to challenge politicians sounding the alarm, the press has contributed to a widespread fear among Americans, especially younger ones that, while they are paying into the system, they never will receive benefits. The news media rarely correct the politicians.

Another example is the failure of the press to explain how the recent bank bailout enabled banks to borrow money from the government for approximately zero percent and lend it back to the government at 3.5 percent. The result: a windfall for banks and little money for small businesses and citizens seeking bank loans. That's a major news story that has been underreported, leaving Americans in the dark about an unintended consequence of the bank bailout. (Later in this chapter we deal in a little more detail with this aspect of the bank bailout and the press failure on Social Security.)

Reporting the Collapse

In July 2009, Henry Banta, a Washington attorney who is a contributor to the Nieman Watchdog Web site, voiced this complaint in an e-mail: "Once again I feel compelled to rant about the media's inability to deal with serious economic issues. . . . We now are headed into a debate of terrifying importance: whether or not the economy needs additional stimulus. What is really frightening is that this debate shows every promise of being conducted on an even lower level than the last round." Banta continued, "Maybe I expect too much from your profession. Perhaps I have never gotten over that as a young government lawyer my heroes were all journalists—you know the names. I know it is unfair of me to be standing on the sidelines screaming 'do something' when I haven't a clue of what to do."

Banta's lament echoed the Nieman Watchdog mission of commissioning experts to offer questions the press should ask, and in that way encourage better reporting on public policy issues. And while the Watchdog project does not have a reporting staff, we made an exception on the story about the economic collapse. We asked a veteran Washington, DC, reporter, John Hanrahan, to work for us for three months covering this story. Hanrahan had worked for the old *Washington Star*, the *Washington Post*, and for UPI, and had been executive director of the Fund for Investigative Journalism. He was not a financial reporter, but over those three months he became one. Others contributed to our series on the economy as well, including Banta and another Washington attorney, Martin Lobel (a law partner with Banta), and Dan Froomkin, the deputy editor of NiemanWatchdog.org and the senior Washington correspondent of the Huffington Post. Together, these journalists wrote twenty-one articles, most of them interviews with distinguished, independent economists, scholars, and activists.

The articles offer many lessons in good financial reporting. They also could run prominently in any news publication. Suggesting lines of coverage, not media criticism, was a main goal of the series, but there were critiques every now and then. Invariably it was the *New York Times* that drew praise. Our purpose was to help the press do a better job on a serious story. Some news organizations have done excellent work in reporting the collapse and subsequent events, and the lessons of our series were not intended for them. Our point is that while there has been good reporting and commentary in the mainstream media, there hasn't been nearly enough. When asked why something wasn't written about, a typical response from both reporters and editors is "We had that." This may be correct, but the answer is still invalid. It's not enough to have run a story or two, or to maintain that readers and viewers don't read or understand or care about financial news; it is negligent of the press not to offer sustained and analytical coverage. The economy has come crushing down on millions of people. It's the obligation of reporters and editors to help citizens understand and care.

It's also not enough for news organizations to hobble themselves with a self-imposed fairness doctrine that gives space and time to disinformation.

In his e-mail, Henry Banta gave an example from a Sunday morning talk show:

> The person being interviewed was Republican John Boehner of Ohio, the House minority leader who denounced the stimulus program of the Obama Administration as "mere spending." This was a splendid opportunity to open an intelligent debate on the subject. A knowledgeable interviewer would have known that in economic terms a recession represents a gap between the falling level of private spending and the level necessary to keep workers employed. The purpose of the stimulus program was to partially fill that gap with government spending.
>
> If Boehner was opposed to government spending just because it was spending, certain obvious questions should have suggested themselves. What was his belief about how markets behave and on what was it based? The questions would have provided an excellent point from which to ask basic questions of the Administration. But nothing like this was ever asked and the opportunity for stimulating a real debate was missed.

Millions of jobs were lost in this Great Recession. Had viewers understood that massive government spending was needed to save and create jobs, Boehner couldn't have gotten away with his uninformed remark and perhaps wouldn't have had the nerve to make it. But there was no push from the interviewer.

We began the series on October 8, 2009, with two stories, one by Banta framing the issues and the other an interview by Hanrahan with the economist James Galbraith. Banta described efficient market theory:

> Government policy makers—from Cabinet members, members of Congress, down to low level lawyers at the SEC— approached the regulation of financial markets with a set of assumptions that were just plain wrong. In the simplest terms, they believed that markets left to their own devices could be relied on to self-correct. They were flat wrong, of course.

By the fall of 2008, Banta wrote, "this efficient market theory was, if not dead, badly wounded. The climactic moment came when Alan Greenspan, former chairman of the Federal Reserve and leading proponent of the efficient market theory, told a congressional committee that its 'whole intellectual edifice collapsed.' Perhaps the most spectacular *mea culpa* in the history of economic thought."

Banta pointed out why many in politics, unlike Greenspan, haven't given up on efficient market theory regardless of the disaster it proved to be. "It fits neatly into the agenda of powerful interests," Banta wrote, noting that while efficient market theory had been shaken to its foundations, only a few writers have told that story. Politicians like House minority leader Boehner continue to call for spending cuts, a call that resonates with many citizens.

Reporters rarely challenge Boehner or others when it is clear their goal is partisanship and obstruction. One explanation is that reporters are reluctant to be critical of sources they rely on. What is needed in addition to tough questioning is to put remarks like Boehner's in context every time he makes them, or, perhaps, not run them at all.

Shortly after President Obama's health care summit on February 25, 2010, David Camp, a representative from Michigan and the ranking Republican on the House Ways and Means Committee, was interviewed by Robert Siegel, host of NPR's *All Things Considered*.[3] Here is an excerpt in which Siegel challenges Camp's assertion that the president's bill is a federal government takeover of health care.

> SIEGEL: The president was at pains to say that his bill is not a federal government takeover of health care. It's a bill, he says, that sets a baseline standard for what you can call a health insurance policy. First, do you accept that this is not a federal takeover of healthcare that he proposes?
>
> REP. CAMP: Well, it very much is a federal-government-centric approach to health care because not only does the federal government set the plans that are in the exchange, but when this bill becomes up full and running, it sets the requirements for all insurance plans all over the country . . .
>
> SIEGEL: But federal-government-centric with heavy regulation from Washington, that's not a federal takeover. Would

you back away from the phrase a federal takeover of the health care system?

REP. CAMP: Well, the problem is because all of the rules and regulations are going to be set in Washington, in essence, unless the plan qualifies under Washington's standards, there's not going to be a plan. So it's going to be very federally centered.

During the 2008 presidential campaign, the *St. Petersburg Times* created PolitiFact to help sort truth from fiction in politics. *Times* reporters and researchers examine statements by members of Congress, the president, cabinet secretaries, lobbyists, people who testify before Congress, and anyone else who speaks up in Washington, and rate the accuracy on the newspaper's Truth-O-Meter—True, Mostly True, Half True, Barely True, and False. The most ridiculous falsehoods get the lowest rating, Pants on Fire. Scott Brown, the new Republican senator from Massachusetts, earned a "Pants on Fire" after asserting that the stimulus bill "didn't create one new job." This project is one example of how a fine regional newspaper has invested in a quest to find out who is telling the truth and who is not; it is a model to monitor truth-telling that other local newspapers might adapt.

"You Can't Tell From the Press That Social Security Is Untroubled and Sustainable"

Reporters and editors must look beyond establishment sources not only to interpret events but for basic facts as well. They should resist allowing political leaders alone to set the news agenda, using their own judgment instead to determine what's important for the public to know and then seek out independent-minded experts for authoritative commentary.

It is the conventional wisdom that Social Security and Medicare, America's two most popular social programs, are fiscally troubled and likely to bring down the American economy in the coming decades. The need to rein in these entitlements has long been a maxim for Republican politicians and for many Democrats as well. An informed voice that has not been well reported on this issue is that of James Galbraith, a highly respected economist at the University of Texas. In the first of John Hanrahan's interviews,

Galbraith said, "Let me make this clear: Social Security is untroubled. It is sustainable." As Hanrahan wrote:

> Galbraith said the press has been subjected to, and has largely bought into, a long-running "massive assault and propaganda campaign by the Wall Street crowd," spearheaded by Peter G. Peterson (fiscally conservative banker, author and politician) and David Walker (president and CEO of the Peterson Foundation), "over the notion that Social Security is unsustainable . . ."
>
> Rather than being a troubled program, Galbraith said that Social Security "merely by the fact of its existence is a major stabilizer in the economy," especially in these tough economic times when seniors' wealth has been hard-hit by the stock market fall affecting retirement income; by the collapse of housing values, and by the drop in interest rates, which reduces interest income. For more and more retired elderly, "Social Security and Medicare wealth are all they have."
>
> Galbraith told Nieman Watchdog that the dire warnings about looming Social Security shortfalls and the need for future cuts ignore the fact that "there is no earthly reason to fund Social Security benefits only from the payroll tax," as is now the case. Rather, he said, benefits could be funded for a time directly from the federal treasury. . . . Summing up, Galbraith has some very basic advice for reporters covering Social Security issues: Separate propaganda from fact.[4]

Galbraith, like other experts Hanrahan spoke to, was unequivocal on the need for massive government spending to deal with the recession and highly critical of much of the press for what he called "confused and ignorant positions" regarding deficits. He was especially critical of the *Washington Post* editorial page, saying, "Their editorials reveal a lack of understanding of the structure of the economy . . . and an indifference to basic accounting. To put the point firmly, they say that the economy is recovering but the deficits are a problem. But the economy is recovering because of the budget deficits. Without these budget deficits, there would be no recovery, because it is the deficits that are helping to put more money into households' pockets. To talk of recovery but to criticize the deficits is ridiculous. The whole point of this thing [stimulus spending] is to add to the deficit. The patient is recovering from a deadly illness and yet the press is attacking the medicine."

Hanrahan asked Galbraith if his criticism held for other news organizations as well and got this response: "I'm not a big reader of editorials in general. But the *Washington Post* is a broken record that one only has to consult occasionally. [Regarding deficits] they think that zero is the middle number and that balance is the same as virtue—convenient and simple beliefs that can be repeated endlessly to the approval of others, equally clueless."

Washington Post editorial writers would no doubt defend their position. But Galbraith's assertion that big deficit spending is the key to economic recovery is widely held by experts and was a basic view shared by all the economists interviewed by Hanrahan.

Nevertheless, in the period following the Nieman Watchdog series, the press emphasized sources expressing serious alarm over deficits but did not explore in depth calls for a second stimulus or any large-scale recovery spending. While some news organizations explained the need for massive deficits, most news coverage in 2009 and early 2010 was mired in standard he-said, she-said reporting with little regard for facts or established economic principles. The *New York Times* columnist Paul Krugman compared press scare coverage of deficits to its "groupthink" coverage during the run-up to the Iraq war. In a February 2010 column, Krugman, a Nobel Prize–winning economist, wrote:

> These days it's hard to pick up a newspaper or turn on a news program without encountering stern warnings about the federal budget deficit. The deficit threatens economic recovery, we're told; it puts American economic stability at risk; it will undermine our influence in the world. These claims generally aren't stated as opinions, as views held by some analysts but disputed by others. Instead, they're reported as if they were facts, plain and simple . . .
>
> The main difference between last summer, when we were mostly (and appropriately) taking deficits in stride, and the current sense of panic is that deficit fear-mongering has become a key part of Republican political strategy, doing double duty: it damages President Obama's image even as it cripples his policy agenda. And if the hypocrisy is breathtaking— politicians who voted for budget-busting tax cuts posing as apostles of fiscal rectitude, politicians demonizing attempts

to rein in Medicare costs one day (death panels!), then de-
nouncing excessive government spending the next—well,
what else is new?

The trouble, however, is that it's apparently hard for
many people to tell the difference between cynical posturing
and serious economic argument. And that is having tragic
consequences.[5]

The Hanrahan articles, like this and other Krugman columns,
report and flesh out ideas that are seldom aired, that are the opposite of what politicians tell us, and that make great common sense.
If there's one thing Americans think they know, for example, it
is that large deficits amount to generational theft, in effect steal-
ing from our children and grandchildren. That argument has been
around for many years; it sounds perfectly reasonable and is widely
accepted as fact. As Hanrahan wrote:

> Galbraith also criticized news and editorial coverage that un-
> questioningly reports the notion "of the relationship of the
> present to the future, the idea that the public debt puts the
> debt on our children and grandchildren. This is not true. If
> I incur a debt personally and die, it comes out of my estate
> or the pockets of my children. The public debt is not like
> that. There is the debt, yes, but there are also assets, namely
> the benefits that accrue to households today [through gov-
> ernment stimulus spending]. Without deficits, people to-
> day will have no assets to pass down to their children and
> grandchildren."
>
> Galbraith said that instead of holding the line on spending
> following the passage of the $780 billion stimulus measure
> earlier this year [2009], "we need more recovery bills" that
> are larger and reflect "the true scale of the emergency."

Another common misperception, Galbraith said, is that once
banks were stabilized, lending to businesses and individuals would
resume. This is exactly backward, he said. "First comes household
recovery and then the credit will flow." He said, "The full restoration
of private credit will take a long time. It will follow, not precede, the
restoration of sound private household finances. There is no way the
project of resurrecting the economy by stuffing the banks with cash
will work. Effective policy can only work the other way around."

Nevertheless, through the $700 billion TARP (Troubled Asset Relief Program), "we've given all this money to the banks, and the only place they can lend it to is back to the government."

Another economist interviewed by Hanrahan, Dean Baker, a macroeconomist and co-founder and co-director of the Center for Economic and Policy Research, also focused on that point. Hanrahan wrote:

> Baker observed that there have been a number of news articles recently about big banks returning to profitability, but most of those stories fail to make the point as to how those banks are becoming profitable—namely, by borrowing money short-term from the Federal Reserve at near zero cost and then loaning that money back to the Treasury by buying U.S. government bonds that pay around 3.5 percent interest.
>
> Baker said this means "we lend the banks the money that they lend back to us, albeit at a considerably higher interest rate"—which is "not exactly a boon for taxpayers." On a trillion dollars of lending, "this will give the banks $33 billion a year in net interest or profit. This is the extra money that the government is paying the banks to borrow back the money that it lent them through the Fed."
>
> Baker would like to see more press attention to this aspect of bank profitability so that citizens can more fully understand how taxpayer largesse produces profits for the banks.

As Hanrahan's reporting drew to a close, Dan Froomkin summarized its findings and added a few conclusions of his own in a striking column titled "Seven Things About the Economy That Everyone Should Be More Worried About Than They Are."[6]

Froomkin noted that the Hanrahan series laid out a broad landscape of economic issues that had been largely overlooked, including "the endemic fraud at the heart of the collapse, the resultant need for a comprehensive dissection of some key financial institutions, how the wars in Iraq and Afghanistan have weakened the economy, the dramatic effects of the crash on domestic poverty and world poverty, and underlying it all, the critically important role of government spending in a recovery, be it through a second stimulus or expanded entitlements or jobs programs, all of which requires that deficits be seen, for the short run at least, as the solution, not the problem."

Each of Froomkin's "seven things" is a line of inquiry for the press:

No. 1: The middle class may never be the same again.

No. 2: The recovery could take a really long time.

No. 3: The recovery could only be temporary.

No. 4: Then what? This time, we don't have the tools to get out of a recession.

No. 5: The "very serious" people in Washington are still obsessed about the deficit.

No. 6: Whatever is making the stock market go up could go away.

No. 7: The hugely irresponsible financial sector remains unchastened.

What the Experts Had to Say

In addition to James Galbraith and Dean Baker, Hanrahan interviewed Linda Bilmes of Harvard, Simon Johnson of MIT, David Moss of Harvard, and Jeffrey Sachs of Columbia University, an authority on poverty.[7]

Each of them had valuable advice for reporters and editors, and commonsense comments about the collapse of the economy and steps needed to deal with it. As noted, each of them—and other experts who took part aside from those interviewed by Hanrahan—agreed on the need for continued, massive deficit spending. Dean Baker, one of the few economists who correctly foresaw the housing bubble years before it burst, is a strong advocate of additional government spending—a second stimulus—to boost the economy and reduce unemployment. He told Hanrahan, "The mainstream news media should make sure that, in any discussion of the deficit, they make it clear that many economists regard the deficit as manageable and favor adding to the deficit by spending more, not less, federal stimulus to reduce unemployment and to bring about a true economic recovery."

Danny Schechter, a 1978 Nieman Fellow who runs a journalism Web site (http://mediachannel.org/) on social and political issues, produces films and writes books, took part in our "Reporting the Collapse" series as a contributor and was highly critical of media coverage. This is from his essay in October 2009:

> But do we know that, even now, much of our media, despite the sheer volume of coverage, may be missing the real story? Do we know that if we want to find missing facts and the real context we have to turn away from the failed media system that never really investigated the failed financial system?
>
> The Project for Excellence in Journalism that examines media trends released a study charging "that the gravest economic crisis since the Great Depression has been covered in the media largely from the top down, told primarily from the perspective of the Obama administration and big business, with coverage reflecting the concerns of institutions more than the lives of everyday Americans."[8]
>
> Why is this? I asked several journalists in making a film and writing a book about the financial crisis as a crime story. A number agreed that the media themselves are "embedded" in the culture and narratives of Wall Street, like reporters embedded in Iraq. Many lack the willingness to be critical of the sources they rely on. Most bring too little perspective and context to their work.

David A. Moss, who teaches business, government, and international economy at the Harvard Business School, came out strongly for regulation of financial institutions and told Hanrahan the media are obligated to dig deeply into the specific proposals for regulation proposed by the Obama administration, Congress, think tanks, and academics such as himself. Moss likened the economic crisis to children leaving a school yard and heading for a dangerous cliff, only to be rescued by school authorities just as they were about to go over the cliff. Financial institutions were about to go over the cliff when the government rescued them. But, said Moss, the government, like the school authorities, should have been minding them beforehand.

As Hanrahan wrote, "For his part, Moss has developed such a comprehensive plan that he said could make the 'school yard' safe as well as regulating those giant financial institutions that are regarded as 'too big to fail.' Without reforms, he said, these institutions have an implicit government guarantee that they will be rescued again if they take foolish risks that precipitate another financial crisis."

One essay in the series, by Martin Lobel and Lee Ellen Helfrich (a law partner with Lobel and Banta), made a case for increasing taxes on the very rich:

> Our economic recovery will be slow because middle-income taxpayers cannot generate the consumer demand necessary to get the economy moving quickly. This is the result of a shift in wealth from middle-income taxpayers to the very rich since the Reagan era, coupled with the high and increasing unemployment rate. The federal government will have to spend about $760 billion more to return the economy to full employment. That cannot be done, however, without increasing the federal deficit, unless the stimulus is accompanied by tax increases on those most able to bear them without significantly impairing spending—that is, the very rich.

Ideas like these from Lobel and Helfrich are obviously worth exploring but are seldom heard in the mainstream media. Also missing from most coverage is any sense of the toll the economic collapse has taken on the poor in America and worldwide, and the crushing burden that the wars in Iraq and Afghanistan have put on taxpayers.

Jeffrey Sachs, a leading expert on global poverty, spoke at length to Hanrahan. Like others interviewed, Sachs had mixed views, most of them sharply critical of press coverage, except for a number of writers and columnists at the *New York Times*, whom he singled out for praise.

Sachs told Hanrahan that he sees some spot-news and feature coverage of poverty-related issues in the mainstream press from time to time, and exceptional op-ed pieces from *New York Times* columnist Bob Herbert. But he sees little comprehensive newspage focus on "the systematic realities of poverty and the tax and spending policies" that need to be reformed to reduce poverty and income inequality.

Sachs told Hanrahan that "it's not only the news media" that generally ignore poverty in the United States. "It is not on the political agenda. I doubt if President Obama has said much about it. The word 'poverty' itself is hardly ever used. Sometimes political leaders refer to the unemployed or low-income wage earners or struggling families, but not poverty. We have no activism around poverty. The political rhetoric is always built around 'the hard-working taxpayer' and not poor people."

Hanrahan interviewed Professor Linda Bilmes, who teaches budgeting and public finance at the Harvard Kennedy School of Government, on the damages two wars have done to the economy. "There are very fundamental flaws in the way most people and the news media look at the cost of wars, "Bilmes told him. "For the press, these are still uncharted waters. The press doesn't always do a good job in connecting the dots. Their stories might be adequate in reporting what different people are saying about a particular issue, but often they don't deal with what might be the economic consequences of doing something or not doing something, as with the costs of going to war."

Bilmes is co-author with Nobel Prize–economist Joseph Stiglitz of two books on the costs of the Iraq war. "The question is not whether the economy has been weakened by the [Iraq] war," they wrote in 2008 in their the second book, *The Three Trillion Dollar War.* "The question is only by how much."

Economist Simon Johnson of MIT, like James Galbraith, called on reporters to be muckrakers who take on the financial institutions that helped cause, and even benefited from, the collapse. "I would like to see serious journalism, blow-by-blow exposés of these [financial institutions] in the manner of Ida Tarbell," Johnson told Hanrahan, referring to the muckraking journalist of the early twentieth century whose most famous story revealed the illegal means used by John D. Rockefeller to monopolize the early oil industry in the United States.

Hanrahan wrote: "As one prime example among many that would be worthy of the Tarbell treatment, Johnson cited the banks' credit card companies. How, he asked, did we get to the point 'where these companies can take such advantage of their customers? Where are the detailed stories that put a human face on this? Who are the people who run these companies? How can they justify what they do?' And who are the customers who suffer because of the credit card industry's practices?"

Worth noting for reporters and editors is a comment Hanrahan inserted at this point in his interview with Simon Johnson: "And, we would add, who are the credit card lobbyists and how do they operate? Which politicians protect the industry and benefit most from its largesse?" Here we have the reporter as a thinking person, interjecting appropriate thoughts of his own to an interview with an expert. Not exactly he-said, she-said, is it? We find this to be a worthwhile lesson for reporters and editors, albeit a somewhat risky one, since not all reporters are as knowledgeable or sure-footed as Hanrahan.

Finding Credible Economists as Sources

The question arises, why did Hanrahan choose these experts for interviews and how do they differ, if at all, from experts the main-stream press calls on frequently? Also, how did Hanrahan, who was not a financial reporter, prepare to discuss complicated issues in interviews with leading economists? What are the lessons here? The first part of the answer is that several of us, including Hanrahan, met and developed our source list carefully. We also received suggestions from Joseph Bower, a Harvard Business School professor specializing in general management who is a member of the Nieman Foundation's advisory board. We then sent notices to the experts we wanted to interview, asking them to take part. In addition, and importantly, Hanrahan made himself familiar with the work of each economist. He telephoned and e-mailed them a description of his proposed line of questioning that was framed on his knowledge of their areas of expertise. These were busy people with projects of their own. More than one of them told Hanrahan that they were not inclined to take part but that they couldn't refuse once they read his e-mail. That is, of course, a tribute to Hanrahan, but there's a lesson in it for all reporters: be prepared.

As for why we sought out these experts and not some others, Henry Banta addressed the issue of experts' credibility in a column for niemanwatchdog.org in February 2010, dividing economists into three groups. The first group, the one most often called on by the media, especially cable TV, Banta said, includes fine, competent economists but ones employed by Wall Street and various commercial interests. It would be unfair to ask any of them for an unbiased opinion when an honest answer might be inconsistent with their employers' or clients' interests. The second group includes those who became so immersed in efficient market hypothesis that they simply couldn't let go of it, even after the great catastrophe that exposed the flaws in the theory and left millions out of work, homes lost, savings gone. These economists often blame government policies for the collapse, although that would be supremely illogical if the efficient market hypothesis were valid. The third group, those with credibility, believes that markets are fallible, vulnerable to irrational speculation and bubbles, and that government has a large role in regulating markets and in establishing monetary policy that helps stabilize them.

These are logical divisions, helpful to reporters and editors looking for credible experts. Unfortunately, there is an obvious complicating factor: many Republicans, including all orthodox Republicans these days, are comfortable with the Wall Street economists and the efficient market economists, and act as though the third group—the credible experts—were created only to thwart them. While a good number of Democrats also hold on to efficient market theory, it is mostly Republicans who do, and they hold onto it deeply. As Banta wrote, "What characterizes the Republican Party at present is a complete failure to recognize the collapse of its basic economic principles. It is locked in a passionate embrace with a corpse."

So one problem for the press is that the more it seeks credibility and the more independent it becomes, the more it will be held to be partisan, part of an anti-Republican conspiracy. That will be true regardless how down-the-middle coverage is, and it is no small problem. Are editors and reporters ready for it? Are publishers and broadcast executives?

ABOUT THE CONTRIBUTORS

Ryan Chittum writes about the business press for the *Columbia Journalism Review*'s The Audit. He is a former *Wall Street Journal* reporter and has written for the *New York Times* and other publications. He lives in Seattle with his wife and twin daughters.

Robert H. Giles is curator of the Nieman Foundation for Journalism, a mid-career fellowship program for journalists at Harvard University. He worked for nearly forty years as a newspaper reporter and editor, most recently as editor and publisher of the *Detroit News*, which he joined in 1986 as executive editor. From 1977 to 1986, Giles was executive editor and then editor at the *Democrat & Chronicle* and the *Times-Union*, in Rochester, NY. His newspaper career began in 1958 at the *Akron* (Ohio) *Beacon Journal*, where he held several reporting and editing positions before becoming managing editor and then executive editor.

As managing editor of the *Beacon Journal*, Giles directed coverage of the campus shootings at Kent State University, for which the newspaper was awarded the Pulitzer Prize. Before coming to Harvard in 2000, he was a senior vice president of the Freedom Forum and executive director of its Media Studies Center in New York City.

Giles is a graduate of DePauw University and the Graduate School of Journalism at Columbia University. He was a Nieman

Fellow in 1966. He received an honorary doctorate in Journalism from DePauw in 1996.

Peter S. Goodman is the business editor at the Huffington Post, and was previously the national economic correspondent for the *New York Times*. His coverage of the origins of the financial crisis of 2008 was part of "The Reckoning," a *Times* series that garnered a Gerald Loeb award—the so-called Pulitzer of business and economic reporting. His book, *Past Due: The End of Easy Money and the Renewal of the American Economy*, chronicles the roots and consequences of the Great Recession, exploring the technology bubble of the 1990s, China's breakneck development, and the American real estate bubble while considering how the nation may construct a new, more sustainable economy, perhaps focused on renewable energy and the life sciences.

Goodman previously spent a decade at the *Washington Post*—as the newspaper's Shanghai-based Asian economic correspondent from 2001 through 2006; before that he covered the technology bubble as the *Post*'s telecommunications writer. He began his career as a freelancer in Southeast Asia, where he chronicled the civil war in Cambodia, the emergence of market-embracing reforms in Vietnam, and the struggle for independence in East Timor.

Goodman is a graduate of Reed College, where he majored in political science, and the University of California at Berkeley, where he gained an MA in Vietnamese history. He lives in Brooklyn.

Chris Roush is the Walter E. Hussman Sr. Distinguished Scholar in business journalism at UNC-Chapel Hill. He is the founding director of the Carolina Business News Initiative, which provides training for professional journalists and students at UNC-Chapel Hill. He is also director of the master's program at the School of Journalism and Mass Communication. In 2010, he was named Journalism Teacher of the Year by the Scripps Howard Foundation and the Association for Education in Journalism and Mass Communication. The judges noted that Roush "has become the expert in business journalism—not just at Chapel Hill, but throughout the country and even in other parts of the world." He is the author of two books about business journalism—*Show Me the Money: Writing Business and Economics Stories for Mass Communication* (second edition, 2010) and *Profits and Losses: Business Journalism and Its Role in Society* (2006). He is the co-author of *The*

Financial Writer's Stylebook: 1,100 Business Terms Defined and Rated (2010). Roush has been quoted about business journalism in publications such as the *New York Times*, the *Wall Street Journal*, *USA Today*, and *American Journalism Review*, and he has written about business journalism in *Columbia Journalism Review* and *American Journalism Review*.

Steve Schifferes is Marjorie Deane Professor of Financial Journalism at City University London and course director for the MA in Financial Journalism. He was previously an economics correspondent for the BBC News Web site, where he also served as Washington correspondent, General Election Issues Producer, and head of the specials team. He has covered major economic crises for the past twenty-five years, from the 1987 crash to the Asian crisis to the dot-com bubble to the collapse of Lehman. He started his journalism career at London Weekend Television. Steve was educated at Harvard and the University of Warwick, and was a Knight-Bagehot Fellow at Columbia and a Reuters Fellow at Oxford.

Anya Schiffrin is the director of the International Media, Advocacy and Communications program at Columbia University's School of International and Public Affairs. She spent ten years working overseas as a journalist in Europe and Asia, writing for a number of different magazines and newspapers. She was bureau chief for Dow Jones Newswires in Amsterdam and Hanoi, and wrote regularly for the *Wall Street Journal*. She was a Knight-Bagehot Fellow at Columbia University's Graduate School of Journalism in 1999–2000, and then a senior writer at the Industry Standard, where she covered banking and finance. She was the founder of the Web site www.journalismtraining.net, which provides training materials for journalists, and has edited three textbooks and manuals for reporters. Schiffrin organizes seminars around the world to strengthen the capacity of journalists in developing countries to cover finance and economics. She has taught in Azerbaijan, China, Indonesia, Moldova, Mongolia, Nigeria, Kazakhstan, South Africa, and Vietnam. She is a member of the sub-board of the Open Society Foundation's Media Program.

Dean Starkman is editor of The Audit, an online critique of financial journalism of *Columbia Journalism Review*, and the magazine's Kingsford Capital Fellow. A reporter for two decades, Starkman was most recently a Katrina Media Fellow with the Open Society Institute, covering the insurance industry's response to Hurricane Katrina, and he spent a year covering white-collar crime on a contract for the *Washington Post*. He spent eight years at the *Wall Street Journal*, where he served as national real estate writer and covered white-collar crime and securities law, as well as the paper industry. A former chief of the *Providence Journal*'s investigative unit, he won numerous national and regional awards and helped lead the team that won the 1994 Pulitzer Prize for Investigations. He is a graduate of McGill University and the Columbia University Graduate School of Journalism.

Joseph E. Stiglitz is University Professor at Columbia. In 2001, he was awarded the Nobel Prize in economics for his analyses of markets with asymmetric information, and he was a lead author of the 1995 Report of the Intergovernmental Panel on Climate Change, which shared the 2007 Nobel Peace Prize. He was the chief economist of the World Bank from 1997 to 2000. From 1994 to 1997 he was member and then chairman of the Council of Economic Advisors under President Clinton.

Stiglitz helped create a new branch of economics, "The Economics of Information," exploring the consequences of information asymmetries and pioneering such pivotal concepts as adverse selection and moral hazard, which have now become standard tools not only of theorists, but of policy analysts. He has made major contributions to macroeconomics and monetary theory, to development economics and trade theory, to public and corporate finance, to the theories of industrial organization and rural organization, and to the theories of welfare economics and of income and wealth distribution. In the 1980s, he helped revive interest in the economics of R&D. His work has helped explain the circumstances in which markets do not work well, and how selective government intervention can improve their performance.

His most recent book was the bestseller *Freefall: America, Free Markets and the Sinking of the World Economy*, published in 2010.

Barry Sussman is the editor of the Nieman Foundation's Watchdog Project (www.niemanwatchdog.org), which aims at encouraging better news media reporting on public policy issues. Previously he was a *Washington Post* editor for twenty-two years, holding the positions of city editor, special Watergate editor, special projects editor/national, pollster and public opinion analyst and columnist for the *Washington Post* national weekly edition.

He is the author of three books. The first, *The Great Coverup: Nixon and the Scandal of Watergate*, was named one of the best books of the year in 1974 by the *New York Times*. His other books are *What Americans Really Think*, published in 1987 and dealing in the main with public opinion and politics; and *Maverick: A Life in Politics*, written with Lowell P. Weicker Jr., and published in 1995. In addition, Sussman has worked as an international news media consultant with assignments at newspapers in Spain, Portugal, and in seven Latin American countries.

Maureen (Moe) Tkacik is a former staff reporter at the *Wall Street Journal* and co-founder of the blog Jezebel. She currently possesses no institutional affiliation, but has written for the *Nation*, the *Baffler*, *Columbia Journalism Review*, Talking Points Memo, the *New York Times*, *New York* magazine, and numerous other publications, many of which are now defunct. She has worked in Hong Kong, Los Angeles, and Philadelphia, and presently lives in Brooklyn.

NOTES

Chapter I: The U.S. Press and the Financial Crisis

1. John Koblin, "Los Angeles Times Cuts Staff for Third Time This Year; 10 Percent of Newsroom Let Go," *New York Observer*, October 27, 2008, Media section, http://www.observer.com/2008/media/l-times-cuts-staff-third-time-year-10-percent-newsroom-let-go (accessed March 15, 2010); Richard Pérez Peña, "Times Says It Will Cut 100 Newsroom Jobs," on Media Decoder, a blog on the Web site of the *New York Times*, posted October 19, 2009, http://mediadecoder.blogs.nytimes.com/2009/10/19/times-says-it-will-cut-100-newsroom-jobs/ (accessed March 15, 2010); Robert MacMillan, "Chicago Tribune Cuts 11 Percent of Newsroom Jobs," Reuters, April 22, 2009, http://www.reuters.com/article/idUSTRE53L66P20090422 (accessed March 15, 2010).
2. Jon Meacham, "A New Magazine for a Changing World," *Newsweek*, http://www.newsweek.com/id/197888 (accessed March 15, 2010).
3. "New York, Oct 26 (Reuters)—The plunge in U.S. newspaper circulation is accelerating, according to the latest figures released on Monday, as more people cancel their subscriptions and publishers cut distribution and sales of discounted copies. Average weekday circulation at 379 daily newspapers fell 10.6 percent to about 30.4 million copies for the six months that ended on Sept. 30, 2009,

from the same period last year, according to the U.S. Audit Bureau of Circulations. The pace of decline more than doubled compared with last year. From September 2007 to September 2008, circulation fell 4.6 percent," Robert MacMillan, "U.S. Newspaper Circulation Plunge Accelerates," Reuters, October 26, 2009, http://www.reuters.com/article/idUSN2633378520091026 (accessed March 15, 2010); "U.S. measured-media ad spending plunged 14.7% in the first nine months of 2009, reflecting a freefall in local advertising (such as auto dealer ads), according to WPP's TNS Media Intelligence. TNS said the nation's 100 largest advertisers cut measured-media spending by 7.9% in the first three quarters," "Ad Spending Heads Into Tepid Recovery," *Advertising Age*, December 28, 2009, http://adage.com/article?article_id=141211 (accessed March 15, 2010).

4. Richard Pérez Peña, "It's Official: 2009 Was Worst Year for the Newspaper Business in Decades," on Media Decoder, a blog on the Web site of the *New York Times*, posted on March 24, 2010, http://mediadecoder.blogs.nytimes.com/2010/03/24/its-official-2009-was-worst-year-for-the-newpaper-business-in-decades/ (accessed March 29, 2010).

5. Leonard Downie Jr. and Michael Schudson, "The Reconstruction of American Journalism," *Columbia Journalism Review*, October 19, 2009, http://www.cjr.org/reconstruction/the_reconstruction_of_american.php (accessed March 15, 2010).

6. Edmund L. Andrews, *Busted: Life Inside the Great Mortgage Meltdown* (New York: W.W. Norton, 2009).

7. Megan McArdle, "The Road to Bankruptcy," *Atlantic*, May 21, 2009, http://www.theatlantic.com/business/archive/2009/05/the-road-to-bankruptcy/17976/ (accessed March 15, 2010).

8. Ben S. Bernanke, "The Economic Outlook," March 28, 2007, Web site of the Federal Reserve, http://www.federalreserve.gov/newsevents/testimony/bernanke20070328a.htm (accessed March 16, 2010).

9. The National Bureau of Economic Research, "Determination of the December 2007 Peak in Economic Activity," http://www.nber.org/cycles/dec2008.html (accessed March 16, 2010).

10. Ben S. Bernanke, "The Economic Outlook," November 8, 2007, Web site of the Federal Reserve http://www.federalreserve.gov/newsevents/testimony/bernanke20071108a.htm (accessed March 16, 2010).

11. Ben S. Bernanke, "At the Greater Austin Chamber of Commerce, Austin, Texas," December 1, 2008, Web site of the Federal Reserve,

http://www.federalreserve.gov/newsevents/speech/bernanke
20081201a.htm (accessed March 16, 2010).

12. Andrew Ross Sorkin, "In Flurry of Big Merger Deals, Signs
of Restored Confidence," *New York Times,* September 29,
2009, Business section, http://www.nytimes.com/2009/09/29/
business/29sorkin.html (accessed March 29, 2010).

13. Richard Pérez-Peña, "Amid Market Turmoil, Some Journalists Try
to Tone Down Emotion," *New York Times,* September 21, 2008,
http://www.nytimes.com/2008/09/22/business/media/22press.html
(accessed March 16, 2010).

14. John Talton, "Journalism's Culpability in the Economic Crisis,"
Britannica Blog, March 4, 2009, http://www.britannica.com/
blogs/2009/03/journalisms-culpability-in-the-economic-crisis/ (accessed March 16, 2010).

15. Rory O'Connor, "Embedded Business Press Misses the Story of the
Century," The Huffington Post, March 21, 2009, http://www
.huffingtonpost.com/rory-oconnor/embedded-business-press
-m_b_167860.html (accessed March 16, 2010); Danny Schechter, "A
Media Failure Compounds Our Financial Crisis," The Huffington
Post, October 7, 2009, http://www.huffingtonpost.com/danny
-schechter/a-media-failure-compounds_b_312404.html (accessed
March 16, 2010).

16. Wayne Parsons, *The Power of the Financial Press.* (Piscataway, NJ:
Rutgers University Press, 1990), 41.

17. Ibid., 12.

18. Mark Frazier, "Five Reasons for Crash Blindness," *British Journalism
Review* 20 (2009): 78–83.

19. Author interview, New York, June 2009.

20. Bethany McLean, "Is Enron Overpriced?" *Fortune,* March 5, 2001,
http://money.cnn.com/2006/01/13/news/companies/enronoriginal
_fortune/index.htm (accessed March 17, 2010).

21. Paul E. Steiger, "Not Every Journalist 'Missed' the Enron Story,"
Nieman Reports 56 (2): 10–13.

22. "Timeline of Enron's Collapse," *Washington Post,* September 30,
2004, http://www.washingtonpost.com/wp-dyn/articles/A25624
-2002Jan10.html (accessed March 29, 2010).

23. Scott Sherman, "Enron: Uncovering the Uncovered Story,"
Columbia Journalism Review, March–April 2002, 24.

24. Author interview, February 2010, New York.

25. Herbert J. Gans, *Deciding What's News: A Study of CBS Evening*

News, NBC Nightly News, Newsweek and Time (Evanston, IL: Northwestern University Press, 2004), 133.

26. Edward S. Herman and Noam Chomsky, *Manufacturing Consent: The Political Economy of the Mass Media* (New York: Pantheon Books, 2002), 22.

27. Robert Skidelsky, *John Maynard Keynes: Economist, Philosopher, Statesman* (London: Macmillan, 2003), xx–xxi.

28. One example is Truman Capote, who befriended the two murderers of the Clutter family while writing his book *In Cold Blood*. Joe McGuiness did the same thing to the murderous Jeffrey MacDonald when he researched his book *Fatal Vision*. While McGuiness was writing the book, he gave MacDonald the impression that he believed in the murder suspect's innocence and wrote him countless empathetic letters when he was in jail awaiting his trial. When the book came out, however, McGuiness clearly took the view that MacDonald was guilty and was sued by MacDonald. Janet Malcolm wrote a book about the case, *The Journalist and the Murdered*, and described the process as one of seduction and betrayal. She was later accused of doing something similar when she won the confidence of Jeffrey Masson as she was researching her book *In the Freud Archives*, which was drawn from her *New Yorker* article about Masson's falling out with Anna Freud. When it came out, Masson was reportedly furious at her portrayal of him as egotistical, irresponsible, and dishonest and sued her for libel.

29. Gabriel Sherman, "The Information Broker," *New York*, November 8, 2009, http://nymag.com/news/media/61870/ accessed on March 7, 2010 (accessed March 29, 2010).

30. Gillian Doyle, "Financial News Journalism: A Post-Enron Analysis of Approaches Toward Economic and Financial News Production in the UK." *Journalism* 7 (4; 2006): 444.

31. Author interview, South Hampton, New York, August 2009.

32. Timothy Crouse, *The Boys on the Bus* (New York: Random House, 2003), 22.

33. For examples see the *New York Times* and *Time* magazine's coverage of Bush's last press conference on January 12, 2009. Sheryl Gay Stolberg, "Mistakes, I've Made a Few, Bush Tells Reporters," *New York Times*, January 12, 2009, http://www.nytimes.com/2009/01/13/us/politics/13bush.html?_r=1&scp=3&sq=Bush&st=nyt (accessed March 29, 2010); Massimo Calbresi, "Bush's Last Press Conference: Full of Disappointment," *Time*, January 12, 2009, http://www.time

.com/time/nation/article/0,8599,1871113,00.html (accessed March 29, 2010).

34. Author interview, New York, February 2009.

35. Author interview, New York, October 2009.

36. Among other stories, see "'Good Jobs in Hard Times" by Louis Uchitelle, *New York Times*, October 3, 1993, which describes how Wal-Mart and others created jobs that paid $5 to $9 an hour.

37. Interestingly, under the ownership of Robert R. McCormick the *Chicago Tribune* in the thirties was very much against President Roosevelt and the New Deal. For more information, see Richard Norton Smith's biography *The Colonel: The Life and Legend of Robert R. McCormick, 1888–1955* (Evanston, IL: Northwestern University Press, 1997), 314, 316, 329, 330, and 342.

38. Special Reports, "Updated Report: Economists Comprised Only 6 Percent of Guest Appearances Discussing Stimulus on Cable News, Sunday Shows," Media Matters for America, http://mediamatters. org/reports/200902240021 (accessed March 28, 2010).

39. The battle over regulation (a story with a true heroine, Brooksley E. Born, sparring with, and ultimately losing to, the concerted efforts of Rubin, Greenspan, and Summers, was poorly reported. That story was "broken" in 2009—years after the fact—by Manuel Roig-Franzia for the *Washington Post* and by *Stanford Magazine* in its March/April 2009 issue, http://www.stanfordalumni.org/news/magazine/2009/marapr/features/born.html.

Chapter 2: The Media and the Crisis: An Information Theoretic Approach

1. University Professor, Columbia University and Chair, Brooks World Poverty Institute, University of Manchester. Financial support from the Hewlett and Ford Foundations is gratefully acknowledged. I am also indebted to Jonathan Dingle and Jill Blackford for research assistance.

2. In 2005, Greenspan said: "There are a few things that suggest, at a minimum there's a little froth in this market." While "we don't perceive that there is a national bubble . . . it's hard not to see that there are a lot of local bubbles." [Craig Torres and Alison Fitzgerald, "Greenspan Says Housing Market 'Speculation' Is Unsustainable," Bloomberg, May 20, 2010, http://www.bloomberg.com/apps/news?pid=newsarchive&sid=azb8fwbe5Fqw.]

3. As late as March 2007, Federal Reserve Chairman Bernanke claimed

that "the impact on the broader economy and financial markets of the problems in the subprime market seems likely to be contained." Statement of Ben S. Bernanke, Chairman, Board of Governors of the Federal Reserve System, before the Joint Economic Committee, U.S. Congress, Washington, DC, March 28, 2007. [Stiglitz, *Freefall*, 19.]

4. As the housing market fell to a fourteen-year low, Bush reassured the nation on October 17, 2007: "I feel good about many of the economic indicators here in the United States." Bush in November 2007: "The underpinnings of our economy are strong, and we're a resilient economy." Bush in October 2008, "We know what the problems are, we have the tools we need to fix them, and we're working swiftly to do so." [Stiglitz, *Freefall*, 28–29.]

5. The Dutch "tulip mania" of the 1630s was one of the most famous early bubbles. In this bubble, the price of tulip bulbs—a product that can be quickly reproduced at low costs—reached 2,500 florins, which would be worth more than $30,000 in today's prices. See Charles P. Kindleberger, *Manias, Panics, and Crashes: A History of Financial Crises* (New York: Basic Books, 1978), and Mark Hirschey, "How Much Is a Tulip Worth?" *Financial Analysts Journal* 54 (4; July–August 1998): 11–17.

6. See, for instance, preface and introduction to *Selected Works of Joseph E. Stiglitz: Volume I: Information and Economic Analysis* (Oxford: Oxford University Press, 2009), ix–lxi and 1–26.

7. Though the role of "belief systems" has long been central to the understanding of sociologists and anthropologists of the functioning of society, until the recent crisis, the dominant school in economics focused on rational expectations, on models in which market participants digested all of the information that was available, using (somehow) the "correct" model of the world. Ironically, of course, what these economists asserted as the "correct" model was shown to be grossly flawed in the recent crisis. More recently, economists have attempted to incorporate broader perspectives concerning belief systems in their models—especially as they affect developmental processes. See Avner Greif, *Institutions and the Path to the Modern Economy: Lessons from Medieval Trade* (Cambridge and New York: Cambridge University Press, 2006); Masahiko Aoki, *Toward a Comparative Institutional Analysis* (MIT Press, 2001); and Karla Hoff and Joseph E. Stiglitz, "Equilibrium Fictions: A Cognitive Approach to Societal Rigidity," *American Economic Review* 100(2) (May 2010): 141–46.

8. The usual advice given to central bankers, which unfortunately many (including those in the United States) did not heed.

9. See, e.g., Jack Hirshleifer, "The Private and Social Value of Information and the Reward to Inventive Activity," *American Economic Review*, 61 (4; September 1971): 561–74 and J.E. Stiglitz, "Using Tax Policy to Curb Speculative Short-Term Trading," *Journal of Financial Services Research* 3 (2/3; December 1989): 101–15.

10. A point brought out forcefully by Lehman's infamous "Repo 105" transactions, which moved some $50 billion off its balance sheet. The use of "creative accounting" is not new; it was one of the distinctive aspects of the scandals of the early years of the century, epitomized by Enron. In the case of Lehman brothers, a firm that claimed to have a net worth of $26 billion just before its collapse turned out to have a negative net worth of –$200 billion). See J.E. Stiglitz, *Freefall*, 156.

11. Remarkably, as Citibank went through its crisis, Citigroup shareholder equity (as reported) continued its growth: it went from $114 billion (December 2007), to $142 billion (December 2008), and onto $153 billion (December 2009), http://www.google.com/finance?q=NYSE:C&fstype=ii.

12. Tony Barber, David Oakley, and Kerin Hope, "Chinese Whispers Drive Up Greek Yields" *Financial Times*, January 26, 2010, http://www.ft.com/cms/s/0/65ac74fc-0aaf-11df-b35f-00144feabdc0.html.

13. Mark Pittman, "S&P, Moody's Mask $200 Billion of Subprime Bond Risk," Bloomberg, June 29, 2007, http://www.bloomberg.com/apps/news?pid=20601087&refer=home&sid=aIzzx2vC10KI and "S&P May Cut $12 Billion of Subprime Mortgage Bonds," Bloomberg, July 10, 2007, http://www.bloomberg.com/apps/news?pid=20601103&sid=aN4sulHN19xc.

14. A U.S. district judge ordered the Federal Reserve to turn over records identifying the companies receiving money through its emergency lending programs in August 2009. Mark Pittman, "Court Orders Fed to Disclose Emergency Bank Loans," Bloomberg, August 25, 2009, http://www.bloomberg.com/apps/news?pid=20601087&sid=a7CC61ZsieV4. In March 2010, the U.S. Court of Appeals in Manhattan upheld the decision that the Fed must disclose its documents. David Glovin and Bob Van Voris, "Federal Reserve Must Disclose Bank Bailout Records," Bloomberg, March 19, 2010, http://www.bloomberg.com/apps/news?pid=20601087&sid=aUpIaeiWKF2s.

15. Jody Shenn, Bob Ivry, and Alan Katz, "AIG 100-Cents Fed Deal

Driven by France Belied by French Banks," Bloomberg, January 20, 2010, http://www.bloomberg.com/apps/news?pid=newsarchive&sid= a__.69Q8BR04.

16. See, for instance, J.E. Stiglitz, *Roaring Nineties* (New York: W.W. Norton, 2003).

17. John Maynard Keynes, *The General Theory of Employment, Interest, and Money* (London: Macmillan, 1936).

18. See George A. Akerlof and Robert J. Shiller, *Animal Spirits: How Human Psychology Drives the Economy, and Why It Matters for Global Capitalism* (Princeton, NJ: Princeton University Press, 2009).

19. George Soros has emphasized that while beliefs are an important part of economic reality, they are not untethered. See George Soros, *The New Paradigm for Financial Markets* (New York: Public Affairs, 2008).

20. See, in particular, J.E. Stiglitz, "Transparency in Government" in *The Right to Tell: The Role of Mass Media in Economic Development*, ed. Roumeen Islam (Washington, D.C.: World Bank Publications, 2002) and J.E. Stiglitz, "On Liberty, the Right to Know and Public Discourse: The Role of Transparency in Public Life," chapter 8 in *The Rebel Within*, ed. Ha-Joon Chang (London: Wimbledon Publishing Company, 2001), 250–78. Also published in *Globalizing Rights*, ed. Matthew Gibney (Oxford: Oxford University Press, 2003), 115–56. (Originally presented as 1999 Oxford Amnesty Lecture, Oxford, January 1999.)

21. See J.E. Stiglitz, *Freefall*.

22. See, for instance, Floyd Norris, chief financial correspondent for the *New York Times* and the *International Herald Tribune;* Gretchen Morgenson, who writes the Sunday "Fair Game" column for the *New York Times;* and the late Mark Pittman of Bloomberg.

Chapter 4: The Financial Press: It's Not as Bad as Its Reputation

1. Stieg Larsson, *The Girl with the Dragon Tattoo.* (New York: Vintage Books, 2009), 102.

2. Marcus Brauchli, personal interview, October 20, 2008.

3. Erin Arvedlund, "Don't Ask, Don't Tell: Bernie Madoff Is So Secretive, He Even Asks Investors to Keep Mum," *Barron's,* May 7, 2001, 26.

4. Howard J. Carswell, "Business News Coverage," *Public Opinion Quarterly* 2 (4; October 1938): 613–21.

5. W.M. Pinkerton, "Businessmen and the Press," *Harvard Business Review 28* (3; May 1950): 25–32.

6. Gerald M. Loeb, "Flaws in Financial Reporting." *Columbia Journalism Review*, Spring 1966, 37–39.

7. Chris Welles, "The Bleak Wasteland of Financial Journalism," *Columbia Journalism Review*, July–August 1973, 40–49.

8. Herbert Stein, "Media Distortions: A Former Official's View," *Columbia Journalism Review*, March–April 1975, 37–39.

9. William McPhatter, "Introduction" in *The Business Beat: Its Impact and Its Problems*, ed. William McPhatter (Indianapolis, IN: Bobbs-Merrill Educational Publishing, 2008), xii.

10. R.E. Cheney, "Cheering on the Scoundrels," *Nieman Reports* 45 (3; fall 1991): 18–19.

11. Merrill Goozner, "Blinded by the Boom: What's Missing in the Coverage of the New Economy?" *Columbia Journalism Review*, November–December 2000, 23–27.

12. Diana B. Henriques, "What Journalists Should Be Doing About Business Coverage—but Aren't," *Harvard International Journal of Press Politics*, 5 (2; 2000): 118–21.

13. Allan Sloan, personal interview, October 17, 2008.

14. Gregory S. Miller, "The Press as a Watchdog for Accounting Fraud," *Journal of Accounting Research* 44 (5; December 2006): 1001–33.

15. Sarah Bartlett, personal interview, October 17, 2008.

16. Gretchen Morgenson, "Mortgages May Be Messier Than You Think," *New York Times*, March 4, 2007, C1.

17. Steve Pearlstein, "Credit Markets Weight Puts Economy on Shaky Ground," *Washington Post*, August 1, 2007, D1.

18. Patrick Barta, "Why Calls Are Rising to Clip Fannie Mae's, Freddie Mac's Wings," *Wall Street Journal*, July 14, 2000, A1.

19. Jathon Sapsford, "Despite the Recession, Americans Continue to Be Avid Borrowers," *Wall Street Journal*, January 1, 2002, A1.

20. Patrick Barta, "Saturation Scenario: Will Fannie Mae, Freddie Mac Hit Limits in Growth?" *Wall Street Journal*, August 6, 2002, A1.

21. Patrick Barta, "Mortgage Mismatch: Home Refinancings Widen Fannie's Risk," *Wall Street Journal*, September 17, 2002, C1.

22. Patrick Barta and Ruth Simon, "Furor Greets Bid to Alter System of Closing Costs on Mortgages," *Wall Street Journal*, August 19, 2003, A1.

23. Patrick Barta, John D. McKinnon, and Gregory Zuckerman,

"Behind Freddie Mac's Troubles: A Strategy to Take on More Risk," *Wall Street Journal*, September 22, 2003, A1.

24. James R. Hagerty and Ruth Simon, "As Prices Rise, Homeowners Go Deep in Debt to Buy Real Estate," *Wall Street Journal*, May 23, 2005, A1.

25. Ruth Simon, James R. Hagerty, and James T. Areddy, "Housing-bubble Talk Doesn't Scare Off Foreigners," *Wall Street Journal*, August 24, 2005, A1.

26. James R. Hagerty, "Millions Are Facing Monthly Squeeze on House Payments," *Wall Street Journal*, March 11, 2006, A1.

27. Ruth Simon and James R. Hagerty, "More Borrowers with Risky Loans Are Falling Behind," *Wall Street Journal*, December 5, 2006, A1.

28. Jesse Eisinger, "Wall Street Requiem," Condé Nast *Portfolio*, November 2007, 178–81.

29. Nik Deogun, personal interview, October 16, 2008.

30. Gretchen Morgenson, "A Coming Nightmare of Homeownership?" *New York Times*, October 3, 2004, C1.

31. Timothy L. O'Brien and Jennifer 8 Lee, "A Seismic Shift Under the House of Fannie Mae," *New York Times*, October 3, 2004, C1.

32. Diana B. Henriques, "Needing Cash, Veterans Sign over Pensions," *New York Times*, December 29, 2004, C1.

33. Diana B. Henriques, personal interview, October 21, 2008.

34. Shawn Tully, "Is This House Worth $1.2 million?" *Fortune*, October 28, 2002, 58–72.

35. Shawn Tully, "Is the Housing Boom Over?" *Fortune*, September 20, 2004, 90–108.

36. Shawn Tully, "Is It Time to Cash Out?" *Fortune*, July 11, 2005, 54–60.

37. Shawn Tully, "Welcome to the Dead Zone," *Fortune*, May 5, 2006, 94–102.

38. Bethany McLean, "The Fall of Fannie Mae," *Fortune*, January 24, 2005, 122–40.

39. Carol Loomis, "The Risk That Won't Go Away," *Fortune*, March 7, 1994, 40–50.

40. Mara Der Hovanesian, "Nightmare Mortgages: They Promise the American Dream," *BusinessWeek*, September 11, 2006, 70–72.

41. Mara Der Hovanesian, "Taking Risks to Extremes: Will Derivatives Cause a Major Blowup in the World's Credit Markets?" *BusinessWeek*, May 23, 2005, 96.

42. Mara Der Hovanesian, "Mortgage Lenders: Who's Most at Risk?" *BusinessWeek*, April 24, 2006, 50–52.

43. Emily Thornton, "Inside Wall Street's Culture of Risk," *BusinessWeek*, June 12, 2006, 52–58.

44. Dean Foust and Peter Coy, "Housing: The Mortgage Trap: Lenders Are Cranking Out an Ever-growing Array of Financing Schemes and Lowering Standards to Keep the Boom Going," *BusinessWeek*, July 27, 2005, 32–36.

45. Peter Coy, "What the Mortgage Next Door Can Tell You," *BusinessWeek*, July 27, 2005, 35.

46. Gary Weiss, personal interview, October 16, 2008.

47. Marcus Brauchli, personal interview, October 20, 2008.

48. The 2009 finalists are listed at http://www.pulitzer.org/awards/2009.

49. Matthew Taibbi, "The Great American Bubble Machine," *Rolling Stone*, July 9, 2009, 52–54, 58–61, 98–101.

Chapter 5: Missing the Moment

1. Dean Starkman, "Boiler Room," *Columbia Journalism Review*, September–October 2008.

2. Andrew Ross Sorkin, *Too Big to Fail: The Inside Story of How Wall Street and Washington Fought to Save the Financial System—and Themselves* (New York: Viking, 2009).

3. Matthew Goldstein, "Bear Stearns' Subprime IPO," *BusinessWeek*, May 11, 2007.

4. Richard Beales, "Structured Debt Investments Aimed at U.S. Retail Investors," *Financial Times*, May 30, 2007.

5. Kate Kelly and Serena Ng, "Bear's Fund Is Facing Mortgage Losses—Bond Sale Set for Today in Attempt to Raise Cash; Woes Could Be Another Sobering Sign for Market," *Wall Street Journal*, June 14, 2007.

6. Michael Hudson, "Debt Bomb—Lending a Hand: How Wall Street Stoked the Mortgage Meltdown—Lehman and Others Transformed the Market for Riskiest Borrowers," *Wall Street Journal*, June 27, 2007.

7. Ruth Simon and James R. Hagerty, "Debt Bomb—Inside the Mortgage Lending Debacle—The Middlemen: Mortgage Mess Shines Light on Brokers' Role—Job-Hopping Mr. Shaikh Left

Trail of Lawsuits, Failed License Exams," *Wall Street Journal*, July 5, 2007.

8. Greg Ip and Jon E. Hilsenrath, "Debt Bomb: Inside the 'Subprime' Mortgage Debacle—Seeds of Excess: How Credit Got So Easy and Why It's Tightening—Responses to S&L Mess, Asian Crisis, Tech Bust All Fed Into the Boom," *Wall Street Journal*, August 7, 2007.

9. Carrick Mollenkamp and Serena Ng, "Wall Street Wizardry Amplified Credit Crisis—A CDO Called Norma Left 'Hairball of Risk'; Tailored by Merrill Lynch," *Wall Street Journal*, December 27, 2007.

10. Jesse Eisinger and Jake Bernstein, "The Magnetar Trade: How One Hedge Fund Helped Keep the Bubble Going," ProPublica, http://www.propublica.org/feature/the-magnetar-trade-how-one-hedge-fund-helped-keep-the-housing-bubble-going.

11. Simon Johnson, "The Quite Coup," *Atlantic*, May 2009.

12. *Squawk Box*, CNBC, February 19, 2009.

13. Mara Der Hovanesian, "Sex, Lies, and Subprime Mortgages," *BusinessWeek*, November 13, 2008.

14. E. Scott Reckard, "Ameriquest Settles 29 Class-action Lawsuits," *Los Angeles Times*, January 27, 2010.

15. "Who's Behind the Financial Meltdown?" Center for Public Integrity, May 6, 2009, http://www.publicintegrity.org/investigations/economic_meltdown/the_subprime_25/.

16. Rick Brooks and Ruth Simon, "Subprime Debacle Traps Even Very Credit-Worthy—As Housing Boomed, Industry Pushed Loans to a Broader Market," *Wall Street Journal*, December 3, 2007.

17. David Heath, "WaMu: Hometown Bank Turned Predatory," *Seattle Times*, October 26, 2009.

18. Gretchen Morgenson, "The Reckoning: Behind Insurer's Crisis, Blind Eye to a Web of Risk," *New York Times*, September 28, 2008.

19. Mark Pittman, "Goldman, Merrill Collect Billions After Fed's AIG Bailout Loans," Bloomberg News, September 29, 2008.

20. Mark Pittman, "Evil Wall Street Exports Boomed With 'Fools' Born to Buy Debt," Bloomberg News, October 27, 2008.

21. Kate Kelly, "Bear CEO's Handling of Crisis Raises Issues—Cayne on Golf Links, 10-Day Bridge Trip Amid Summer Turmoil," *Wall Street Journal*, November 1, 2007.

22. Kate Kelly, "How Goldman Won Big on Mortgage Meltdown—A Team's Bearish Bets Netted Firm Billions; A Nudge From the CFO," *Wall Street Journal*, December 14, 2007.

23. Mark Pittman, "S&P, Moody's Mask $200 Billion of Subprime Bond Risk," Bloomberg News, June 29, 2007.

24. Ryan Chittum, "Audit Interview: Mark Pittman," *Columbia Journalism Review*, The Audit, February 27, 2009, http://www.cjr .org/the_audit/audit_interview_mark_pittman.php.

25. Carrick Mollenkamp, Susanne Craig, Jeffrey McCracken, Jon E. Hilsenrath, "The Two Faces of Lehman's Fall—Private Talks of Raising Capital Belied Firm's Public Optimism," *Wall Street Journal*, October 6, 2008.

26. Eric Dash, "Fed Helped Bank Raise Cash Quickly," *New York Times*, March 12, 2010.

27. Planet Money, "Elizabeth Warren Checks In," May 8, 2009, http:// www.npr.org/blogs/money/2009/05/hear_elizabeth_warren_ checks_i.html.

28. *This American Life*, "The Giant Pool of Money," May 9, 2008, http:// www.thisamericanlife.org/radio-archives/episode/355/The-Giant -Pool-of-Money.

29. Matt Taibbi, "Inside the Great American Bubble Machine," *Rolling Stone*, 1082–83, July 9–23, 2009.

30. Heidi N. Moore, "Will Everyone Please Shut Up About Goldman Sachs?" The Big Money, July, 29, 2009, http://www.thebigmoney .com/articles/judgments/2009/07/29/will-everyone-please-shut -about-goldman-sachs.

31. Charles Gasparino, "Stop Blaming Goldman Sachs," The Daily Beast, August 2, 2009, http://www.thedailybeast.com/blogs-and -stories/2009-08-02/stop-blaming-goldman-sachs/.

32. Megan McArdle, "Matt Taibbi Gets His Sarah Palin On," *Atlantic* online, July 10, 2009, http://www.theatlantic.com/business/ archive/2009/07/matt-taibbi-gets-his-sarah-palin-on/21084/.

33. Jay Rosen, "Karl Rove and the Religion of the Washington Press," PressThink, August 14, 2007, http://journalism.nyu.edu/pubzone/ weblogs/pressthink/2007/08/14/rove_and_press.html.

34. Elizabeth Warren, "America Without a Middle Class," The Huffington Post, December 3, 2009, http://www.huffingtonpost .com/elizabeth-warren/america-without-a-middle_b_377829.html.

35. "The Reckoning," series, *New York Times*, September 28–December 28, 2008, http://topics.nytimes.com/topics/news/business/series/ the_reckoning/index.html.

36. Richard Pérez-Peña, "Wall Street Journal Aims to Win Over the New York Times's Local Audience," *New York Times*, March 22, 2010.

37. Greg Gordon, Goldman Sachs series, McClatchy Newspapers, October 18–November 4, 2009.

38. Binyamin Applebaum, Lisa Hammersly Munn, Ted Mellnik, "Sold a Nightmare," March 1–4 and March 18–21, 2007.

39. Jack Dolan, Matthew Haggman, Rob Barry, "Borrowers Betrayed," *Miami Herald*, 2008.

40. Jesse Eisinger, "Wall Street Requiem," Condé Nast *Portfolio*, November 2007.

41. Claire Hoffman, "Barely Legal," Condé Nast *Portfolio*, November 2008.

42. Arianna Huffington, Testimony to the U.S. Senate Subcommittee on Communications, Technology, and the Internet, "Future of Journalism" hearing, May 6, 2009.

43. Tyler Durden, "How Lehman, With the Fed's Complicity, Created Another Illegal Precedent in Abusing the Primary Dealer Credit Facility," Zero Hedge blog, March 13, 2010, http://www.zerohedge .com/article/how-lehman-feds-complicity-created-another-illegal -precedent-abusing-primary-dealer-credit-f.

44. Kathy Chu, "Banks' 'Courtesy' Loans at Soaring Rates Irk Consumers," *USA Today*, July 10, 2009.

45. Andrew Martin, Ron Lieber, Keith Bradsher, Lowell Bergman, "The Card Game," series, September 9, 2009–January 4, 2010.

46. Louise Story, "The Reckoning: On Wall Street, Bonuses, Not Profits, Were Real," *New York Times*, December 18, 2008.

Chapter 6: The Quiet Crisis

1. Chairman Ben S. Bernanke, "The Housing Market and Subprime Lending," a speech to the 2007 International Monetary Conference in Cape Town, South Africa, June 5, 2007. Transcript available online at http://www.federalreserve.gov/newsevents/speech/bernanke 20070605a.htm.

2. Jonathan Stempel, "New Century, Subprime Lenders Rebound a Bit," Reuters News, March 6, 2007.

3. Peter S. Goodman, *Past Due: The End of Easy Money and the Renewal of the American Economy* (New York: Times Books, 2009), 214.

4. In 1973, the average rank-and-file American worker—about 80 percent of the American workforce—brought home about $330 a week, in inflation-adjusted dollars. By 1996, those same weekly earnings had dipped below $260, in inflation-adjusted terms. By early 2008,

they were at about $280 a week, or roughly the same level as in 1983. In other words, a quarter century had come and gone with average weekly earnings stuck in place. There are caveats to this data: large numbers of women and immigrants entered the workforce in these years, which tends to bring the numbers down. But the basic truth of these numbers cannot be dismissed. For more analysis of this, see my book, *Past Due*, 9–14.

5. Census Bureau data, as cited in David Leonhardt, "For Many a Boom That Wasn't," *New York Times*, April 9, 2008, C1.

6. Paul Osterman, "Improving Job Quality," in *A Future of Good Jobs?*, ed. Timothy J. Bartik and Susan N. Houseman (Kalamzoo, MI: W.E. Upjohn Institute for Employment Research, 2008), 204.

7. Ed McKelvey, "U.S. Daily: More Evidence for the Hiring Strike," Goldman Sachs U.S. Economic Research, January 3, 2008.

8. Peter S. Goodman, "Homeowners Feel the Pinch of Lost Equity," *New York Times*, November 8, 2007, A1.

9. Goodman, *Past Due*, 149.

10. Peter S. Goodman, "On Every Front, Anxious Questions and Uncomfortable Answers," *New York Times*, July 19, 2008, A10.

11. President George W. Bush, speech to the nation, September 24, 2008, transcript available at http://www.nytimes.com/2008/09/24/business/economy/24text-bush.html?pagewanted=1&_r=2.

12. See Peter S. Goodman, "Taking Hard New Look at a Greenspan Legacy," *New York Times*, October 8, 2008, A1, available online at http://www.nytimes.com/2008/10/09/business/economy/09greenspan.html.

13. Edmund L. Andrews, "Greenspan Concedes Error on Regulation," *New York Times*, October 23, 2008.

14. Peter S. Goodman and Gretchen Morgenson, "Saying Yes, WaMu Built Empire on Shaky Loans," *New York Times*, December 27, 2008, A1.

15. Testimony by Henry M. Paulson Before the House Committee on Oversight and Governance Reform, January 27, 2010, available online at http://www.scribd.com/doc/25877513/Henry-M-Paulson-Jr-s-Prepared-Remarks-for-A-I-G-Hearing; Testimony by Secretary Timothy F. Geithner, House Committee on Oversight and Governance Reform, January 27, 2010, available online at http://www.scribd.com/doc/25899750/Geithner-s-A-I-G-Testimony.

16. Peter S. Goodman, "Experts See a Need for Punitive Action in Bailout," *New York Times*, September 22, 2008, A1.

17. I was then the Asian economic correspondent for the *Washington Post*.
18. "U.S. Treasury Chief Urges China to Open Up Its Financial Markets," *South China Morning Post*, September 22, 2006, 6.
19. Treasury press release, "Statement by Treasury Secretary Henry M. Paulson Jr., on Comprehensive Approach to Market Developments," September 19, 2008, available online at http://www.ustreas.gov/press/releases/hp1149.htm.

Chapter 8: The Financial Crisis and the UK Media

1. The UK budget deficit ranked fourth largest in OECD countries, behind Iceland, Greece, and Ireland, according to OECD estimates for 2009. See OCED, *Interim Economic Outlook*, April 2010 accessed at http://www.oecd.org/document/13/0,3343,en_2649_33733 _44938317_1_1_1_1,00.html. On IMF estimates for the global cost of the bailouts, see Steve Schifferes, "$10 Trillion Credit Crunch cost," July 31, 2009, accessed at http://news.bbc.co.uk/2/hi/8177814 .stm.
2. Walter Bagehot's classic book on banking crises, *Lombard Street* (New York: Wiley, 1999 reprint), originally published in 1873, has been much cited during the current crisis.
3. On the revamp of the BBC's business coverage, see *The Report of the Independent Panel for the BBC Trust on the Impartiality of BBC Business Coverage* (the Budd report), April 2007, accessed at http://www.bbc .co.uk/bbctrust/assets/files/pdf/review_report_research/impartiality _business/business_impartiality_report.pdf.
4. For the postwar transformation of the City, the definitive account is David Kynaston, *The City of London: A Club No More 1945–2000* (London: Pimlico, 2002). For the recent developments see Larry Elliott and Dan Atkinson, *The Gods That Failed* (London: The Bodley Head, 2008).
5. The biggest critic of the role of the Financial Services Agency in the crisis is its current chairman, Adair Turner. See among other speeches, "The Financial Crisis and the Future of Financial Regulation," The Economist Inaugural City Lecture, January 29, 2009, accessed on FSA Web site at http://www.fsa.gov.uk/pages/ Library/Communication/Speeches/2009/0121_at.shtml.
6. Among the considerable literature on the rise of New Labour, see Andrew Rawnsley, *Servants of the People: The Inside Story of*

New Labour (London: Penguin, 2001) and Anthony Seldon, *Blair's Britain: 1997–2007* (Cambridge: Cambridge University Press, 2007). For insider accounts, see Phillip Gould, *The Unfinished Revolution* (London: Abacus, 1999) and Peter Mandelson, *The Blair Revolution Revisited* (London: Politico's, 2004).

7. On the struggle to maintain London's supremacy as a financial center, see James Faulconbridge, "London and Frankfurt in Europe's Evolving Financial Centre Network," *Area* 36 (3; 2004): 235–44 and City of London Corporation, *The Competitive Position of London as a Financial Centre*, April 2005, accessed at http://www.cityoflondon .gov.uk/NR/rdonlyres/131B4294-698B-4FAF-9758080CCE86 A36C/0/BC_RS_compposition_FR.pdf.

8. See Will Hutton, "Sarkozy is Absolutely Right: The City Has to Be Cut Down to Size," *Observer*, December 6, 2009, accessed at http:// www.guardian.co.uk/commentisfree/2009/dec/06/will-hutton-city -finance-budget.

9. Gillian Tett, "Unease Bubbling in Today's Brave New Financial Markets," *Financial Times*, January 19, 2007, accessed at http://www .ft.com/cms/s/0/92f7ee6a-a765-11db-83e4-0000779e2340.html. Gillian Tett's account of her full investigation of structured credit derivative markets is contained in her book *Fool's Gold* (London: Little, Brown, 2009).

10. Martin Wolf was speaking in conversation with Professor Joseph Stiglitz at the conference Facing the Fracture: The Media and Economic Understanding held on April 6, 2010, at the School of International and Public Policy, Columbia University, New York.

11. For an excellent comparative account of the politics of the recent housing boom, see Herman Schwartz and Leonard Seabroke, *The Politics of Housing Booms and Busts* (London: Palgrave MacMillan, 2009).

12. Channel 4's panoply of housing programs went on to include *Grand Designs, The Restoration Man, Country House Rescue, Kirstie's Homemade Home, The Home Show*, and *Relocation: Phil Down Under*. The television regulator Ofcom recently criticized Channel 4 for showing more repeats of *Relocation, Relocation* than other any show.

13. Robert Peston, "Media Complicit in Talking up Debt," *Press Gazette*, November 10, 2008, accessed at http://www.pressgazette .co.uk/story.asp?storycode=42410.

14. Mervyn King, speech at the Lord Mayor's Banquet for Bankers and Merchants at the Mansion House, June 20, 2007, Bank of England press office, accessed at http://www.bankofengland.co.uk/

publications/speeches/2007/speech313.pdf. Among politicians perhaps the most prescient one was the Liberal Democrat Treasury spokesman Vince Cable. See his book *The Storm, The World Economic Crisis and What it Means* (London: Atlantic, 2010).

15. See "ECB Moves to Help Banking Sector," BBC News Web site, August 9, 2007, accessed at http://news.bbc.co.uk/2/hi/business/ 6938425.stm.

   The statement by BNP Paribas that caused the crisis was the following: "The complete evaporation of liquidity in certain market segments of the U.S. securitization market has made it impossible to value certain assets fairly regardless of their quality or credit rating."

16. The best general account of the fall of Northern Rock is Alex Brummer, *The Crunch* (London: Random House, 2008). For Robert Peston's broader views on the role of regulators and bankers in causing the crisis, see his book *Who Runs Britain—and Whose Responsible for the Mess We're In?* (London: Hodder, revised edition, 2008).

17. "Northern Rock Gets Bank Bail-out," BBC News Web site, September 13, 2007, accessed at http://news.bbc.co.uk/2/hi/business /6994099.stm.

18. The UK eventually revised its deposit insurance scheme to cover £50,000 of savings without any portion being penalized. However, the crisis in October 2008 revealed the need for European-wide minimum standards of deposit protection. That was because under the EU single market financial institutions had the right to establish branches in any EU country, but the level of deposit insurance was determined by the prevailing law in their home country. In the UK, savers in the Icelandic banks were particularly affected by this provision, and the UK has engaged in a long legal struggle with Iceland to ensure its depositors are repaid following the collapse of the Icelandic banking system.

19. The governor of the Bank of England made his position clear during his testimony to the House of Commons Treasury Committee on September 20, 2007. See Treasury Committee, session 2006–7, uncorrected Oral Evidence testimony of Mervyn King, Sir John Gieve, and Paul Tucker, September 20, 2007, Q5, accessed at http:// www.publications.parliament.uk/pa/cm200607/cmselect/cmtreasy/ uc999-i/uc99902.htm.

20. Robert Peston testimony, House of Commons Treasury Committee, Session 2008-9, *Banking Crisis: Oral evidence*, Febru-

ary 4, 2009, Q1504, accessed at http://www.publications.parliament
.uk/pa/cm200809/cmselect/cmtreasy/144/09020401.htm.

21. See Peter Thai Larson, "Sir Fred's Heady Firsts," *Financial Times*,
October 4, 2007. The first sentence reads: "Sir Fred Goodwin is on
the verge of completing the impossible."

22. Steve Schifferes, "Foreclosure Wave Sweeps America," BBC News
Web site, November 5, 2007, http://news.bbc.co.uk/2/hi/business
/7070935.stm; Steve Schifferes, "Housing Meltdown Hits U.S.
Economy," BBC News Web site, November 9 2007, http://news
.bbc.co.uk/2/hi/business/7078492.stm; Steve Schifferes, "Carnage
on Wall St. as Loans Go Bad," BBC News Web site, November 13,
2007, http://news.bbc.co.uk/2/hi/business/7086909.stm.
    The author was economics correspondent for the BBC News Web
site from 1999 to 2009.

23. Clare Oldfield, *The Credit Crunch Commentariat* (London: Editorial
Intelligence, 2009) from which quotations for this section are
drawn.

24. Anatole Kaletsky, "The End of Homo Economicus," *Prospect
Magazine*, April 2009.

25. Decca Aitkenhead, "Storm Warning," *Guardian*, August 30, 2008,
http://www.guardian.co.uk/politics/2008/aug/30/alistairdarling.
economy; see also "Economy at 60-year Low—and It Will Get
Worse," *Guardian*, August 30, 2008, http://www.guardian.co.uk/
politics/2008/aug/30/economy.alistairdarling.
    Decca Aitkenhead wrote about the circumstances of the interview
in a profile piece, "Budget 2010: Darling's Last Stand?" *Guardian*,
March 21, 2010, http://www.guardian.co.uk/uk/2010/mar/23/
alistair-darling-budget-profile.

26. Darling's remarks that "the forces of hell were unleashed against
me" were made on Sky News on February 26, 2010. The story was
denied by Prime Minister Gordon Brown the next day. See "PM:
I Never Unleashed Hell on Chancellor," http://news.sky.com/
skynews/Article/201002115558080.

27. Phillip Webster, "Alistair Darling's Job on the Line After Recession
Blunder," *Times*, September 1, 2008.

28. See Andrew Rawnsley, *The End of the Party* (London: Viking, 2010),
for the continuing tension between no. 10 and no. 11 Downing
Street (the offices of the prime minister and chancellor of the
exchequer).
    Ironically, it was not until some months later that it became clear
that the chancellor had been right and the UK had actually entered

a recession in the summer of 2008. The official government figures initially put the growth rate in that quarter at 0 percent, which delayed the official recognition that the UK had experienced two quarters of negative growth until well into 2009, when they were finally revised downward.

29. On the role of the British government in the Lehman crisis, see Henry Paulson, *On the Brink: The Race to Save the Global Financial System from Collapse* (New York: Business Plus, 2010), Andrew Ross Sorkin, *Too Big To Fail* (New York: Viking, 2009), and David Wessel, *In Fed We Trust* (New York: Crown Press, 2009). See also the interview with the chancellor for the BBC News Aftershock series on the first anniversary of the Lehman crash at http://news.bbc .co.uk/2/hi/in_depth/business/2007/creditcrunch/default.stm.

30. See Robert Peston blog, "Lloyds to Buy HBOS," September 17, 2009, BBC News Web site, accessed at http://www.bbc.co.uk/blogs/ thereporters/robertpeston/2008/09/lloyds_to_buy_hbos.html.

31. The article that sparked the panic in UK shares was "Banks to Ask Chancellor for Capital," Peston blog, October 7, 2008, BBC News Web site, accessed at http://www.bbc.co.uk/blogs/thereporters/ robertpeston/2008/10/banks_ask_chancellor_for_capit.html.

32. The Bank of England later revealed its secret emergency support operations for HBOS and RBS, providing up to £60 billion ($100 billion) in short-term funds in October 2008. See comments on the Peston blog, "Why Did the Bank of England Keep Shtoom?" November 24, 2009, http://www.bbc.co.uk/blogs/thereporters/ robertpeston/2009/11/why_did_bank_of_england_keep_s.html.

33. Of the many accounts of the UK financial crisis, as well as the works by Peston, Brummer and Elliott already cited, see also for the banking perspective Alistair Milne, *The Fall of the House of Credit* (Cambridge: Cambridge University Press, 2009) and Paul Mason, *Meltdown: The End of the Age of Greed* (London: Verso, 2009).

34. See *Daily Mail*, October 8, 2008.

35. David Gauke MP in the committee debate on banking regulation. (House of Commons Bill Committee, October 22, 2008, accessed at http://www.publications.parliament.uk/pa/cm200708/cmpublic/ banking/081021/am/81021s06.htm.

36. Richard Lambert, Director-General, CBI, speech at the Reform Media Group Dinner, December 2, 2008, CBI Press office, accessed at http://www.cbi.org.uk/pdf/20081205-Richard-Lambert-speech -Reform-Media-Group.pdf.

37. Roy Greenslade, "Critics May Carp but Media Did a Good Job Exposing Crunch," *Evening Standard*, February 12, 2009.

38. Treasury Committee, Inquiry into the Banking Crisis, session 2007–8, Oral Evidence, February 4, 2009, q1510 at http://www.publications.parliament.uk/pa/cm200809/cmselect/cmtreasy/144/09020403.htm.

39. Treasury Committee, q1516, 1520.

40. Treasury Committee, q1540. See also Jeff Randall, "Royal Bank of Scotland Chiefs to be Forced Out in Bail-out Deal," *Daily Telegraph* October 8, 2008.

41. Jenkins, 2009 Treasury Commitee hearings, Role of Journalists in the financial crisis, question 1519.

42. Personal communication, Tim Weber, business editor, BBC News Web site, December 2008.

43. For the source of press quotes on bankers, see *The Credit Crunch Commentariat*.

44. For the archbishop of Canterbury Rowan Williams's interview on the first anniversary of the collapse of Lehman Brothers on BBC TV's Newsnight program, on September 18, 2009 and reactions, see http://news.bbc.co.uk/2/hi/programmes/newsnight/8260059.stm.

45. The UK government's elaborate media campaign included a sophisticated Web site of its own, http://www.londonsummit.gov.uk/en/.
   For comprehensive overview of the G20 London summit, see BBC News Web site G20 Summit special coverage, http://news.bbc.co.uk/2/hi/in_depth/business/2009/g20/default.stm.

46. Much of the domestic coverage of the G20 summit focused on the issue of overzealous policing of the protests in central London, which resulted in one death and several injuries.

47. Professor Goodhart was speaking at a seminar at City University London entitled Saints or Sinners: The Role of the Media in the Financial Crisis on December 2, 2009. See http://www.city.ac.uk/whatson/2009/12_dec/021209-media-financial-crisis.

48. Larry Elliott, speaking at the Saints and Sinners conference.

49. Martin Wolf, Facing the Fracture conference, April 6, 2010.

50. Alex Brummer, quoted in James Robinson, "Why Didn't City Journalists See the Crisis Coming?" *Observer*, October 18, 2008. For the history of financial crises, and the forgetfulness of policymakers, see Kenneth Rogoff and Carmen Reinhardt, *This Time It's Different: Eight Centuries of Financial Follies* (New York: Little Brown, 2009).

Chapter 9: What Would Good Reporting Look Like?

1. Bethany McLean, "Is Enron Overpriced?" *Fortune*, March 5, 2001.
2. Howard Kurtz, "The Enron Story That Waited to Be Told," *Washington Post*, January 18, 2002.
3. "GOP Leader Weighs in on Health Summit," *All Things Considered*, National Public Radio, February 25, 2010, www.npr.org.
4. John Hanrahan, "Rein in Entitlements? No. Increase Them, Says James Galbraith," October 8, 2009, http://www.niemanwatchdog .org/index.cfm?fuseaction=background.view&backgroundid=00397.
5. Paul Krugman, *New York Times*, February 2010, http://www .nytimes.com/2010/02/05/opinion/05krugman.html?pagewanted= print.
6. Dan Froomkin, "Seven Things About the Economy That Everyone Should Be More Worried About Than They Are," http:// niemanwatchdog.org/index.cfm?fuseaction=background .view&backgroundid=00427.
7. Galbraith, the author of seven books, holds the Lloyd M. Bentsen Jr. chair in government/business relations and is a professor of government at the University of Texas, Austin. Baker is co-director of the Center for Economic and Policy Research and was one of the few economists to recognize the housing bubble and warn of it on a regular basis, having spotted it as early as 2002 when he wrote a paper entitled, "The Run-up in Home Prices: Is It Real or Is It Another Bubble?" Bilmes is a lecturer in Public Policy at the John F. Kennedy School of Government at Harvard University. She teaches budgeting and public finance. Johnson is a professor of global economics and management at MIT's Sloan School of Management. Moss is the John G. McLean professor of business administration at the Harvard Business School. Sachs is director of Columbia's Earth Institute and special adviser to United Nations Secretary-General Ban Ki-moon on the Millennium Development Goals to fight global poverty.
8. http://www.journalism.org/analysis_report/covering_great _recession.